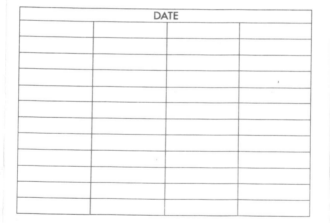

DATE			

The Politics of Airline Deregulation

The Politics of
Airline Deregulation

Anthony E. Brown

THE UNIVERSITY OF TENNESSEE PRESS/KNOXVILLE

The paper in this book meets the minimum requirements of the
American National Standard for Permanence of Paper for Printed
Library Materials. ∞ The binding materials have been chosen for
strength and durability.

Library of Congress Cataloging-in-Publication Data

Brown, Anthony E.
  The politics of airline deregulation.

  Bibliography: p.
  Includes index.
  1. Aeronautics, Commercial—United States—
Deregulation. 2. Airlines—United States—
Deregulation. 3. Aeronautics, Commercial—Law
and legislation—United States. I. Title.
HE9803.A4B68 1987   387.7′1   86-30888
ISBN 0-87049-532-1 (alk. paper)

Contents

Contents

Tables

Preface

It must be considered that there is nothing more difficult to carry out, nor more doubtful of success, nor more dangerous to handle, than to initiate a new order of things. For the reformer has enemies in all those who profit by the old order, and only lukewarm defenders in all those who would profit by the new order, this lukewarmness arising partly from fear of their adversaries, who have the laws in their favour; and partly from the incredulity of mankind, who do not truly believe in anything new until they have had actual experience of it. Thus it arises that on every opportunity for attacking the reformer, his opponents do so with the zeal of partisans, the others only defend him half-heartedly, so that between them he runs great danger.

Machiavelli, *The Prince*

One of the most fascinating aspects of the public policy disputations I have participated in during the last four years is the widespread acceptance of the notion that the burden of proof rests always with the advocates of change—that even if one is dealing with manifestly irrational, if not idiotic, arrangements, the advocate of moving in the direction of rationality is called upon to predict exactly how the process will work out and to prove beyond all doubt that it will work perfectly.

Alfred Kahn, *Applying Economics to an Imperfect World*

Deregulation first emerged as a politically acceptable reform alternative during the decade of the 1970s, and a number of industries were affected by the movement to curtail the scope of regulatory intervention. Reforms in regulatory policies governing the economic operations of the securities, banking, energy, communications, and transportation industries were adopted, and these reduced and, in some cases, removed traditional regulatory controls.

Commercial aviation was one of the first industries affected by the deregulation movement. In 1978, President Carter signed into law the Airline Deregulation Act, which restricted the authority of the Civil Aeronautics Board (CAB) to regulate commercial airlines for the first time since 1938. The law provided for the eventual termination of airline economic regulation and the CAB.

The following analysis examines how deregulation came to be an acceptable reform alternative in the field of government aviation policy. Government documents, including congressional hearings and reports, a variety of contemporaneous reports, public speeches, and memoranda, were principal sources for the study. Book-length studies of airline regulation provided background information and historical perspectives on the deregulation initiative. Journal articles, news journals and papers, and trade journals were also consulted. Finally, the documentary sources were supplemented by personal interviews with participants in the reform process.

Two major conclusions emerge from this study. First, it becomes evident that several features of the process and politics of airline deregulation contradict conventional assumptions about the dynamics of the policy process in general and the character of regulatory politics. Treatments of the policy process that insist on the stability, perpetuation, and incremental elaboration of existing policy frameworks are not compatible with the facts of the airline case. Aviation reform was a case in which a policy termination proposal was not defeated. On the contrary, deregulation became increasingly popular during the reform process. Furthermore, the regulatory agent served as an advocate of deregulation in this case rather than as an opponent—a role generally assigned to it by most studies of regulatory politics. Administrative deregulation played a major part in passage of the reform bill.

A second argument that will be developed is that the adoption of the deregulation alternative was not the result of a major transformation in the politics of regulation. Rather, the politics of deregulation is seen as being a continuation of the politics of regulation. Traditional political relationships characteristic of airline regulation were not fundamentally altered in order to make deregulation an acceptable policy alternative. Airline deregulation is explained as having resulted from several interest group techniques, referred to as deregulation strategies, in contrast to the emphasis being placed on interest group structure. The manner and conditions under which deregulation advocates sought change were more critical to the success of policy reform than were the number of interest groups or the intensity of their opposition. Six strategies and the conditions associated with their development will be identified and discussed. They are: the articulation of a policy alternative, policy evaluation, political packaging, strategic compromise, strategic staffing, and administrative deregulation.

Several individuals provided assistance during preparation of the manuscript. I am especially grateful to David M. Welborn for initially suggesting the research topic and for his assistance and encouragement during the project. I am also grateful to Dan Nimmo for enriching my graduate school experience. My research was influenced by insights into the political process gained from seminars he conducted at the University of Tennessee. Comments and suggestions from a number of other colleagues including Paul Quirk, James E. Anderson, Kenneth J. Meier, Sharon Tunstall, Mark Petracca, and Joseph Stewart were very helpful. Julie Marengo provided excellent technical assistance in preparing an early draft of the manuscript. Of course, the research would have been difficult, if not impossible, without the unselfish assistance of those who consented to be interviewed. Finally, the book represents many years of support and encouragement provided by my wife Donna and my parents.

The Politics of Airline Deregulation

1 | The Significance of Airline Deregulation

INTRODUCTION

Regulatory reform emerged as a central issue in national politics in the 1970s. The increased demand for reform in part represented a reaction to major expansions in the national regulatory structure that were initiated in the late 1960s and early 1970s. The appearance of new regulatory agencies such as the Environmental Protection Agency and the Consumer Product Safety Commission reflected the expansion and consolidation of national regulation in the areas of health, safety, and environmental quality. Problems associated with the novelty of the new regulatory endeavors as well as with the magnitude of their programs stimulated demands for reform.[1]

Reform agitation was also fueled by critics of regulation, who blamed national economic problems on regulatory intervention. Pointing to the distress in the private sector during the 1970s, many critics charged that government regulations contributed to inflation, created shortages and misallocations of resources, reduced productivity, and hampered the ability of private industry to respond effectively to changing economic conditions.[2]

A unique feature of regulatory reform in the 1970s was the unprecedented "official recognition of the limits and perils of regulation."[3] Deregulation was accorded a degree of political respectability not granted in previous reform movements. The drive

for deregulation was based on the assumption that problems associated with regulation cannot be remedied short of terminating regulatory policies, programs, and administrative machinery that have
been in place for decades. Many recent reforms of the national
regulatory structure parallel the traditional organizational and procedural remedies for regulatory problems. Some reforms in the
1970s and early 1980s, however, went beyond incremental adjustments to established regulatory frameworks. During the Ford and
Carter administrations, reforms in several regulated sectors "restricted regulation itself, rather than simply adjusting or extending
agency prerogatives."[4]

One of the first regulatory regimes to be affected by the deregulation trend was that governing the domestic operations of the commercial aviation industry. On October 8, 1975, President Ford
proposed legislation that would reduce the authority of the Civil
Aeronautics Board (CAB) to regulate the industry.[5] The Aviation
Act of 1975 was based on the conclusion that the airline industry
had outgrown the need for "protective regulation." In his message
transmitting the bill to Congress, Ford stated that "the rigidly
controlled regulatory structure now serves to stifle competition,
increase cost to travelers, makes the industry less efficient than it
could be and denies large segments of the American public access to
lower cost air transportation."[6] To remedy these problems, he
proposed that Board controls over the availability and pricing of
airline services be relaxed.

In 1975, the prospect of curtailing government control over an
industry that had virtually grown up under the hand of regulation
was given little chance of succeeding. In most quarters, the expecta-
tion was that Ford's proposal would "go down the drain" because it
would "shake up too much opposition."[7] However, it eventually
"shook up" too much support. Three years later, only ten congressmen voted against an amended version of the Ford bill.[8] On October 24, 1978, President Carter signed the Airline Deregulation Act
of 1978 and announced that "for the first time in decades we have
deregulated a major industry."[9]

The legislation was significant in that it restricted government
control over the economic operations of airline firms for the first
time since regulatory controls were imposed by the Civil Aeronautics Act of 1938.[10] The 1978 bill, however, did not mandate the
immediate and total deregulation of the industry as President Car-

ter had suggested. Rather, it redesigned the existing regulatory regime to ease the transition to eventual removal of regulatory controls.

During a transition period, the CAB was directed to promote airline competition, and its authority to supervise airline pricing and route decisions was curtailed. The remaining powers of the Board to regulate carrier service routes were scheduled to terminate on December 31, 1981, rate regulation on January 1, 1983; and by January 1, 1985, the CAB's residual responsibilities were to be transferred to other agencies and the Board abolished.[11]

The phased deregulation schedule was not blocked by Congress; and by January 1, 1985, the economic operations of the industry were no longer subject to public-utility-type controls administered by an independent commission. The industry was transferred to a new control regime guided by existing antitrust laws, and the CAB was abolished. Commercial aviation became the first industry successfully transferred from classical regulatory supervision to less restrictive methods of control.

Airline deregulation raises a question of fundamental significance: How are changes in mature governmental arrangements effected? The framework for administrative regulation of the airline industry was implemented in 1938. Not until the mid-1970s, however, was administrative supervision of the industry seriously challenged. At that time, deregulation passed from a policy alternative to a policy mandate, and incremental policy changes gave way to a major reformulation of the traditional regulatory framework. The legislation altered more than four decades of accumulated government policy and signaled the dismemberment of a mature policy subsystem.

In the following pages, the conditions culminating in passage of the Airline Deregulation Act of 1978 are examined. The central question guiding the analysis is how a substantive change in regulatory policy was effected. A response to that question must include both a historical analysis of CAB regulatory policy as well as an examination of the problems, conditions, and strategies associated with the promotion and adoption of airline deregulation.

The analysis that follows suggests that the politics of deregulation was in large part an extension of the politics of airline regulation. Several conditions facilitated adoption of deregulation. One of the most important was the cyclical dynamic of CAB regulatory policy, which fluctuated between a competitive and anticompetitive approach to regulation. The regulatory policy cycle worked to the advantage of groups supporting statutory codification of the traditional competitive approach to airline regulation. Deregulation advocates influenced the legislation by using several strategies that served to discredit the regulatory framework and promote deregulation as a policy alternative. Furthermore, it is argued that the process of airline deregulation contradicts conventional assumptions about the politics of regulatory reform and the role of the regulatory agent in the reform process.

THE PROBLEM

Contemporary reforms in airline regulation pose a challenge to both historical and theoretical formulations about regulatory politics. Both the history of regulatory reform and various theoretical treatments of regulatory politics suggest that proposals to alter regulatory controls by curtailing the authority of the regulator will generate substantial political opposition. Thus, it is often predicted that the most politically acceptable remedies for regulatory failure will be those that prescribe strengthening or expanding existing regulatory arrangements. In other words, if regulatory reform is accomplished, it will be incremental and not decremental in character.[12] The case of aviation reform, however, challenges both the historical and theoretical bases for this general hypothesis.

Historically, the legislation represents a dramatic change in the thrust of regulatory reform. Until 1978, statutory reforms served only to build upon the basic regulatory framework established by the Civil Aeronautics Act of 1938. The 1978 legislation reflected a shift from an incremental to a decremental approach to regulatory reform in that it prescribed relaxation and eventual termination of classical regulatory controls. Unlike previous reform efforts, deregulation was seriously considered as a policy alternative and significantly affected the substance of airline regulatory reform.

Theoretically, it is difficult to incorporate the occurrence of deregulation into dominant conceptualizations and reigning assumptions about the nature of the policy process in general and the regulatory process in particular. In both cases, theorists assume that the continuation, stability, or at most the incremental elabora-

tion of established policies and patterns of behavior are the dominant characteristics of the policy process. However, the politics of
regulatory reform during the 1970s led one observer to note that
"what everybody 'knows' about the politics of regulation is no
longer so, if indeed it ever was."[13]

Stated implicitly if not explicitly in treatments of the regulatory
process is a theory of politics that may be useful perhaps in explaining stability or incremental changes in political arrangements. Traditional characterizations of the regulatory process, however, are
often inadequate and misleading when applied to a situation characterized by decremental change or significant reformulation of
established political arrangements. Consequently, "few economists
[and] scarcely any political scientist [were] prepared for the events
of recent years."[14] In sum, contemporary aviation reform challenges much of the conventional wisdom about the politics of the
regulatory process.

HISTORICAL SIGNIFICANCE OF AIRLINE DEREGULATION

The Airline Deregulation Act of 1978 represents a significant departure from a traditional reform strategy which sought to preserve
the basic system of administrative regulation. Until the 1970s,
changes in the airline regulatory scheme consisted of incremental
adjustments within a broader regulatory framework. A 1974
congressional staff study reviewing the history of airline regulation
concluded that "no concurrent resolution or general statutory reform concerning economic regulation has been voted up or down by
Congress." Since 1938, congressional expression took the form of
"committee hearings and reports and congressional *changes to
specific parts of the regulatory scheme* [emphasis added]."[15] In other
words, airline regulatory reform was based on the premise that it
was appropriate and necessary to employ regulation as a tool for
controlling the industry.

In this regulatory climate, those advocating curtailment of regulation never enjoyed substantial political support for their proposals. On the contrary, the Civil Aeronautics Act signed by President
Roosevelt on June 23, 1938, articulated a regulatory framework
that was to remain basically unaltered for more than forty years.

There were changes made in some provisions of the Act in the following years. Prior to the 1970s, however, reforms served to refine and expand the scope of economic regulation rather than to replace or dismantle it.

Although beginning of government economic regulation of civil aviation is usually traced to the 1938 Act, the basic features of the regulatory scheme incorporated in the Act began to emerge earlier.[16] By 1925, the government had come to exercise a loose, de facto form of control over the industry's basic economic components—market entry, service routes, and rates. Two developments were responsible for the government's assuming this role . First, in 1918, the Army and Post Office cooperatively initiated air mail service in the United States. The Air Mail Act of 1925 (the Kelly Act)[17] authorized mail carriage by commercial airlines. This ended the practice of flying the mail exclusively with Army personnel and equipment. The Post Office was directed to determine mail routes and award mail contracts. Second, in the absence of a developed passenger transport market, private carriers came to depend heavily on government contract payments for their operating revenues. In effect, the 1925 legislation tied the economic fortunes of the aviation industry directly to government policies and laid the groundwork for government regulation.

In the ensuing years, the government's regulatory involvement in the industry was strengthened and expanded. Subsequent amendments in the Kelly Act in 1926, 1928, and 1930[18] strengthened the mail contract as an instrument for subsidizing airline development. They also increased the postmaster general's authority over air mail route determinations and made mail contracts more lucrative by extending the contract period from four to ten years. In 1926, public funding of airport development and navigational aids was provided by the Air Commerce Act.[19] The legislation also initiated government regulation of airline safety, designating the Department of Commerce as enforcement agent.

By 1934, the haphazard and piecemeal development of government aviation policy precipitated economic and political problems that came to a climax under the administration of Postmaster General Walter F. Brown. These problems led to a Senate investigation into charges of maladministration by the Post Office, cancellation of all mail contracts by President Roosevelt, and a disastrous attempt to continue air mail service using Army personnel and equipment.[20] The Black-McKeller Act of 1934[21] sought to bring order to this chaotic situation, and it set the stage for a comprehensive examination of government aviation policy.

The 1934 legislation further refined and extended government control of the aviation industry. Regulation of the airline industry was assigned to three agencies. Competitive bidding by private carriers for mail contracts was reinstated with administration assigned to the Post Office. Authority of the postmaster was curtailed by making the Interstate Commerce Commission responsible for determining ceilings for mail rates. Finally, the Department of Commerce, through its Bureau of Air Commerce, the predecessor of the Federal Aviation Agency, was to regulate the safety, maintenance, operation, and development of the industry.

Regulatory arrangements established by the Black-McKeller Act, however, proved ineffective in coping with industry problems. Confusion in government responsibilities resulted from the dispersal of regulatory functions among three agencies. Loopholes in the bill were exploited, rendering the mail contract ineffective in maintaining financial stability in the industry.[22] Consequently, new legislation was passed in 1938 that sought to remedy these problems.

The Civil Aeronautics Act of 1938 crystallized aviation policies that had evolved during the previous two decades. In formulating the bill, legislators drew upon the government's experience with railroad and trucking regulation and the twenty years of government participation in the development and control of the aviation industry. Recommendations from the Federal Aviation Commission also provided guidance. The Commission had been created and directed by the Black-McKeller Act to review government aviation policies and propose changes. One of its recommendations was to place economic regulatory responsibilities under a single administrative body. Acting on this proposal, Congress created the Civil Aeronautics Authority, the predecessor of the Civil Aeronautics Board.

To remedy administrative confusion, the legislation established clearer lines of administrative responsibility for the regulation and development of aviation safety, airline facilities, and the economic practices of the industry. These responsibilities were initially transferred from the Post Office and Interstate Commerce Commission, where they previously were performed, to the Civil Aeronautics Authority, a Civil Aeronautics Administrator, and an Air Safety Board.

The Authority was composed of five members, appointed for staggered six-year terms by the president with the advice and consent of the Senate. No more than three members could be appointed from the same party, and the president was authorized to designate a chairman annually. The Authority was created as an independent commission whose members could be removed by the president only in the case of their malfeasance in office. Its responsibilities included both economic and safety regulation.

An Administrator also was to be appointed by the president with advice and consent of the Senate. The Administrator's term of office, however, was not set, and his tenure was left to the discretion of the president. The Administrator's primary duties included the promotion and development of aviation landing and navigation facilities.

Finally, the Air Safety Board consisted of three members responsible for the investigation of aviation accidents. It was also enabled to make recommendations for improved safety regulations. However, the power to make rules regarding safety was reserved to the Authority.

The first reform of the original regulatory framework came as a result of two executive orders issued in 1940.[23] Both orders resulted in the reorganization of the nine-member organization responsible for the regulation and development of the aviation industry. Relying on his newly acquired reorganization authority, President Roosevelt transferred the Civil Aeronautics Administrator to the Department of Commerce, placing him in charge of a new agency, the Civil Aeronautics Administration (CAA). The Administrator and the CAA were charged with the development and operation of air navigation facilities, aircraft registration and flight personnel licensing, and the enforcement of safety rules. Furthermore, the Civil Aeronautics Authority and the Air Safety Board created by the 1938 legislation were abolished and some of their functions transferred to a new, independent commission, the Civil Aeronautics Board. It was to be headed by a five-member board appointed for fixed terms by the president with senatorial advice and consent.

Economic supervision of the commercial aviation industry was centralized in the CAB. It was granted regulatory authority over individual firms concerning their entry into and exit from routes. The controversial mail contract was replaced by a certification system administered by the Board as a means for regulating market entry and airline services. Each firm was required to apply for an operating certificate which stipulated the routes to be served and the type of airline service the carrier could provide. In addition, the administration reforms gave the CAB regulatory authority over airline rates by requiring Board approval of airline proposals for fare changes. Finally, the financial operations of the airline companies were made subject to regulatory controls by the Board. Airline acquisitions and mergers required Board approval. To strengthen coordination of the operations of the aviation industry, the Board was granted authority to exempt carriers from prosecution under the antitrust laws. Taken together, these measures assured substantial government control over the aviation industry.

These reforms initiated by the Roosevelt administration shortly after passage of the Civil Aeronautics Act are typical of the direction taken by regulatory reforms in the post-1938 period. For the most part, subsequent changes in the regulatory framework were designed to provide for more effective management of airline competition and to ameliorate problems associated with the rapid growth of commercial aviation. For example, in 1949 the Board extended its certification requirements to cargo carriers in response to growth in that segment of the airline industry.[24] In 1962, Congress passed legislation requiring CAB certification of supplemental carriers that were primarily engaged in chartered airline service.[25] Such a measure reflected the growing demand for this type of service after World War II.

Increased aviation traffic and associated safety problems resulted in the transfer of most of the CAB's safety responsibilities to the Federal Aviation Agency in 1958. After the 1940 reorganization, the CAB retained the right to make safety rules and investigate aviation accidents. Safety regulation, however, was transferred from the CAB to the Federal Aviation agency with passage of the Federal Aviation Act of 1958. After 1958, the CAB's only direct responsibility in the safety area was the investigation of accidents involving regulated carriers. This last remnant of its safety jurisdiction was removed in 1966 when the Department of Transportation Act[26] assigned all investigative responsibilities to the National Transportation Safety Board. The 1966 Act also changed the autonomous status of the Federal Aviation Agency by replacing it with the Federal Aviation Administration and locating it in the new Department of Transportation.

These and other reforms to check the excesses or correct the deficiencies of regulatory policies and agency actions were formulated without seriously addressing the more fundamental question of whether regulation was necessary.[27] Rather, reform proposals were aimed at tidying up the procedural and organizational instruments of regulation and providing administrative relief in specific circumstances. Until the reform effort in the 1970s, the problem in airline regulation was one of perfecting the existing regulatory framework, not questioning its existence. The relaxation of economic controls legislated in 1978 represents an aberration when placed against the backdrop of the government's traditional relationship to the aviation industry. On its face, the historical thrust of regulatory reform appears to offer no direct explanation for the sudden trend toward deregulation.

The shift in direction of regulatory reform is examined in chapter 2, where it is argued that three distinct approaches to the issue of government regulation of industry can be identified in contemporary reform debates. Prior to the 1970s, an incremental approach to regulatory reform dominated policies affecting airline regulation. The Airline Deregulation Act of 1978, however, codified a decremental approach and mandated eventual deregulation of the industry. Decremental and deregulatory approaches differ significantly from the more traditional incremental approach in their assumptions about the regulatory process and their prescriptions for correcting regulatory failure.

THEORETICAL SIGNIFICANCE OF AIRLINE DEREGULATION

The argument that the Airline Deregulation Act of 1978 is historically significant rests on the premise that the Act represented a markedly different policy framework from that guiding government control of the industry during the previous four decades. However, the legislation represents more than a reversal in the direction of reform in a regulated sector, as significant as that may be. Broader theoretical implications are indicated by the case. The type of policy change adopted and the dynamics of the policy process preceding adoption, particularly the behavior of the regulatory agent in that process, contradict much of the conventional wisdom about the dynamics of regulatory politics.

Deregulation as Policy Termination

The type of reform adopted in the field of airline regulation bears the mark of deregulation proponents. Deregulation implies reduction in government intervention and termination of existing policies, programs, and/or agencies. Consequently, deregulation can be viewed as a termination policy. The fact that deregulation won political acceptance as a policy alternative contradicts two commonly accepted descriptions of the general policy process as well as trends in the development of regulatory policy.

A traditional view of the policy process

While deregulation implies reductions in the scope of government intervention, many academic studies of the policy formation process assume that the natural tendency is toward growth and expansion on the part of national government programs. The trend toward more programs, more agencies, and more expenditures is offered as evidence of a policy-formation process that significantly and inexorably increased the scope of intervention by the national government during this century.

Many studies of government policymaking also emphasize the perpetuation of existing programs, policies, and agencies as opposed to instances of termination. Many analysts stress the incremental character of the policy process and the political conditions which obstruct policy termination and promote continuation. Conditions promoting termination and the features of a decremental approach to policy change are given relatively little attention.[28]

In one sense it is unremarkable that policy analysts emphasize the growth and expansion of government. Much evidence points to its importance. In general, assessments of the policy process agree that developments in this century have yielded a larger national government as measured in terms of expenditures and number of agencies. For example, Herbert Kaufman offers support for the popular belief that government organizations are indeed "immortal" and that growth and not decline best characterizes the development of national government structures. He concluded that of the 175 national government agencies in existence in 1923, only 15 percent were phased out by 1973. And most of these had been terminated by simply transferring their programs to another agency. Furthermore, he found that the agency population had expanded from 175 to 394 in the same time period.[29]

The scope of regulation is also characterized in terms of its expansion. Particularly striking is the growth in the fields of environmental, health, and safety regulation that occurred during the latter part of the 1960s and continued into the 1970s. Creation of the "new" social regulatory agencies such as the Consumer Product Safety Commission, Occupational Safety and Health Administration, Equal Employment Opportunity Commission, and the Environmental Protection Agency are indicative of the trend. Observers also point to the larger amount of public expenditures channeled through these agents as well as to the substantial increase in the number of federal regulations as a measure of the growth of government intervention.[30]

Perpetuation is often presented as another dominant feature of the policy process. That policies are continued, with incremental adjustments, rather than being terminated or reduced in scope is viewed as being the dominant trend because of the existence of significant political obstacles to change. Many studies of the policy process accept the proposition "that the longer a policy, program, or agency remains in existence, the less likely it is to be terminated. Accommodations are made and support develops that enable them to survive."[31] The author of another frequently cited analysis of the policy process reaches a similar conclusion that "more impressive than the number of policy systems that go out of existence is the number that survive and expand. Once policy cycles have developed in a particular issue-area, stopping the process is a major assignment. Too many commitments by too many people exist at that point for a clear cut-away to occur."[32] As these statements suggest, a commonly accepted generalization is that the political dynamics in the policy process reinforce the status quo.

An emphasis on the continuation of existing policies and the unlikelihood of major reform is particularly evident in descriptions of regulatory politics. As in other fields of policy analysis, many students of the regulatory process are often pessimistic about the prospects of significant regulatory reform, particularly if the proposal is for deregulation.

In his analysis of the development of the administrative structure in the United States, James Q. Wilson concludes that much of the growth can be attributed to the creation of clientele and regulatory agencies. An important consequence of this trend is that it has resulted in a significant shift of political power to the administrative structure. The political resources of clientele groups combine with the agencies' broad grant of administrative discretion to insure policy continuance and to block attempts to terminate the agency. Wilson pessimistically concludes that "Congress could change what it has devised, but there is little reason to suppose it will."[33] Similarly, after considering the conditions necessary for the termination of existing regulatory policies, Emmette Redford argues that "only a major revolution in technology, interests, and/or beliefs can change the shorelines of the environmental sea or agitate the whirlpool enough to create new shorelines on the main policy stream."[34]

As the preceding statements indicate, the dominant assumptions about the character of the regulatory process are even more pessimistic about the prospects of radical policy change than are general descriptions of the policy process. The political arena for resolving regulatory issues is often presented as a closed system dominated by the regulated economic groups. According to this view, the regulated join with the regulatory agent and congressional subcommittees to form an "iron triangle" that monopolizes the political resources necessary to alter traditional regulatory controls. Furthermore, it is unlikely that these resources will be used to terminate existing arrangements because those in strategic positions of control over regulatory policy are the beneficiaries of regulation. Reform may come but only if no objections are raised by the regulated and only if they are convinced that the changes will improve the existing system of administrative control. Opposition to reform is almost guaranteed if it entails deregulation because of the vested interest in the regulatory regime.

A critique of the traditional view

Growth and perpetuation, however, is only one feature of the policy process. Policies are also terminated. Furthermore, policy growth and expansion does not always characterize the regulatory process. A variety of public sector trends point to the growing salience of policy termination. Deregulation represents such a trend in the field of regulatory policy. Here policy developments include the termination of traditional regulatory policies and not merely their incremental reform. As in the case of airline regulation, the policies, programs, and administrative machinery that had been in place for decades came under attack in the 1970s. As political changes have increased the incidence and visibility of policy terminations, "there has developed in recent years a large discrepancy between social science and reality"[35] both in the field of regulatory politics and in other policy areas.

Some analysts are critical of dominant assumptions and conclusions about the policy process. The prevailing emphasis on policy perpetuation is viewed by some analysts as imposing limitations on a broader understanding of the policy process by directing attention away from cases that violate the trends of policy growth and expansion. The critics examine instances of policy termination and the processes involved in the "deliberate conclusion or cessation of specific government functions, programs, policies, or organizations."[36] Robert P. Biller speaks for other analysts when he proposes that the phenomenon of policy termination is "a wrongly underattended issue that receives little overt scrutiny by policy analysts."[37]

Critics of the traditional treatment of the policy process conclude that most inquiries tend to be dominated by concerns flowing from government intervention in new policy areas, the genesis and expansion of public programs and organizations, and the perpetuation of existing policies. In most cases, analysts are concerned with vexing problems attending the initiation, legitimization, and implementation of new and expanded forms of government intervention. The conspicuousness of the problems stems largely from the extraordinary growth of the public sector during the last two decades. Cases of policy discontinuance, if considered at all, are often accorded anomalous status, dismissed as aberrations in the general trend of policy perpetuation, and treated as deviant cases rather than as the potential source of analytical insights into ongoing policy processes. Despite the assumed rarity of the phenomenon, however, termination does occur and is therefore a feature of the larger political process. The central question that remains "is not whether a given policy or organization shall end, but rather where and when and under what circumstances."[38]

This line of criticism has led some students of the policy process to give more serious attention to the processes and consequences of policy discontinuance. Questions such as how termination occurs, the character of termination politics, why discontinuance is rarely attempted, and the conditions facilitating cessation have been addressed. If for no other reason, research efforts are pursued on the assumption that "it is precisely the rarity of the phenomenon that makes it important."[39] Other evidence suggests, however, that policy termination is not as rare as the infrequency of its study indicates.

Current trends in some public sectors indicate the growing incidence of policy termination. For example, inflationary pressures working in tandem with concerted efforts to reduce public spending and taxation are contracting government revenue bases. Declining revenues indicate the prospect, and in many cases the necessity, of terminating established policies and programs.

Development of nonincremental approaches to policy making and resource allocation attest to the significance of termination phenomena. The attractiveness of management technologies such as zero-based budgeting and sunset legislation can be explained in part because they facilitate the management of decline by establishing decision priorities and routinizing policy review and termination. These techniques are accompanied by calls to increase productivity and develop "cutback management" skills.[40]

Growing awareness of the incidence of policy termination has contributed, in some circles, to the reassessment of dominant theories. In his appraisal of organization theory, William Scott concludes that the common denominator of various theories about organization processes is the assumption of growth and expansion.[41] Taking his cue from Scott's proposition, Charles H. Levine states that "public management strategies are predicated on the assumptions of continuing enlargement of public revenues and expenditures."[42] Consequently, "management and policy paradigms will have to be replaced or augmented by new frameworks" that take into account "the reality of zero growth and absolute decline."[43] In other words, the incidence of policy termination is forcing management theorists to confront cutback and decremental planning situations which in turn point out the deficiencies, if not the basic fallacies, of prevailing theoretical assumptions.

Studies of the regulatory process parallel the trends emphasized in other policy areas. Much of the literature on regulation focuses on the conditions associated with intervention and the problems associated with the administration of regulatory policies and not their termination. By the 1960s, a protectionist or "capture" interpretation of regulatory politics dominated much of the thinking about the regulatory process. This perspective stems from a research tradition primarily concerned with investigating the phenomenal expansion in regulatory intervention by the national government during this century. "Capture," "iron triangles," and a "propensity to regulate" offered convenient shorthand explanations for a regulatory environment characterized by the expansion and perpetuation of traditional regulatory controls. Consequently, the phenomenon of deregulation did not receive systematic attention.[44] It was a non-event and virtually not an issue, in that regulatory reforms proceeded from the basic assumption that regulation was the appropriate means for solving economic and social problems. The direction of incremental change in the existing system, rather than termination, was the object of study and the issue in reform politics.

Recent developments in regulatory reform, however, question the utility of traditional interpretations of regulatory politics. Agitation for regulatory reform increased during the 1970s. One of the most unusual features of the reform movement was the popularity of deregulation as a reform alternative. In some regulated sectors, attention of policy makers turned from the traditional task of modifying regulatory systems to a search for alternatives to direct control by administrative agent. There was growing political support for the view that dissatisfaction with regulatory policies could only be remedied by terminating administrative regulation itself rather than by attempting to perfect that which is imperfectible.

In sum, the reform of airline regulation adopted in 1978 raises theoretical issues simply because of the type of policy change mandated by the legislation, i.e., deregulation. One would expect, given the traditionally accepted trends of regulatory growth, expansion, and perpetuation of existing policies, that any attempt to deregulate the airline industry would fail. However, overwhelming support for deregulation developed by 1978.

The Political Dynamics of Deregulation

Certain characteristics of the airline case challenge two other commonly accepted propositions about the political dynamics of seeking a major policy change. The first proposition concerns the bargaining process leading to formal adoption of the policy change. The second concerns the behavior of the regulatory agent in that process when the policy change calls for deregulation.

Many analyses of policy making subscribe to an incremental model of the process.[45] Incrementalism emphasizes the necessity of compromise. As a result of the bargaining process, policy innovators achieve a degree of change, but not as much as originally sought. Concessions must be made and bargains struck during the policy process in order to achieve legitimate policy change. As a result, provisions in a policy proposal that depart from established courses of action are compromised and moderated in order to mollify the opposition and enhance the possibilities of at least some degree of policy change. In sum, it is commonly presumed that the initial proposal will be more radical, as measured by the degree it differs from existing policy, then the policy change finally adopted, assuming the proposal for change succeeds.

Support for deregulation in the airline case, however, accelerated rather than diminished as policy makers grappled with the issue. Initially, legislative proposals only advocated relaxing the application of regulation by limiting the Board's authority to regulate airline routes and rates. Termination of direct controls and abolition of the CAB were not proposed. Deregulation was not included in legislative proposals until very late in the reform process. In this sense, the reform process escalated, progressing from a proposal to curtail regulatory control to one mandating its termination.

Another feature of the policy process commonly emphasized in treatments of regulatory politics concerns the role of the regulatory agent. A common presumption is that the regulated group has significant political resources which are used to control the behavior

of the regulatory agent. It is assumed that the actions of the regulators mirror the policy preferences of the regulated group. A variety
of reasons are generally given for the propensity of the regulator to
avoid taking positions that risk alienation of the regulated group.
Some attribute the beneficient behavior of the regulator to its
legislative mandate, others to organizational senility, and still
others attribute capture to agency dependence on the regulated
group for political support.[46] More current perspectives offered by
political economists attribute regulator-regulated collaboration to
rational self-interest, which includes the desire of regulators to
maintain the stability and survival of their agency.[47]

The CAB's performance between 1975 and 1978, however,
violated much of the conventional wisdom about the behavior of
regulatory agents. The proposition that bureaucratic behavior is
motivated by organizational survival was challenged as the CAB
became progressively committed to the idea of deregulation. Board
support for deregulation presented the unusual spectacle of administrative officials advocating reductions in their agency's authority.
The agency pursued policies in 1978 that were antithetical to its
traditional mission. On its own initiative, the CAB implemented
policies that resulted in some defacto deregulation undermining the
source of the Board's reason for existence. Furthermore, the
Board's support for deregulation and its policies promoting it were
pursued over the objections of its regulated clientele, violating the
presumption of regulator-regulated collaboration.

Traditional perspectives on regulatory politics do not easily
accommodate the deregulation movement of the 1970s. As one
commentator noted, "According to the political science of regulation, this movement for deregulation simply shouldn't exist."[48]
Furthermore, the behavior of parties to the regulatory scheme
violated many of the premises and corollary hypotheses of the
dominant "theory" of regulatory politics. The Airline Deregulation
Act of 1978 and the politics culminating in its passage challenge the
traditional paradigm of regulatory politics.

ORGANIZATION OF STUDY

Several arguments raised in the above discussion of the historical
and theoretical significance of airline deregulation will serve to

organize the chapters that follow. First, the argument that the 1978 changes in the regulation of commercial aviation reflect a significant shift in regulatory reform is elaborated in chapter 2. Regulation and deregulation are defined by differentiating between regulatory and nonregulatory forms of government intervention. Deregulation is then considered as one of three major types of regulatory reform. A survey of reform trends in the 1970s suggests variations in the adoption of incremental, decremental, and terminal types of regulatory reform. Finally, the implications for treating deregulation as a termination policy will be examined. Chapter 2 concludes with a discussion of the concept "deregulation strategy" and its usefulness in analyzing the adoption of deregulation.

Chapters 3 and 4 focus on the policies and dynamics of airline regulation from 1938 until 1970, shortly before the move to deregulate began to develop. In chapter 3, the argument that alterations in the regulatory framework developed incrementally during the three decades of CAB regulation is more fully developed. This includes a description of the Board's authority, regulatory instruments, and legislative mandate. Attention is then given in chapter 4 to policy trends in CAB regulation. A variability in CAB policy toward competition among airline firms is identified in the course of describing how the Board implemented regulatory control during the 1938–1970 period. The CAB restrictions on airline competition fluctuated with the financial condition of the major air carriers. In late 1969, the agency began returning to the anticompetitive phase of the regulatory cycle.

The significance of the regulatory policy cycle for the deregulation movement is discussed in the first part of chapter 5. Reform agitation coincided with CAB restrictions on carrier competition. Policies designed to stabilize the industry proved politically unpopular, damaging the credibility of the regulatory agent and enhancing the prospects for deregulation. The chapter is more generally concerned with the chronology of the airline deregulation movement. Critical junctures in the reform process from 1970 until passage of the legislation in 1978 are described. The adoption process proceeded from a relatively modest to a stronger, more deregulation-oriented bill than that originally proposed in 1975.

Analysis of the airline deregulation process is continued in chapter 6. The factors contributing to the escalation of support for deregulation and the methods used to counteract opposition to airline deregulation are examined. Events chronologically presented in the previous chapter are analyzed from the perspective of political strategies and conditions that enhanced their effectiveness. Six distinct deregulation strategies associated with adoption of regulatory reform are discussed and illustrated.

Chapter 7 concludes the study by analyzing the theoretical implications of the deregulation process for the analysis of regulatory policy making. The argument developed in the chapter is that traditional characterizations of the regulatory process represented by "capture theory" and characterizations of the regulatory process illustrated by deregulation politics and the earlier "public interest" view of regulation reflect two contradictory dimensions of the same process. Both perspectives are necessary to an adequate understanding of the regulatory process. What is required is a framework or approach to the analysis of regulatory politics that provides for the integration of the two dimensions of regulatory behavior. The concept of strategic behavior is discussed as such an integrating approach.

2 | Regulatory Reform and Deregulation

INTRODUCTION

The unique character of contemporary regulatory reform is related to a major issue in regulatory policy making—the scope of regulatory intervention. In other respects, agitation for reform in the 1970s was not substantively different from past efforts. For example, the traditional problems of insuring equitable and efficient administration of regulatory authority were the impetus for many reform proposals during the decade and into the 1980s. A more fundamental question, however, dominated much of the reform debate in the 1970s: What private decisions should be subject to review and control by government agencies? Attention to the appropriateness of regulatory intervention sets contemporary regulatory reform apart from previous periods which were preoccupied with problems of regulatory administration.

More importantly, proposals to terminate regulatory intervention in some areas were adopted, prompting some to characterize the current reform movement as the "revolution that occurred in federal regulation."[1] Efforts to deregulate were most successful in the field of economic regulation. Commercial aviation was only one of several industries affected by the deregulation movement. Reforms also were adopted in the securities, banking, energy, communications, railroad, bus, and trucking industries, all of which reduced and, in some cases, removed traditional regulatory controls.[2]

REGULATION AND DEREGULATION

In order to understand what deregulation means when applied to the airline case, the more general question of what constitutes deregulation and how it differs from other types of regulatory reform is important. The definition of regulation and deregulation used in subsequent chapters is based upon a distinction between regulatory and nonregulatory forms of government intervention.

There is much variety in the literature regarding the meaning of regulation and deregulation. For example, Mel Dubnick and Alen Gitelson identify five "definitions in use" for regulation.[3] In some cases, regulation is simply equated with governmental activity of any sort. Others define regulation in terms of the subjects being regulated—such as polluters, natural monopolies, or essential service industries like transportation. Regulation is also described in terms of what the regulatory agent does. Other analysts view regulation as one of several strategies used to alter the behavior of individuals or organizations. Finally, there are functional definitions in which regulation is viewed as the performance of activities that are considered to be regulatory in character—regulation is price control, licensing, and so on.

Those seeking a definition of deregulation confront a similar variety of meanings. Barry Mitnick notes that the concept is defined with respect to the stated purpose or intended consequences of deregulation; the type of activity which is to be deregulated; the object to be removed in order to effect deregulation such as a specific program, regulation, or organization; or factors contributing to de facto deregulation such as lax enforcement.[4]

Much of the controversy and subsequent confusion about the meaning of deregulation in the 1970s can be traced to definitions of the concept based on the intended consequence of deregulation. For example, Herman notes in his analysis of deregulation efforts in the 1970s that "one set of interests, generally represented by industry, means by 'deregulation' the removal of government obstacles to profit making. . . . The other set of interests, generally represented by economists, means by 'deregulation' the removal of governmental and other obstacles to price competition. . . ."[5] Even economists have difficulty agreeing on a definition of deregulation because of "an inability to choose between the proposition that deregulation would produce more competition, and the more obvious proposition that deregulation would produce a closer approximation to laissez-faire."[6]

Defining deregulation in terms of its intended consequences introduces strong ideological connotations that make it difficult to use the term for analytical purposes. A more useful definition of deregulation can be formulated by asking a different question. The question is *termination of what?* instead of *termination for what purpose?* This approach is functional and requires defining regulation by specifying the tools or instruments of regulation and differentiating them from other forms of government intervention in private relationships. Deregulation can then be defined as the termination of a specific method of control.

Regulation Defined

Both Alan Stone and Barry Mitnick offer general definitions of regulation which serve as the basis for the definitions of regulation and deregulation used in this study. Stone defines regulation as "a state-imposed limitation on the discretion which may be exercised by individuals or organizations, which is supported by the threat of sanction."[7] Mitnick's definition also stresses restrictions imposed on the discretion of parties subject to regulation. "Regulation is a process consisting of the intentional restriction of a subject's choice of activity, by an entity not directly party to or involved in that activity."[8] Deregulation can be broadly defined as "the removal of such a choice restriction."[9]

The definitions are made more specific by identifying the means that are used to restrict discretion. Stephen Breyer refers to these means as "classical regulation" or "forms" of regulatory activity.[10] Emmette Redford refers to them as "substantive types of regulatory action."[11] In the following discussion, the means used to restrict the discretion of regulated firms are referred to as regulatory instruments. Each instrument is classified under one of the following categories: (1) price controls, (2) production controls, or (3) standard controls.[12]

Price controls include cost-of-service rate making and historically based price regulation. Under the cost-of-service approach, the regulatory agency estimates the firm's operating and capital costs and allows the firm to set prices adequate to cover costs. Historically based price regulation restricts firms to the prices charged at some point in the past.

Production controls involve the allocation of the right of an individual or firm to provide a good or service. One method of allocation is licensing or granting a certificate of convenience and necessity. Applicants satisfying a minimum set of standards compete for the right to provide a good or service. The regulatory agent awards a license to one or more of the competing applicants, usually after a comparative hearing.[13] Historical use is another method for allocating goods and services. The standard for determining whether an individual or firm should have the right to receive or deliver a good or service is based on historical delivery or receipt patterns and not qualification standards.

Finally, standard controls involve the application of standards to guide the conduct, operation, or service of regulated firms. This method is most characteristic of health, environment, and safety regulation. Standards are formulated and the regulated entity is monitored for compliance. Standard setting also may be used to supervise individual or organizational practices relating to financial matters. In this case, it involves the prescription of specific reporting and accounting practices. Limitations may also be extended to financial relationships with other organizations or individuals regarding such matters as stock issues, mergers, or acquisitions. Individualized screening is another method for standards control. It is used in situations where it is difficult to formulate precise standards, and case-by-case scrutiny by the regulatory agent becomes necessary. Examples include the licensing of professionals, drugs, food additives, and pesticides.

Classical modes of regulation are commonly referred to as "administrative," "direct," "positive," "hands-on," "public-utility type," or "command-and-control" regulation. Emmette Redford defines regulation as "a system in which public authorities stand above private management to restrain or direct its actions. It is a system which concentrates certain decisions and activities in public agencies and leaves the remainder to private directorates."[14] Classical regulation stresses the prevention of potential problems.[15]

Private management is required to receive administrative clearance before taking certain actions, and the agency is usually granted broad discretion to implement corrective measures and supervise an industry or an aspect of its operation.

Alternatives to Regulation

It is important to recognize that regulation is only one form of government intervention. Like all forms, the purpose of regulation is to alter the behavior of individuals or organizations. However, regulation differs from other forms of government intervention in the means it employs to alter behavior. The distinguishing feature of regulatory intervention is its ultimate reliance on coercion.[16] Regulation prescribes or proscribes certain behavior, and these directives are backed by sanctions. In contrast, nonregulatory forms of government intervention are relatively noncoercive. The distinction can be illustrated by identifying the alternatives to regulation.

Interventionist alternatives to regulation are (1) antitrust enforcement, (2) information disclosure, (3) taxes and subsidies, (4) market-based incentives and allocation, (5) bargaining, (6) liability rules and private litigation, and (7) public ownership or nationalization.[17] Antitrust enforcement is sometimes considered a form of regulatory intervention. However, here it is treated as an alternative because antitrust enforcement seeks to achieve the conditions of a competitive marketplace, whereas regulatory intervention seeks to replicate the results of competition or correct for its defects. Public utility regulation employing several of the instruments previously discussed is the traditional response to natural monopolies or industries in which the production of goods or services is done most efficiently by one firm. On the other hand, antitrust is designed primarily to preserve competition in industries that are already structurally competitive.

Information disclosure is an alternative to regulatory intervention because it does not restrict the influence of individual choice in the marketplace. Like antitrust enforcement, it is intended to bolster market competition but does so by enhancing the rationality of consumer choice. It does not dictate behavior beyond that of providing information.

Taxes and subsidies are common forms of intervention different from regulation. Manipulation of the tax structure, including the use of special deductions and credits, can be employed to discourage undesirable behavior or to recapture or prevent windfall or monopoly profits. Subsidies provide for direct payments usually to insure provision of desirable goods and services that would not be adequately provided under normal market conditions. Taxes and subsidies are nonregulatory interventions because they do not prohibit the right to engage or not to engage in an activity. Rather, they make it more or less profitable.

A market-based form of intervention is another alternative to regulation. It first limits the level of an activity and then awards the right to engage in the activity on a competitive basis. Such an approach frequently utilizes lotteries or auctions to allocate among competitors the right to engage in an activity. A variation of this approach was adopted by the Environmental Protection Agency in 1979. Some polluting firms were allowed to bank their right to pollute for later use if their current pollution levels were below permissible emissions. The approach also is commonly used to allocate hunting rights. Sportsmen seeking the right to participate in limited hunts on state or federal lands are selected by lottery.

Bargaining relies on negotiations between private parties to reach agreements about appropriate behavior. It avoids the adversarial or directive character of regulation. Intervention based on bargaining is limited to setting parameters around the negotiation process but stops short of dictating the outcome of the process. Examples include minimum wage and labor legislation and restrictions against discriminatory contracts and agreements.

Private litigation and reliance on liability rules represent another alternative to regulatory intervention. The assumption underlying this approach is that undesirable behavior such as the production of unsafe products or of environmental pollution can be discouraged by increasing the risk of liability. Such an approach relies on the judicial system and tort law to regulate behavior.

Finally, public ownership represents an alternative to regulation. Regulatory intervention can be viewed as a compromise between the extremes of nonintervention (laissez-faire) and nationalization. The latter is not a popular alternative in the United States. However, arguments are sometimes made for the nationalization of infrastructure services such as energy on the grounds that it would eliminate the adversarial relationship between regulator and firm.

All of the above represent alternatives to regulatory intervention. Frequently they are referred to as "indirect" or "hands-off" forms of government intervention. As these terms imply, the methods are considered less restrictive than direct regulation. Managerial decision making is not shared with an administrative agency, and private management is afforded greater discretion in complying with public policy goals. Control is exercised post facto, frequently through court litigation, rather than a priori through administrative clearance.

Deregulation Defined

Specification of the common forms of regulatory intervention and alternative interventionist methods that are nonregulatory provides the basis for a definition of deregulation. In the following analysis of regulatory reform in commercial aviation, deregulation is defined as the simultaneous termination of a regulatory instrument and adoption of a nonregulatory form of intervention. In this sense, deregulation is both an end and a beginning. Put another way, deregulation is the transfer of governmental control over a subject or activity from a control regime dominated by regulatory instruments to a regime that relies on nonregulatory methods of control. This definition rejects the view that deregulation is the termination of all forms of government intervention in an area subject to public control, a definition implying that the opposite of regulation is laissez-faire. The termination of one type of control does not result in the discontinuance of all other modes of governmental restraint on private actions.[18] For example, the lifting of oil price controls did not exempt petroleum companies from antitrust restrictions on collusive pricing practices.

The view that deregulation involves the transfer of control to a different interventionist regime also was suggested by the character of the deregulation debate in the 1970s. The debate was less concerned with the legitimacy of public control over the undesirable consequences of private actions than with the appropriate means for controlling those consequences.[19] More specifically, the issue of

deregulation centered on the appropriateness of regulatory controls. The arguments for deregulation of specific industries suggested that the real alternative to direct regulation was antitrust
enforcement and not laissez-faire.[20] Proposals for environmental,
health, and safety deregulation generally called for replacing the
system under which the government set standards for industry with
noncoercive alternatives such as the provision of economic incentives, rather than simply terminating government action in these
problem areas.

CONTEMPORARY REGULATORY REFORM

In order to sort out the complexities of contemporary reform activism, it is useful first to identify the types of regulatory reform that
were proposed and legislated during the period. They can be characterized as incremental, decremental, and terminal or deregulatory. Previously, deregulation was treated in relation to alternate
forms of government intervention. Here it is viewed as one of three
types of regulatory reform. Deregulation can be distinguished from
incremental and decremental modes of regulatory reform because,
unlike them, it prescribes the termination of regulatory intervention and not simply its modification. The reform types lie on a
continuum between the extremes of laissez-faire and nationalization.

Incrementalism, Decrementalism, and Deregulation

Incremental reform prescribes procedural and organizational solutions to remedy regulatory problems. It enhances the authority of
the regulatory agency either by increasing the agency's discretion
and flexibility in the application of its regulatory instruments or by
expanding the activities or subjects under its jurisdiction.

Reforms that are incremental are usually justified in terms of
what Roger Noll calls an "error by incompetence" view of regulation. This view attributes imperfections in regulation to "externally
imposed difficulties such as coercion by politicians, improper structure of the agency, a bad legislative mandate, inadequate means for
obtaining information, general political support, and coordination

with other agencies."[21] Accordingly, proponents of the "error by incompetence" view prescribe procedural and organizational solutions for regulatory problems.

In contrast, reform through deregulation is based on a very different approach. The major premise of proponents of deregulation is that regulation itself and not its maladministration is the source of regulatory problems. Deregulation advocates adopt an "error by design" explanation that assumes that "inherent in the regulatory process is a persistent tendency to make socially undesirable policy."[22] Procedural and organizational correctives cannot improve the equity and efficiency of the regulatory process because incremental reforms do not attack the root cause of regulatory problems. Inefficient and inequitable regulation can only be remedied through the termination of regulatory intervention, according to this approach. Indirect modes of control such as economic incentives are promoted as more effective methods for addressing economic and social problems.

Finally, decremental reforms move in the direction of deregulation but stop short of terminating regulatory instruments and adopting nonregulatory forms of intervention. Decremental reform has the effect of reducing the authority of the regulatory agent by restricting its discretion and flexibility in the application of regulatory instruments. Regulatory functions are left intact, but the conditions that trigger their operation are limited. An example of decremental reform was the adoption of a "zone of reasonableness" to guide rate regulation by the CAB during the transition to airline rate deregulation. The CAB was prohibited from intervening to block or influence rate changes by air carriers so long as the new rates fell within a specified range. The Board retained its authority to regulate rates, but its opportunity to exercise that authority was limited.

Reform Orientations

In addition to specific types of regulatory reform, it is also helpful to distinguish among different reform orientations or paradigms at work in the 1970s. David Welborn identifies three that were evident in the reform movement. He refers to them as traditionalist, populist, and restrictivist orientations toward reform.[23]

Incremental reform is most frequently associated with a traditionalist view of regulation. This view is based on the assumption that regulatory instruments are viable and appropriate means for controlling social and economic problems and that effective remediation of public problems is possible through efficient and equitable administration of regulation. Regulatory problems are attributed to deficiencies in the implementation of regulatory instruments, not in the instruments themselves. Consequently, reforms advocated by traditionalists tend to be incremental in that they represent adjustments to or extensions of regulation rather than its replacement with nonregulatory controls.

Both deregulation and decremental reform prescriptions are most closely associated with a restrictivist orientation. Proposals including deregulation, the substitution of economic incentives for administrative controls, and the application of economic rationality to regulatory decision making are the hallmarks of the restrictivist position. Restrictivists are philosophically opposed to regulatory intervention and, on economic grounds, view it as a poor substitute for alternative forms of intervention that more closely approximate a free market model.

A third and final reform orientation identified by Welborn is the populist. It is distinguished by its suspicion of corporate power. Regulation is advocated and supported if it appears to favor the consumer and advances desirable social goals. It is opposed if regulatory controls are seen as aiding corporate interests. Consequently, populists are not as consistently aligned with one of the three types of regulatory reform. In some cases they advocate deregulation or decremental reform while incremental reforms are prescribed elsewhere.

Social Versus Economic Regulation

During the 1970s, the incidence of terminal, incremental, and decremental reforms was not uniform across regulated sectors. Irregularities in the incidence of deregulation can be explained in part by distinguishing between regulation of the economic and that of the social type.[24] The distinction also is useful in understanding the mix of reform orientations and their relationship to reform prescriptions of the 1970s.

James Landis provided an early elaboration of the distinction between social and economic regulation in his discussion of promotion and policing types of administrative agencies.[25] He concluded that agencies are primarily related to a specific industry in one of two ways. Some agencies are charged with the supervision of a specific industry, whereas others perform a policing function across industries. Landis referred to supervisory agencies as promotional in character because they are typically made responsible for the economic welfare and development of an industry.

Landis viewed the activities of agencies such as the Federal Trade Commission and the National Labor Relations Board as examples of policing regulation. Agency jurisdiction of the policing type relates less to a single industry than to an activity or problem that cuts across a vast number of businesses and occupations. Agencies responsible for regulating problems such as environmental pollution are primarily engaged in a policing function rather than in promoting the orderly economic development of a specific industry.

A variety of other terms have been used to refer to Landis' distinction between promotional and policing regulation. Synonyms for his definition of promotional regulation include "economic," "cartel," "old-style," and "vertical" regulation. Other terms for the policing type are "product-process," "social," "consumer," "new-style," and "horizontal" regulation.

Environmental, health, and safety regulation fall into the social category. Social regulation focuses on the conditions under which goods and services are produced. The common regulatory instruments are standard setting and enforcement, and the agency is granted discretion to formulate specific standards through rule-making procedures. Jurisdiction is described as horizontal because agencies are organized along functional lines with their rules and regulations applied across industries. Regulatory authority is limited to that segment of a firm's operations that fall under the agency's jurisdiction such as safety in the work place.

Economic regulation encompasses the more traditional agencies such as the Interstate Commerce Commission, Federal Maritime Commission, and the Civil Aeronautics Board. The agency usually is granted direct control over industry rates and prices, certification and licensing of firms in the industry, and their financial practices. Economic regulation is vertically oriented in that agencies are organized by industry rather than across industries. Their authority extends to several operations of an industry and is not limited to one as in social regulation.

Industries subject to economic regulation can be placed into two categories. First are the natural monopoly industries, which are commonly referred to as public utilities. They include the natural gas, electric, and telephone industries. Typically, only one firm is authorized to provide the service to an area because competitive provision of the services would be highly inefficient and costly. On the other hand, other industries are considered to be structurally competitive in that a large number of firms are in the industry and they do not have the high fixed capital costs of public utilities. Nonetheless, they are subjected to economic regulation because they provide essential services. The transportation and banking industries are included in this category.

Variations in Reform Proposals

Differences in social and economic regulation help to explain the variation in reform prescriptions proposed during the 1970s. Table I presents the types of regulatory reforms according to reform orientation and type of regulation.

In the 1970s, traditionalists were more consistent in their prescription for incremental changes in regulation. Regardless of whether the object of reform was economic or social regulation, they emphasized the need for continual improvement in the regulatory process. In contrast, both restrictivist and populist reformers varied their prescriptions according to the type of regulation under consideration. Both restrictivists and populists advocated deregulation of structurally competitive industries, such as airline and trucking, in opposition to traditionalists who argued for continued regulation with reforms limited to procedural aspects of regulation. On the other hand, traditionalists and populists allied against restrictivists on the issue of social regulation. While the former advocated expanding and reinforcing health, safety, and environmental regulation, restrictivists argued for alternatives such as tax incentives or at least for less agency discretion in the setting of standards.

Table I also illustrates the unique and not so unique character of regulatory reform in the 1970s. The influence, and in some areas the dominance, of incremental reform suggests that contemporary de-

Table 1 Types of Regulatory Reform Proposals in the 1970s According to Type of Regulation and Reform Orientation

	Type of Regulation		
	Economic		*Social*
	Structurally Competitive Industries	*Natural Monopoly Industries (Public Utilities)*	
Reform Orientation:			
Traditionalist	Incremental	Incremental	Incremental
Restrictivist	Deregulation	Incremental	Decremental
Populist	Deregulation	Incremental	Incremental

Source: The table was developed from information presented in David M. Welborn, "Taking Stock in Regulatory Reform," paper presented at the annual meeting of the American Political Science Association, Washington, D.C., Sept. 1977; and David R. Berman, "Consumerism and the Regulatory System: Paradigms of Reform," *Policy Studies Review* 1, no. 3 (Feb. 1982): 454–62.

velopments are not significantly different from previous reform episodes. However, the impact of populist and especially restrictivist orientations suggest that the decade of the 1970s may be viewed in the future as a watershed in the development of national regulatory policy.

A Historical Perspective

Historically, major reform proposals as well as modifications in the national regulatory structure have been guided primarily by a traditionalist orientation and dominated by incremental reforms.[26] For the most part, statutory reforms and proposals to improve the equity of the regulatory process, increase administrative efficiency, and alter the scope of regulation assumed the viability of, or at least the lack of significant opposition to, regulation. Many changes in the regulatory process that occurred during the 1970s reflect a continuation of this trend.[27]

In the history of national regulation, the earliest and most comprehensive reforms concerned the equity of regulatory decision making. Administrative procedural due process became an important issue following the assumption of expanded regulatory responsibilities and the concurrent growth of national regulatory agencies in the early decades of the 1900s. The Administrative Procedure Act of 1946 became the hallmark of reform efforts to judicialize the regulatory process. In the 1970s, restrictions on the relationship between agency officials and regulated groups as well as procedural and organizational modifications affecting access to and control over agency decision making were part of the on-going efforts to improve the fairness and impartiality of direct regulation without terminating the same.

Writing in the early 1960s, Emmette Redford noted "a shift from the movement toward further judicialization to interest in simplification, expedition, and use of expert aid."[28] First the Landis and then the Ash Council Reports proposed reform programs aimed at improving regulatory efficiency. Reformers seeking to improve the managerial efficiency of regulatory programs were reacting in part to earlier reforms that judicialized the regulatory process. They assumed that the regulatory process could be improved through such measures as hiring more competent and specialized agency personnel, clarifying agency standards and policies, and instituting a more definite separation between the judicial and policy functions of the agency, and more centralized management control over agency decisions.

Many reform proposals considered in the 1970s reflected the traditional concern of reformers for improving the efficiency of regulatory agency management and procedures. Particular attention was given to the problem of regulatory lag or delays in administrative decision making. Consequently, some reforms were designed to expedite agency procedures. Incremental reform intended to enhance regulatory efficiency also came in the guise of increased presidential oversight. Mechanisms first implemented during the Ford administration were refined and expanded under the Carter presidency. Regulators were required to submit their own version of an environmental impact statement to justify their regulations. The Regulatory Analysis Review Group was created under Carter and authorized to review and veto proposed regulations. Also, a Regulatory Council was created and made responsible for coordinating the activities of thirty-five regulatory agencies in the executive branch.[29]

In the 1970s, however, the list of incremental reforms intended to improve equity and efficiency in regulatory administration was expanded to include the rationalization of agency decision making in accordance with economic criteria. Economists, in particular, argued that "objective" regulatory decisions should be sought through the application of cost-effective and cost-benefit analysis to agency rule-making procedures.[30] Agencies involved in setting standards for health, safety, and environment regulation were the principal targets of such reform. However, the primary thrust of change was toward improving the application of regulatory instruments (standard setting) and not deregulation.

Opponents of cost-benefit analysis viewed it as an attempt to subvert regulation on the part of groups that opposed government intervention in business affairs. The debate and controversy surrounding cost-benefit analysis in the 1970s was strikingly similar to earlier debates over proposals to judicialize or improve the efficiency of agency procedures. In earlier reform periods, those supporting the need for regulatory intervention distrusted the motivations of so-called reformers. They suspected that efforts to judicialize or expedite regulatory administration were actually veiled attempts to curtail government regulation.[31]

An incremental approach is also evident in traditional responses to the question of what the scope of government regulation should be. Historically, the question of what means are most appropriate for attacking social and economic problems has been decided in favor of regulation. The tendency is "to deal with the continuing shortcomings and dissatisfactions with the business system by further government involvement in economic activity."[32] Social and economic regulators such as the Interstate Commerce Commission (1887), Food and Drug Administration (1906), and Federal Trade Commission (1914) were followed in the 1930s by the proliferation of regulatory agencies such as the Federal Communications Commission (1934), Securities and Exchange Commission (1934), Federal Maritime Commission (1936), and Civil Aeronautics Board (1938).

In the 1970s, a third wave of regulatory expansion and consolidation occurred in the fields of health, safety, and environmental quality. Creation of agencies such as the Consumer Product Safety Commission (1972), Environmental Protection Agency (1970), and Occupational Safety and Health Administration (1971) testified to the continuation of the belief that regulation was an appropriate means for controlling social and economic problems.

It is also in regard to the issue of scope that decremental and deregulatory prescriptions for reform are most relevant. In the 1970s, the issue was not resolved entirely in favor of expanding and consolidating direct regulation. Academic and administration economists were the principal advocates of deregulation and relaxation of regulatory controls. Influenced by the Chicago School of economic theory,[33] some economists cast their argument for reform in a microeconomic paradigm that stressed the application of cost-benefit analysis to regulatory policy and the search for more cost-efficient methods for achieving policy goals.[34] Economists as well as other opponents of regulation applied these criteria to argue that regulation was costly, arbitrary, inflexible, and in some cases unnecessary.

Restrictivists came closest in the 1970s to having their proposals for deregulation adopted as policy in the field of economic regulation. Congress and several regulatory agencies adopted policies that restricted the use of regulatory instruments or, as in the case of civil aviation, specified dates for their termination.

Proposals for deregulation were not seriously considered in most policy discussions or actions regarding social regulation. The replacement of standard setting with alternatives to regulation such as economic incentives was not vigorously pursued. Both the Ford and Carter administrations adopted a safer political strategy for reforming social regulation, stressing better management of regulation through strengthened presidential oversight and the use of cost-benefit analysis.[35]

Deregulation efforts also were restricted to regulated industries considered to be structurally competitive. The rule, as stated by one economist, was: "When any industry or economic activity can be as effectively regulated by competitive forces as those industries or activities we now leave to competitive regulation under antitrust, the case for public control over rates and entry and exit disappear."[36] Conventional public utilities did not fall under this rule, and no strong case for their deregulation was made. Reform was limited to changing methods of rate regulation and making other adjustments in the existing regulatory apparatus.[37]

In "competitive" regulated industries such as transportation, economists maintained that regulation "constitutes a form of protection for existing firms in an industry and serves as a barrier to the entry of new firms. Entrenched firms are thus shielded from new competition."[38] Regulation was criticized because "the vigorous competition antitrust policy has sought to foster in the economy is precisely the sort of competition public regulation has been designed to prevent."[39]

Populists joined with economists of the restrictivist persuasion in arguing for the deregulation of competitive industries such as commercial aviation. However, while economists objected to regulation because it fostered restrictions on competition, populists objected on the grounds that it violated a public obligation. As one consumer advocate testified regarding airline regulation: "Economic regulation has become a disease, insidiously destroying the long term potential of the air transportation industry, the affordability of air travel by a large majority of the population, and the faith of citizens in their government."[40] From the populist view, regulation is the use of government authority to protect and further corporate interests at the expense of the general public.[41]

Whether advocated by restrictivists or populists, deregulation only meant the termination of "protective" regulation and not the discontinuance of all forms of intervention. Regulation would be replaced with litigation, according to their proposals, and a policy of deregulation would "dismantle the apparatus regulating entry and prices in nonmonopolistic industries and reassign them to governance by antitrust."[42] Under an antitrust regime, control would be exercised "by a forum that is completely outside the traditional bilateral relationships between the industry and the agency. . . . Suddenly competitive policy decisions are going to be made by judges and not by regulators."[43]

DEREGULATION AND THE ADOPTION PROCESS

Deregulation also is a policy. Unlike other policy proposals that call for the creation of new programs, deregulation proposals prescribe the removal of existing programs and organizations. Because it is a termination policy, formidable obstacles lie in the path of those seeking adoption of deregulation.

The politics of deregulation can be viewed as a special case of the process of policy adoption. As Barry Mitnick explains: "Deregulation of a policy, program, agency, and so on, is itself a policy that must reach an institutional agenda, be subject to decision on that agenda, and experience implementation."[44] Deregulation is also "a policy about a policy"[45] in that its substance entails the elimination of another policy. As suggested in chapter 1, deregulation can be viewed as a termination policy—a policy designed to terminate another policy.

The infrequency of planned and deliberate terminations of national programs and agencies usually is blamed on the strongly resistant and conservative pressures at work in the policy process. The incremental character of political decision making is used to explain why it is difficult to achieve much beyond modest changes in established policy areas. Walter Rosenbaum, in discussing reform of environmental regulatory policy, comments that, "especially for the reformer, incrementalism is frequently a cross to bear because the demand for reform is almost always a demand to alter the status quo in ways costly to vested interests."[46]

Obstacles to Deregulation

Since deregulation prescribes policy termination, its proponents must maneuver around obstacles similar to those that threaten the acceptance of termination policies in general. Peter deLeon suggests six reasons why policy termination is particularly difficult to plan and execute in the policy arena. He defines them as (1) intellectual reluctance, (2) institutional permanence, (3) dynamic situation, (4) anti-termination coalitions, (5) legal obstacles, and (6) high start-up costs.[47] For these reasons, the political act of policy termination is extremely difficult to achieve.

The notion that "intellectual reluctance" constitutes an obstacle is based on the assumption that people are reluctant to recognize policy deficiencies. To do so would force the individual to pursue the often distasteful and painful task of dismantling a program or abandoning a policy. DeLeon's point can be elaborated by noting the uncertainty associated with termination. Policy continuance means the avoidance of the unanticipated reverberations of terminating the incumbent policy itself as well as the possible unintended consequences and problems created by the new policy which replaces the old.

Both "institutional permanence" and "dynamic situation" as impediments to policy termination are based on the premise that survival is the dominant bureaucratic imperative. The notion of institutional permanence is based on the assumption that government organizations are designed to survive because they represent the institutionalization of long-term service demands. In addition, organizations are dynamic and adaptive entities. Not only are organizations designed to resist termination, they can adapt to changing circumstances by altering their clientele, objectives, and policies. Adaptive strategies can undercut termination efforts based on the argument that the organization has outlived its usefulness. Furthermore, structural termination does not necessarily mean policy termination. For example, proponents of policy termination may be stymied by the transfer of the policy function to another organization.

A common reason cited for the failure of policy termination is the development of antitermination coalitions both within the agency itself and among groups affected by the incumbent policy. Opponents of termination within the agency will obstruct the proposal through procrastination, compromise, or simple refusal to accept it. Personnel may also call upon political allies outside the agency for protection. The same political maneuverings are used by opponents to block the creation of a new policy. However, opponents of policy termination are in an especially advantageous position in the politics of termination as opposed to the politics of initiation.

DeLeon offers two arguments to support the proposition that it is easier to obstruct a termination proposal than to attempt to create a new program or policy. First, termination opponents within the bureaucracy are well entrenched in that they have easy and regular access to powerful government allies. During the life of the organization, policy, or program, the administrators have had the opportunity to develop political allies who can be mobilized to oppose the termination proposal. Secondly, the supporters of policy continuance are in a stronger advocate position relative to termination proponents simply because they are receiving concrete benefits from the status quo. The threatened loss of benefits provides a tangible and easily understood focal point from which arguments can be developed and around which termination opponents can become organized. In contrast, those seeking to initiate a new policy through the termination of an established one can only lobby on the basis of expectations regarding the benefits of termination. In other words, the consequences of termination are frequently unknown quantities, and it may be difficult to obtain concrete examples to dispel the speculative aspects of the termination proposal. What is readily available to termination proponents is evidence of deficiencies in the incumbent policy. Consequently, the evidence that most strengthens the position of the advocate of policy termination is negative in character, e.g., the advocate can maintain that the incumbent policy fails in some respect or produces undesirable consequences. However, to promote a policy simply by critiquing the existing policy is generally not the most effective strategy for securing policy adoption. An acceptable alternative to the status quo must also be offered and promoted. It is in the pursuit of this task that termination proponents are most often at a disadvantage.

The problem of uncertainty confronting termination advocates may be ameliorated if there are precedents convincingly similar to the proposed termination to allow for comparisons and credible predictions about the probable consequences of discontinuing a particular policy. This was the case for airline deregulation because all-cargo air carriers had been deregulated in 1977, and there were airlines operating in Texas and California that were not regulated by the CAB. This point will be discussed further in chapter 5.

The two remaining obstacles to policy termination cited by deLeon are legal constraints and high start-up costs. Legal obstacles include restrictions on arbitrary and capricious actions and the emphasis placed on due process in the American policy process. Opponents of change often use the courts to block termination acts. Equity problems attend termination because of vested interests in the status quo.

Finally, the obstacles of intellectual reluctance, institutional permanence, dynamic situation, anti-termination coalitions, and legal constraints described above result collectively in high start-up costs for termination proponents. The obstacles to termination favor supporters of the status quo and place the burden of proof upon those who support major policy change. Considerable political and economic resources are necessary to overcome and redirect the momentum of an incumbent policy.

In sum, deLeon and others argue that the political actor seeking to terminate an existing policy or program confronts a unique set of obstacles that frustrates success. Implied if not stated in their arguments is the proposition that the process of policy, program, or organizational creation can be differentiated from the process of termination in that greater obstacles to change are inherent in the latter. The proposition is intuitively attractive but untested. Its verification would require an analysis comparing the political process culminating in policy terminations with the process associated with policy and institution creation. Such an analysis falls outside the scope of the current study. The purpose in the following pages is not to develop a theory of policy termination, rather, it is to explain how advocates of airline deregulation overcame the obstacles to policy termination. The analysis identifies patterns of behavior that emerged from the activities of various groups seeking adoption of the deregulation proposal. These behaviorial patterns are referred to as "deregulation strategies."

Deregulation Strategy

The concept of "deregulation strategy" is used in the following analysis of the airline case because it focuses on how deregulation proponents counteracted the obstacles to policy termination. In chapter 6, the adoption of airline deregulation and the synergistic character of the termination process is presented in terms of the effective use of termination strategies in conjunction with conditions enhancing their effectiveness. The approach resembles the traditional process-description approach to research on policy making and influence.[48]

A major task in researching the airline case was to determine who interacted with whom, in what manner, and with what consequences—a major feature of case descriptions of a decision process. However, the research goes beyond a simple case description by identifying "the devices used to move from conflict to conflict resolution."[49]

In this case, the "devices" for conflict resolution are the types of political behavior exhibited by deregulation advocates. In this study they are labeled deregulation strategies. An analysis of strategies goes beyond describing the coalitions in support and in opposition to deregulation and the rationales for their positions. Such a task, however, is prerequisite to answering the key question of how proponents of deregulation sought to develop support for their position. The question directs attention to the political behavior and conditions associated with a successful effort to marshal political support for a radical policy change.

Deregulation strategies refer to behavior aimed at building a coalition to support the termination of regulatory functions. Strategies are the behavioral patterns engaged in by deregulation advocates in order to resolve or manage conflicts with the opponents of deregulation and to counteract obstacles to deregulation. Strategies reflect the intended or rational forms of political behavior in the policy process in that they are designed to solicit, organize, and direct political resources toward a specified end.

Obviously, not all factors contributing to the success or failure of a termination effort are planned or controlled. As a result, the effectiveness of deregulation strategies is contingent upon the proponents' ability to identify opportunities to employ the strategies. The ability to identify favorable opportunities is significant because given conditions may enhance or detract from the effectiveness or even the feasibility of implementing a strategy.

The significance of opportunity identification underscores the importance of timing in the policy process as well as the contingent features of political action. Both dimensions of the opportunity-identification process are reflected in the concept of "natural points [which] suggests that there are times and places during a policy's life-span that are more conducive to termination than others."[50] In sum, opportunity identification refers to decisions made about how and when to use strategies in the course of the termination effort. It is a concept that stresses the necessity of recognizing the accidental, fortuitous, and "irrational" aspects of the policy process. Deregulation strategies refer to the calculated behavior of deregulation proponents seeking to build support for their position by either discrediting the incumbent policy, promoting the deregulation proposal, or both.

SUMMARY

In the preceding discussion, the concept of deregulation was considered from three vantage points. First, regulation was viewed as a form of government intervention in order to arrive at a definition of deregulation. Regulatory instruments as well as alternative modes of intervention were described. Deregulation from this perspective was found to involve the termination of a regulatory instrument and the adoption of some alternative to regulation.

Deregulation was then considered as one of three types of regulatory reform. Historically, reform trends in the field of national regulation were dominated by a traditionalist orientation toward regulatory problems. Reforms included wider application of regulatory instruments and only incremental adjustments to established regulatory policies. Reform trends in the 1970s, however, were significantly influenced by those who blamed problems associated with regulation on regulatory intervention itself. In some cases, reform initiatives fell short of terminating regulatory intervention. Though traditional incremental trends continued in some areas, decremental reforms restricting the application of regulatory instruments were prescribed elsewhere. Finally, those of a restrictive bent successfully advanced deregulation proposals in economic regulation where the regulated industry consisted of numerous and potentially competitive firms.

Lastly, we have examined deregulation as a policy, arguing that deregulation proponents confront significant obstacles in winning adoption of their proposal because deregulation involves the termination of an established policy. The major purpose in analyzing the airline case is to identify the strategies used in overcoming the opposition to airline deregulation and the conditions associated with their effectiveness. Before moving to an analysis of the strategies relevant to the airline case, the context and conditions under which the deregulation strategies were developed and employed will be characterized. This is the task of the next three chapters.

3 | The Regulatory Regime

INTRODUCTION

This chapter and the next will attempt to characterize the politics of airline regulation that preceded the movement to deregulate the industry. The politics associated with the implementation of regulatory control over the industry will be examined in the following chapter, but a prerequisite to such an examination is an understanding of the regulatory system and its development. The purpose of this chapter is to characterize the regulatory framework governing the airline industry as it was administered and developed by the national government from 1938 until 1970. This period was selected because it was in the early 1970s that the economic and political developments in airline regulation converged, setting the stage for the deregulation movement. An analysis of post-1970 developments in aviation regulation and their relationshp to the deregulation movement is reserved for chapter 5.

Two questions will serve to organize our examination: First, what was the character and extent of CAB regulatory authority over the industry? Drawing on the distinctions developed in the previous chapter, we will examine in more detail the dimensions of classical regulation as applied to the commercial aviation industry, describing the CAB's scope of authority, regulatory instruments, and policy mandate. The Board was granted significant authority to intervene and regulate the operations of airline firms. Furthermore, Congress required the CAB to pursue several objectives as it exercised its regulatory authority. Essentially, the CAB was directed to provide some degree of competition among airline firms as it fulfilled its dual responsibility of promoting and regulating the aviation industry. Airline competition, according to the Board's legislative mandate, was to be used as a tool for industry development and a criterion for regulatory decisions.

The second question to be examined in this chapter concerns the development of the regulatory framework. Major trends in the development of the airline regulatory system are distinguished by focusing on CAB implementation of its licensing authority. It was noted in chapter I that statutory changes in the regulatory framework prior to the 1970s served only to build upon the regulatory system established in 1938. Legislative action was directed toward perfecting the existing framework and not terminating it. In this chapter, the argument is extended to the exercise of regulatory discretion by the CAB. It is argued that from 1938 until the early 1970s the Board acted to expand and develop the regulatory framework incrementally. Economic control over the industry by the CAB was refined, consolidated, and expanded. The incremental character of airline regulation is illustrated by the Board's development of the carrier classification scheme. Board initiatives in the decades before the deregulation movement contrast sharply with its efforts to deregulate the industry in the mid-1970s.

THE REGULATORY REGIME

Three principal objectives of government intervention specified in the Civil Aeronautics Act of 1938 were to improve airline safety, to insure economic stability of the industry, and to promote industry development. As noted in chapter I, the CAB's responsibility for safety regulation was first curtailed by administrative reorganizations in the 1940s, diminished further by legislation in 1958, and finally transferred to the Federal Aviation Administration in 1966. However, Board promotional and economic regulatory responsibilities were not altered significantly and remained intact until passage of the Airline Deregulation Act in 1978.

The Scope of CAB Authority

The Board's regulatory authority was extended to almost all facets of airline operations including service routes, pricing, service quality, inter- and intra-industry economic relationships, and many aspects of airline management. The following discussion is limited to the domestic operations of commercial carriers. Special provisions governed CAB regulation of carriers engaged exclusively in international transportation. The Board's authority over the international operations of carriers paralleled that over domestic operations except in two cases. It was not authorized to prescribe rates for carriers serving foreign routes nor could it review foreign air carrier rates to determine their reasonableness. However, it was authorized to approve or disapprove agreements among carriers which established rates on international routes. In practice, the Board ratified rates proposed by the International Air Transport Association, whose members were carriers engaged in international transport. A second variation in the CAB's authority over foreign as opposed to domestic operations concerned carrier routes. Section 1461 of the 1938 Civil Aeronautics Act authorized the president to review and veto any Board action affecting the routes of a carrier engaged in international transport.[1]

There were three major statutory limits placed on the Board's authority over domestic carrier operations. First, air carriers engaged exclusively in the intrastate transport of passengers or cargo were exempted from CAB regulation. Exceptions to this rule were intrastate carriers in Alaska and Hawaii. Airlines in this category were accorded special status by the Board because of their isolation from the continental air transport network. State involvement in industry regulation was limited because most firms offered interstate service. When intrastate carriers did operate, the states were usually more interested in promoting rather than regulating air service.[2]

In addition to exempting intrastate carriers from regulation, the legislation also sought to reserve some discretion for the managers of regulated carriers. Board licensing authority was restricted by the stipulation that "no term, condition, or limitation of a certificate shall restrict the right of an air carrier to change schedules, equipment, accommodations, and facilities for performing the authorized service and transportation."[3]

Finally, Board authority was restricted by provisions for obtaining judicial relief from administrative action. Board orders could be challenged by parties having a substantial interest in an order. Relief was made available through a federal appellate court after administrative remedies were exhausted. Court review of Board decisions was to be guided by the rule of substantial evidence, and the court was authorized to either affirm, modify, set aside, or to remand the order to the Board for further proceedings.

Instruments for Regulation and Promotion

Regulatory instruments granted the Board were modeled after those included in the 1887 Act to Regulate Commerce, its subsequent amendments, and other public utility legislation. Regulatory control was to be effected through: (1) licensing, (2) rate making, (3) certification of carrier agreements, (4) granting of regulatory exemption, and (5) investigation and enforcement.

Carrier licensing requirements served as the cornerstone of the regulatory framework. The legislation stipulated that air carriers could not provide any transportation service unless certified by the Board. Certification enabled the Board to control the participation of air carriers in the commercial transport system, to affect the level and type of air service available on a specific route, and ultimately to determine the structure of the commercial aviation industry.

Two forms of carrier entry into commercial aviation were controlled by the CAB through its certification authority. First, new firms seeking entry into commercial aviation required certification, a practice that enabled the Board to control the total number of firms in the industry. Secondly, existing or certificated carriers required Board approval to serve a particular route or "city-pair" market. Consequently, the Board was able to control the number of carriers providing service on the same route.

Board control over air carrier routes was also extended to exit or abandonment of service. Carriers could not abandon any route unless the Board approved. Though given extensive control over air carrier entry, the Board was limited in its ability to revoke a license. Revocation was possible only if the carrier failed to comply with the conditions stipulated in its certificate. Furthermore, the Board was required to afford the carrier an opportunity to remedy the violation before terminating its license.

Board control over the level and types of service offered by a certificated carrier was another consequence of its licensing authority. The Board was allowed to stipulate in a carrier's certificate the terms, conditions, and limitations on its operations. For example, in granting operating authority between two cities, the Board might require the carrier to make stops at intermediate points, thereby denying it the right to provide nonstop service. Furthermore, the Board was authorized to prescribe a minimum amount of service a carrier was expected to provide on its route because of its mandate to insure adequate service to the traveling public.

As a result of its classification authority, the Board also controlled the type of service a carrier provided. Its authority to assign carriers to a category in a classification scheme affected both new and existing carriers. A new carrier seeking entry into the industry was also seeking entry into a particular service classification. On the other hand, a carrier certificated for cargo transport was required to obtain a new certificate before engaging in passenger transport. Consequently, the Board was able to determine the structure of the airline industry.

Through entry control and specification of the type of service to be offered by the carrier, the Board was able to differentiate among types of carriers. Authority to develop a carrier classification scheme based upon the nature of the services performed was specifically granted in the Board's enabling legislation. The authority to classify carriers permitted the Board to differentiate among carriers that only transported cargo (all-cargo carriers), carriers that provided scheduled passenger service on a demand basis (supplemental or charter carriers), and carriers that provided scheduled passenger service (scheduled airlines).

Second only in importance to its licensing authority was the Board's control over carrier revenues. A peculiarity of revenue regulation by the CAB was its dual responsibility of setting rates to be charged to the public and determining the mail pay and subsidy element in revenues.[4]

Carriers were required to file tariffs with the Board specifying their rate schedules. Tariff changes could be initiated by a carrier at its own discretion, by the Board on its own initiative, or by the Board in response to a complaint from a third party. Pending a Board ruling on the proposed rate, the CAB was authorized to suspend its implementation for a maximum of 180 days.

In addition to this review and suspension authority, the CAB was authorized to fix maximum and minimum rates. It could prescribe a rate if it ruled that an existing fare was "unjust or unreasonable." Or, the Board could simply revoke an existing or proposed rate, forcing the carrier to modify its existing rates or apply to the CAB for rate revision.

Rate regulation included the fixing of government payments to carriers for the transport of mail. Prior to 1938, the mail contract was used as a means for subsidizing airline operations. During most of the period, contracts were awarded on a competitive bidding basis. After 1938, the mail contract was continued as a vehicle for direct subsidization of airline operations by the government. The competitive bidding approach was discontinued, and the Board was authorized to award mail contracts as part of its normal licensing duties. The postmaster general was given the responsibility for scheduling mail deliveries. Carriers were authorized to receive mail subsidy payments by the CAB through its certification authority. The Board was authorized to fix mail rates according to the economic needs of each air carrier and to insure the maintenance and continual development of the air transportation system. Drawing on this authority, the Board developed and implemented its subsidy program.

Initially, no distinction was made between the actual costs for carrying mail and the amount needed to subsidize a carrier's operations to keep it economically viable and to "maintain and continue the development of air transportation." Direct subsidy channeled through mail contracts was included in the legislation to compensate carriers for their "duty to serve" obligation and to develop the infant industry for reasons of national interest.

The Board was also granted extensive authority to control the relationships a regulated carrier might develop with other certificated airlines and with common carriers such as trucking firms. Board control over the external relations of an airline firm was exercised in two areas. One concerned financial and corporate control of a regulated airline and the other, intercarrier operating agreements. No carrier could consolidate, merge with, or acquire control of another airline or common carrier without Board approval. The clearance requirement included any purchase, lease, or contract agreement among carriers. Board approval for interlocking directorships was also required.

Board control over intercarrier agreements also extended to cooperative working agreements. Contracts or agreements among carriers which pooled or regulated earnings, losses, traffic, service, equipment, or schedules required Board approval. Numerous features of carrier operations were consequently controlled by the Board. Carrier agreements involving baggage handling, joint equipment maintenance and ownership, and passenger ticketing services provided through travel agencies were industry operations subject to Board approval, or veto if found to be "adverse to the public interest."

The authority to regulate intercarrier financial and operation agreements was supplemented with the authority to exempt carriers from otherwise illegal intercarrier agreements as well as from the Board's own rules and regulations. In the event a financial transaction or cooperative agreement among carriers was approved by the CAB, the affected carriers were exempted from relevant antitrust laws. The CAB also was granted discretion to relieve carriers from the burden of its own regulations. It was authorized to exempt any carrier or carrier class from existing rules and regulations if the Board determined that their enforcement would be unusually burdensome.

A final set of authorizations enabled the Board to enforce its orders and regulations and to monitor compliance. Carriers were required to provide the CAB with information about their operations. The CAB was authorized to require special reports from any air carrier and to prescribe the form of records each carrier was to maintain. Rounding out its investigative authority was the Board's access to carrier records and facilities and its right to investigate the management of any air carrier.

Board enforcement of its rules and regulations was effected through the federal courts. Civil and criminal penalties were provided for carrier violations such as certificate forgery, unauthorized ticket rebates, and other prohibited activities. Assessment of penalties, however, was dependent on judicial action in response to a Board petition. The Board depended upon a district attorney working under the direction of the attorney general for the enforcement of its orders and regulations. In sum, the CAB was made dependent on the Department of Justice for legal aid and on the courts for legal enforcement.

The CAB's Policy Mandate

In implementing its regulatory authority, the Board was directed to base its decisions on several objectives. For the most part, the criteria that were intended to guide Board policies were enumerated in a "Declaration of Policy" included in the enabling legislation.

In the exercise and performance of its powers and duties under this chapter, the Board shall consider the following, among other things, as being in the public interest, and in accordance with the public convenience and necessity: (a) The encouragement and development of an air-transportation system properly adapted to the present and future needs of the foreign and domestic commerce of the United States, of the Postal Service, and of the national defense; (b) The regulation of air transportation in such manner as to recognize and preserve the inherent advantages of, assure the highest degree of safety in, and foster sound economic conditions in, such transportation, and to improve the relations between, and coordinate transportation by, air carriers; (c) The promotion of adequate, economical, and efficient service by air carriers at reasonable charges, without unjust discriminations, undue preferences or advantages, or unfair or destructive competitive practices; (d) Competition to the extent necessary to assure the sound development of an air-transportation system properly adapted to the needs of the foreign and domestic commerce of the United States, of the Postal Service, and of the national defense; (e) The promotion of safety in air commerce; and (f) The promotion, encouragement, and development of civil aeronautics.[5]

The CAB's policy mandate was often criticized in subsequent analyses because of the multiple and potentially discordant objectives the Board was directed to pursue. In effect, the policy declaration "identifies a number of desirable goals and leaves it up to the Board to choose which ones it will pursue."[6] Nevertheless, policy choices were made within a regulatory scheme that combined two overall objectives—the promotion of the airline industry as well as its regulation. The dual charge of promotion and control contributed to the unique character of airline regulation and colored the developments and problems in its history. The resulting government-industry relationship was characterized by one study as "no less than familial in character. The government has provided the industry with parental support and protection, while exercising in turn, a strong measure of parental control."[7]

In one sense, the distinction between promotion and regulation is artificial. Regulation and promotion in practice were interdependent issues and not treated as mutually exclusive operations by the Board. In addition to direct subsidies, regulatory instruments such as service and pricing controls were also used for promotional purposes. Consequently, a less visible form of industry promotion was made possible by granting the Board extensive economic controls. Under CAB regulation, it was often difficult to determine where promotion ended and control began, a problem commonly found in the analysis of economic regulation.[8]

The task of balancing regulation and promotion was complicated by the status accorded competition in the regulatory scheme. At several points in the statute, reference was made to competition. In its declaration of policy, the Board was directed to consider "competition to the extent necessary to assure the sound development of an air transportation system." Competition as a tool for industry development and a criterion for Board regulatory decisions was reiterated in other provisions of the Act. For example, Section 408 stated that the CAB could not approve any consolidation, merger, purchase, lease, operating contract, or acquisition of control which would restrain competition. Section 409 of the statute prohibited restrictions on competition regarding interlocking relationships, and Section 411 authorized the CAB to prohibit unfair competitive practices.

Legislative emphasis on competition as a tool for industry development reflected the view that the airline industry was not a natural monopoly. Rather, it consisted of privately owned and often competing firms. Some of the distinct characteristics of the industry were summarized in a congressional committee report in 1957.

In many significant ways, however, the airline industry and regulation of the industry is different from the normal public utility. In the first place, the typical public utility statute does not have developmental and promotional objectives, nor does it usually affirmatively recognize competition as being an element in determining the public interest. Further, the airline industry does not have the physical limitations of a natural monopoly. Unlike the situations where the requirements of efficiency permit only one operating factor, as in dam sites, railroads or pipeline right-of-ways, or municipal power distribution systems, in air transportation many competitors can utilize the same airport facilities and operate over the same airlines. In the typical public utility, relatively large investments are required to purchase the equipment and construct the facilities necessary to go into business. The air transport industry is substantially different. There is an absence of large fixed investments. There are no right-of-ways to buy nor are the operators required to bear the expenses of installing and maintaining the ground connections between the various facilities. There are no roads or rails to be built between stations involving the expense of surveys through remote distances or tunneling through mountains. On the contrary, the flexibility of aircraft permits a maximum ability to connect widely separated markets with a relatively small initial expenditure.[9]

The legislative requirement that some degree and form of competition be used in the regulatory scheme, coupled with the economic characteristics of the industry that make competition possible, suggests that the regulatory framework can best be understood as a system of "regulated competition."[10] Redford supports this view in his conclusion that "management of the system of competition has been the chief task of regulation" under the CAB.[11]

In addition to integrating the goals of promotion and control, the CAB was also confronted with the issue of competition and its place in the regulatory scheme. Richmond observed that, "the Civil Aeronautics Board . . . has always been faced with the problem of determining just what does constitute the 'competition' envisioned by the Act, and further, of defining the amount of competition which constitutes the 'extent necessary' referred to in the Act."[12] And Gellman concluded in his analysis that "nowhere in performing its two basic functions (regulation and promotion) does the Board meet conflict as frequently as it does in specifying and controlling the level and character of competition that will prevail over the myriad routes operated by the industry."[13]

The mandate of "encouragement and development of an air transportation system [and] the promotion of civil aeronautics, . . . promotion of adequate, economical, and efficient service by air carriers at reasonable charges," and "competition to the extent necessary to assure the sound development of an air transportation system" suggested several directions CAB policy could take. Trends in CAB regulation of airline competition between 1938 and 1970 indicate how the regulator confronted the problem of blending the

objectives of control, promotion, and competition outlined in its
legislative mandate.

DEVELOPMENT OF THE CARRIER
CLASSIFICATION SCHEME

Development of the regulatory framework proceeded incrementally. Furthermore, the CAB was not a passive participant in the
expansion and consolidation of the regulatory system adopted in
1938. A broader regulatory net was cast by the Board in response to
problems and developments in the industry. Incremental and not
decremental changes in the scope of regulation were the norm.

Through its certification authority, the CAB significantly influenced the structural development of the airline industry. By the
mid-1950s, a variety of distinct carrier groupings had evolved as a
result of Board actions and industry growth. Table 2 presents the
type of carriers recognized by the CAB in 1970. The carrier classes
are the product of a dominant trend in CAB regulatory policy in years
immediately following the 1938 Act. Initially, the CAB responded by
promoting greater service specialization within the industry as service demands increased and the industry grew rapidly. By creating
new service classifications, the Board in effect was extending its
regulatory authority to more and more firms. It sought to segregate
carrier operations according to the type of service provided, thereby establishing a separate air transportation role for each type of
carrier. The policy of air carrier class segregation played a dominant
role in CAB implementation and significantly shaped the politics of
regulation.

The Civil Aeronautics Act of 1938 mandated the first class of
carrier by requiring the Board to certify airlines operating when the
Act was passed. Sixteen carriers were "grandfathered" into the
regulatory framework and assigned the trunk classification. The
trunk line segment of the industry, traditionally including most of
the largest air carriers, was primarily engaged in scheduled passenger transport. Trunk carriers were also authorized to transport
cargo and provide charter service. By 1970 the 11 trunk carriers
accounted for approximately 90 percent of the domestic passenger
market.[14]

Table 2 Air Carriers by Service Classification (1970)

Service Classification	Number of Carriers	Date Authorized	Percent of Total Industry Revenue
Trunk	11	1938	86.5
Local Service	9	1955	10.3
Supplemental	13	1962	1.3
All-Cargo	2	1949	0.7
Commuter	179	1952	Financial data not reported to CAB)
Air Taxi	1425	1952	Financial data not reported to CAB)
Helicopter	3	1947	0.1
Intra-Hawaii	2		0.6
Intra-Alaska	4		0.4

Source: Adapted from tables in George W. Douglas and James C. Miller III, *Economic Regulation of Domestic Air Transport: Theory and Policy* (Washington, D.C.: Brookings, 1974), 110, 193; and *Civil Aeronautics Board Reports to Congress, Fiscal Year 1971.*

Shortly after passage of the Act and creation of the trunk classification, the CAB exercised its exemption authority and excluded from regulation all air carriers not engaged in scheduled air service. The non-scheduled or irregular segment of the airline industry included carriers engaged in charter passenger service and cargo transport. The initial exemption of non-trunk carriers was a temporary measure taken by the Board so that it could give its full attention to problems posed by the major air carriers.[15] Until the end of World War II, most of the CAB's efforts were limited to trunk regulation with little attention directed to the non-scheduled carriers.[16]

Beginning after World War II and continuing through the 1950s, the CAB pursued a policy of carrier segregation by carving out of the irregular industry six additional domestic carrier classes. Special classifications also were created for carriers operating exclusively in Hawaii and Alaska. In addition, some carriers were designated as international carriers and restricted to routes serving foreign countries. The addition of carrier classifications to the regulatory scheme represented an extension of CAB regulatory control over the industry, guided by a policy of service differentiation among classes of carriers. Regulatory extension paralleled the dramatic growth of the commercial aviation industry.

The policy of carrier segregation evolved over time as the Board responded to regulatory problems posed by non-trunk carriers. As early as 1941, the policy began to take shape. In the Delta Airline Case, the Board closed further carrier entry into the trunk classification. In its decision, the Board concluded that

the number of air carriers now operating appears sufficient to insure against monopoly in respect to the average new route case, and we believe that the present domestic air-transportation system can by proper supervision be integrated and expanded in a manner that will in general afford the competition necessary for the development of that system in the manner contemplated by the Act. In the absence of particular circumstances presenting an affirmative reason for a new carrier there appears to be no inherent desirability of increasing the present number of carriers merely for the purpose of numerically enlarging the industry.[17]

Subsequent to this decision, no carrier was granted entry into the trunk class.

Rather than granting trunk status and privileges to new carriers, the Board responded to industry growth and regulatory problems by promoting service specialization within the industry. For the most part, creation of new carrier classifications was justified on the grounds that carriers operating at that time outside the bounds of CAB economic regulation were better suited to provide a needed type of airline service than the trunk carriers were either willing or able to provide. It was on the basis of this reasoning that the local service, large irregular, small irregular, and all-cargo carrier groups were carved out of the non-trunk segment of the industry shortly after World War II.

On July 11, 1945, the Board initiated its "local service airline experiment" after it became convinced that the trunks lacked the capacity to meet growing demands for air service to smaller communities not located in the trunk route system.[18] In 1943, the CAB had announced its intention to investigate the feasibility of expanded airline service to small communities. Faced with the choice of allowing the existing trunks to provide the new service or authorizing carriers in the irregular segment to initiate it, the Board chose the latter course. It adopted the hearing examiner's recommendation that a new class of carrier be created specializing in air service to short-haul, low passenger-density markets characteristic of routes designed to serve small communities. Pointing to the long-haul, high-density characteristics of trunk routes, the examiner noted that small community air service represented a significant departure from the type of service provided by the trunks. The Board accepted the conclusion that "different standards of operation can best be developed by new carriers organized for such a purpose."[19] Interchangeably referred to as feeder, regional, or local service carriers, airlines in this class were viewed by the Board as a means to provide more economical service to low-density, short-haul routes than was feasible with the larger planes operated by the trunks. A related role of the carriers was to feed passengers from outlying areas into major cities served by the trunks.

By 1950, sixteen local service carriers had been granted entry into the regulated industry and given temporary certificates to serve routes designated by the CAB. Provisions in their certificates reflected both the specialized role of the carriers intended by the CAB and its desire to minimize direct competition between a local service carrier and a trunk carrier on a route. The method used to insure specialization and prevent trunk-local competition for passengers was to deny nonstop service for locals between major cities served by trunks. Certificate restrictions required them to stop at intermediate cities on the route segment, thereby denying them the more attractive nonstop service between major points while simultaneously feeding passengers into the route network of the trunks.

The intended distinctions between trunk and local carrier services were sumarized in a 1952 CAB decision regarding the certificate renewal of a local service carrier.

When created, local carriers were initially identified as "feeder" operators, indicative of their anticipated role of feeding traffic to the trunkline carriers for long-haul travel. The experience of the local carriers indicates that the major traffic they serve is local in character between smaller points and their trade centers, and to a lesser degree between the smaller points and themselves. The present line of demarcation between the services of local and trunkline carriers in some respects is not always clear. Many trunkline routes contain small cities between major points, comparable to local service routes. However, the principal distinction appears to be that local service carriers generally are required to serve each point in the order designated on their certificates in each flight over a particular route segment. On the other hand, trunkline carriers are free to schedule service to smaller points on a skip stop or local basis as they see fit, subject only to the adequate service requirement of Section 404 of the Act.[20]

As will be discussed later in this chapter, the strict segregation described above began to deteriorate soon after local carriers were granted temporary certificates. However, despite departures from the intended role of the local carriers, Congress directed the CAB to grant them permanent operating certificates in 1955.

The issue of local carrier service was part of a broader problem associated with the irregular carrier industry. Previously, the irregular or non-scheduled carrier industry, which had been exempted from CAB rate and route restrictions, did not pose a regulatory problem. However, the postwar influx of pilots and the availability of cheap surplus warplanes resulted in substantial growth in non-scheduled carrier operations, drawing Board attention to this segment of the industry.

Trunk carriers blamed a postwar slump in their earnings in part on the unregulated operations of the non-scheduled industry. The trunks asserted that the exemption of non-scheduled carriers from pricing and routing restrictions and the scheduled nature of supposedly non-scheduled operations enabled them to raid trunk routes and "skim the cream" off their passenger markets.[21]

In response to trunk charges of unfair competition, the CAB moved to more closely monitor and restrict operations of the irregular carriers. In 1946, the exemption first granted the irregulars in 1939 was renewed with no additional restrictions.[22] However, the following year the CAB moved toward a more stringent definition of irregular carrier operations and required the carriers to register with the Board. For administrative and registration purposes, irregular carriers were classified as (1) large irregular, (2) small irregular, and (3) all-cargo carriers.[23]

Exemption from CAB economic regulations was removed from some irregulars when an "all-cargo" class of carrier was created in 1949. Eventually, three types of carriers emerged out of the remaining carriers in the small irregular group. In 1947, helicopter transports were granted certificates and added to the Board's classification scheme. The remaining small irregular carriers came to be designated as air taxis and commuters when, in 1952, the Board continued its exemption of irregular carriers if they operated equipment that did not exceed a specified take-off weight. The weight restriction was designed to prevent the air taxis and commuters from purchasing larger aircraft that would enable them to compete with local and trunk carriers. Both commuters and air taxis were authorized to provide unrestricted connecting services to points not served by the larger scheduled carriers. Nor were they required to acquire prior Board approval for their route and rate decisions. Commuters operated on a scheduled basis, whereas taxi operators provided service on demand.[24] Helicopter carriers, commuters, and air taxis came collectively to be referred to as "third-level carriers."

Finally, the last major carrier classification, the supplemental carriers, was created in 1962. Having incorporated all-cargo carriers into the regulatory framework, certificated the locals, and exempted the small irregular carrier group from CAB economic regulation, the Board was left with the problem of the large irregular carriers. Legally restricted to charter service, they presented the most significant competitive challenge to trunk operations. Free to select their own routes and set their own rates, the charters exercised a flexibility in their operations denied the trunks. To resolve the trunk-charter conflict, the Board first moved to deal with irregular carriers on a case-by-case basis to determine any violation of their operating restrictions. Managerial problems attending this approach led to the Large Irregular Investigation which eventually resulted in legislation mandating that large irregular carriers be certificated and renamed supplemental carriers.[25]

Certification of supplemental carriers in 1962 rounded out the major features of the airline industry. Changes in the regulatory framework and CAB policy trends prior to 1970 can be described in terms of the carrier classification scheme. In subsequent years, significant changes did occur in CAB regulation of carrier relationships both within a class as well as between classes. The changes reflect policy developments regarding the regulation of carrier competition by the CAB which provide the framework for the analysis of the politics of regulation in the next chapter.

SUMMARY

The CAB was granted significant authority to control the economic operations of the industry in 1938, and it used its authority during the three decades surveyed in the foregoing chapter to develop the regulatory framework incrementally. The typical agency and legislative response to regulatory problems confronted in the management of airline competition was to contain them by casting a broader regulatory net over the industry. This was done by using the government's certification authority to carve the industry up into specialized carrier groups which were initially segregated and regulated according to a service classification scheme. As the industry and the variety of air services it offered grew, the regulatory framework expanded to accommodate the growth. Soon after creation of the trunk classification, local service, supplemental, air taxi, commuter, all-cargo, and helicopter carrier classifications were added to the regulatory scheme. The next chapter will examine the politics of regulating the carrier groups.

4 | The Politics of Airline Regulation[1]

INTRODUCTION

A politics of deregulation assumes a politics of regulation. An important question raised by the airline case is the relationship between a political process supporting the maintenance and perpetuation of an existing policy as opposed to a political process associated with its termination. From this perspective, the politics of regulation differs from the politics of deregulation in that the goal of political action in the former is to perpetuate and manage the regulatory framework; whereas, in the latter the objective is to terminate the framework. Despite differing objectives of political action, the question still remains whether or not the political relationships guiding industry regulation contributed to the development of political support for deregulation and, if so, exactly how.

Throughout its history, the CAB confronted a plurality of competing political demands made on behalf of regulated firms, consumers of airline service, and other groups with a stake in the development of commercial aviation. The various prescriptions for regulatory action tended to support one of two general approaches to airline regulation. In one approach, the Board was encouraged to promote competition among air carriers. In the other, carrier competition was to be restricted in the interests of protecting and stabilizing the financial condition of the industry. Both factions could find support for their position in the CAB's policy mandate.

A cyclical pattern in CAB policy behavior associated with competitive and anticompetitive approaches to regulation developed over the years. The Board alternately shifted from a procompetitive to an anticompetitive policy stance. This regulatory policy cycle was due in part to the sensitivity of the airline industry to general economic conditions and the business cycle. The policy cycle also developed in response to the two policy factions confronting the CAB. Carrier competition was promoted by the Board during periods of industry prosperity, placating those favoring competitive regulation. However, as the economy worsened and passenger traffic declined, competitive policies were blamed for deteriorating financial conditions in the industry. Consequently, the Board implemented anticompetitive policies in an attempt to bolster industry profits and placate critics of the competitive phase of the regulatory policy cycle. As the economy once again improved and carrier profits increased, the CAB's anticompetitive policies came under attack. Increased demand for airline service rendered an anticompetitive posture less defensible and facilitated readoption of less restrictive regulatory policies.

CONTENDING POLICY PRESCRIPTIONS

The prescriptions for regulatory policy pressed upon the Board by various groups affected by airline regulation represent two major and inconsistent positions regarding the primary goal of regulatory intervention. Both positions had become well developed by the late 1940s.[2] On one side were those who adopted a pro-industry or producer approach to the question of airline regulation. It was argued that CAB actions should be designed to produce a self-sufficient industry not dependent upon government subsidy. The primary purpose of regulation was to insure the financial health and economic stability of the industry. In contrast to this emphasis on industry promotion, there were other groups, especially consumer and small business, who argued that regulation should produce low-cost air service that was widely available to the public.

Each position regarding the goal of regulatory intervention yielded its own distinct and disparate set of policy prescriptions. Those arguing from a promotional standpoint favored an anticompetitive approach to regulation. Policies acting to curtail carrier

profits were opposed by this group because of their desire to minimize the need for government subsidies. For the same reason, price
competition and competition among carriers for passenger traffic
was to be discouraged. Competition as a tool of regulation was to be
used cautiously because of its potentially destabilizing influence on
carrier operations and profit levels. Service to unprofitable markets
was to be curtailed to prevent carrier losses. Where service suspension was not politically feasible, the carrier should be allowed
higher profits on some routes to compensate for losses on unprofitable routes. Segregation of carrier classes should be maintained to
insure against competition and protect a carrier's market from the
encroachment of another carrier class. This position was most
consistently advocated by the major trunk carriers, the financial
community, and others with a large stake in the financial security of
the major airline firms.

In contrast, those who supported a procompetitive approach to
airline regulation advocated a very different set of policies. The
regulator should encourage price competition among carriers as a
means of insuring the lowest possible fares. More efficient carriers,
those able to underprice their competitors, should not be penalized
by regulatory policy, and competitive pricing strategies should be
encouraged. Competition among carriers on the same route should
be allowed and encouraged through liberal route entry policies. In
regulatory actions, the public need for air service should take
priority over the desire to minimize subsidies if subsidy reduction
entailed restricting access to air service. Low-cost air service such as
that offered by supplemental carriers should be promoted by the
regulator and not restricted in an effort to bolster the profits of the
larger scheduled carriers. Consumers of airline services, including
freight shippers, business and recreation travelers, air travel clubs,
and municipalities, were common advocates of this procompetitive
position.

Board efforts to manage the two competing sets of expectations
about the functions of regulatory action cannot be understood in
the simplistic terms of clientele capture. The CAB actions in the long
term were not compatible with the thesis that regulatory policy is
designed exclusively to protect and promote the interests of a
particular carrier group. There were more complex influences at
work, including congressional and presidential pressure and the
Board's own efforts to articulate its dual mandate of promotion and

regulation. Nor was the CAB erratic and inconsistent in its management of the competitive system. Consistent and predictable responses to regulatory problems were developed in the decades after 1938 as the regulators worked to cope with the competing demands placed on the regulatory framework. How the CAB traditionally responded to the disparate set of policy demands is important to an understanding of why deregulation was adopted in the 1970s.

In the previous chapter, it was argued that the structure of the airline industry as well as provisions in the CAB's mandate suggest that the Board's task was the management of a system of competition. Consequently, both the character of the politics engaging the regulatory agent and the agent's methods of coping with the political aspects of regulation are considered in terms of the forms of competitive relationships possible among regulated air carriers.

In the regulation of most forms of carrier competition, the CAB alternated between an anticompetitive and a procompetitive approach to regulation. The phases were synchronized with the financial condition of the industry. In periods of rising industry profits and high passenger demand, the agency responded to those calling for relaxed restrictions on carrier competition. However, declining carrier profits eventually triggered a period of retrenchment in which the CAB discouraged carrier competition. Furthermore, the policy cycle had the long-term effect of integrating the classes of carriers rather than consistently improving the competitive advantage of any one class over another.

REGULATING COMPETITION

The central method developed by the CAB to manage the airline industry was a classification scheme designed to provide a separate air transportation role for each type of carrier. Each carrier class was to be limited to a specific type of air service through certificate restrictions on carrier operations or by means of qualifications a carrier must meet in order to avoid economic regulation by the CAB.

Four distinct types of competition among airline firms were made possible by the development of the classification scheme and regulatory responsibilities assigned the CAB. The four modes were interclass route, intraclass route, price, and service competition. Table 3 presents the four types and their distinguishing characteristics.

Table 3   A Typology of Competition among Regulated Carriers

	Type of Competition			
	Interclass Route	*Intraclass Route*	*Price*	*Service*
Competitors:	Carriers in different service classifications	Carriers in the same service classification	Carriers in the same service classification serving the same route	Carriers in the same service classification serving the same route
Primary regulatory instrument:	Certification (entry into a service classification)	Certification (entry into a specific route)	Rate making	Certification and rate making; proscription of unfair methods of competition

Interclass and intraclass route competition correspond to two different dimensions of CAB entry regulation. In any given route case, two distinct forms of entry could be at issue. The case might involve the question of carrier entry into a service classification or it might involve the question of entry into a specific route or city-pair market. The CAB's decision on the former issue affected interclass route competition whereas intraclass route competition was affected by the latter.

The issue of interclass competition arose when an uncertificated carrier requested a license or a certificated carrier sought permission to be transferred to another service classification. The decision in such cases forced the Board to determine what number of carriers in a class was sufficient to provide adequate service without damaging the economic viability of incumbent carriers in the classification. The character and level of interclass competition was determined by the Board's treatment of this issue.

In the previously discussed Delta Airline Case, for example, the Board determined that the number of carriers in the trunk class was sufficient to provide adequate scheduled long-haul service. On the other hand, the Board proceeded to create new service classifications enabling the development of interclass competition and conflict within the industry. In subsequent years, interclass competition spawned a variety of conflicts and regulatory problems. For example, conflict between trunk and supplemental carriers ran throughout the history of airline regulation as supplementals pressed for authority to provide schedule passenger service and scheduled carriers pressured the Board to restrict charter operation. These and other developments in CAB regulation associated with interclass competition will be discussed more thoroughly in following sections.

In sum, interclass competition refers to policies and conflicts related to entry into a particular service classification and Board policy regarding its operationalization of class distinctions and maintenance of class boundaries. Interclass competition existed as a result of the Board's early attempts to segregate carriers according to a service classification scheme.

Intraclass route competition, in contrast, refers to the competition and conflict among carriers in the same service classification. In some route cases, the carrier request was not for initial certification or recertification into a different service classification. Rather, the petition was for authority to alter the route system over which it was previously allowed to provide a service. In this case, entry is defined in terms of a specific route and not a service classification. Basically, the CAB's task was to determine how many carriers providing the same type of service could operate profitably on one route segment. The level of competition was measured by the number of carriers in the same class serving the same route. A competitive route was served by two or more carriers or was not dominated by one carrier, whereas a monopoly route was served by only one carrier or dominated by one. Conflicts were restricted to carriers of the same class and resulted when a carrier sought to expand its route system by requesting authority to serve a route already served by another carrier.

The two remaining forms of competition regulated by the CAB were price and service. Both forms were possible between two or more carriers providing the same type of service on the same route. Price or rate competition was regulated by the CAB through its authority to prescribe minimum and/or maximum air fares and to rule on rate changes proposed by the regulated carriers. Through rate regulation, the Board determined the rate structure and rate level.

Carriers also competed for customers through service differentiation. Service competition occurred in four basic areas: (1) equipment, (2) flight scheduling, (3) airplane seating configurations, and (4) on-board and ground services available to customers. The offering of new and modern aircraft and the convenience of frequent flight service were common methods used to attract customers away from a competing carrier. More spacious and comfortable seating configurations, as well as provisions of amenities such as free meals and discounts on rental cars, were used to increase a carrier's share of the passenger market on a route.

Regulation of some forms of service competition was restricted by the CAB's legislative mandate. Included were the type and frequency of equipment purchases and flight frequencies in excess of mininum service levels prescribed by the Board. Nevertheless, service competition could be influenced by the CAB in two ways. First, the Board was authorized under Section 411 of the Act to investigate any practice suspected of being discriminatory or constituting an unfair or deceptive method of competition.[3] Second, there were instances where control over carrier rates and route systems was used to influence the level and character of service competition.

THE REGULATORY POLICY CYCLE

Board regulation of route, price, and service competition during the 1938-70 period tended to assume alternately an anticompetitive and procompetitive character. Table 4 presents the policies associated with each approach according to the type of competition regulated by the Board. Approximate dates when the procompetitive and anticompetitive phases were operative are also listed. The dates correspond to financial cycles in the industry. Anticompetitive policies were adopted during or shortly after periods of low passenger demand and declining industry profits. Procompetitive policies were implemented to manage a different set of economic and political problems associated with periods of high industry profits and passenger demand. Board regulation of each type of competition illustrates the dynamics of airline regulation and how

Table 4 Anticompetitive and Procompetitive Airline Regulatory Policies According to Type of Airline Competition

Phases in CAB Regulation and Approximate Dates	Type of Competition			
	Interclass Route	Intraclass Route	Price	Service
Anticompetitive: 1946–55 1960–65 1969–74	*Boundary Maintenance:* segregation of route systems among competitors and restrictions on types of service provided	*Route moratorium and interchange agreements:* limiting the number of competitors on a route by restricting carrier route expansions; authorizing route adjustments by incumbent carriers	*Discrimination approach:* disapproval of discount pricing strategies	*Intervention:* restrictions on level and type of service improvement and differentiation allowed carriers
Procompetitive: 1941–46 1955–60 1965–69 1975–78	*Boundary deterioration:* integration of route systems among competitors and removal of service restrictions	*Competitive route awards:* promotion of multicarrier service on specific routes	*Experimental approach:* approval of temporary discount pricing strategies to generate new passenger traffic	*Nonintervention:* laissez-faire approach to product improvement and differentiation by carrier management

Sources: The table was developed from data presented in the Civil Aeronautics Board's *Annual Reports to Congress* and other sources cited in the text. The competitive-restrictive swings in CAB regulatory policy also are documented and discussed in Basil Mott, "The Effect of Political Interest Groups on CAB Policies," *Journal of Air Law and Commerce*, 19 (Autumn 1952): 379–410.

the CAB coped with political demands representing competing pre-scriptions for regulatory action.

Interclass Route Competition

Initially, the Board relied upon two criteria to differentiate among classes of carriers providing passenger service. First, some carriers were segregated according to their route characteristics. Local service carriers and the air taxi–commuter group were intended to serve low-density, short-haul routes providing nonstop service between major cities. The second criterion was the regularity of service on a route. Supplemental carriers were restricted to charter operations and limited to a maximum number of flights on a specific route. The restriction did not apply to scheduled carriers like the trunks, locals, and some commuters.

Two policy trends were significant in CAB regulation of the relationship between classes of carriers from 1938 until 1970. Each trend can be described in terms of the criteria adopted by the Board for segregating carrier classes. The route characteristic criterion was eventually compromised and in some cases abandoned by the Board as a guide to route decisions. Consequently, retention of a distinct transportation role for each class of carrier authorized to provide scheduled passenger service on domestic routes deteriorated during the 1950s and 1960s. The lines segregating the operations of trunk, local service carriers, and the exempted air taxi–commuter group became fuzzy. On the other hand, the scheduled/non-scheduled criterion continued to be enforced by the CAB. Hostility between the scheduled carriers and the supplemental group was a key component of the politics of regulation during the period. Nevertheless, the CAB did allow the supplemental industry to expand in response to growth in recreational travel and the popularity of charter travel in the 1960s, and expansion increased the incidence of trunk and supplemental competition.

Substantial desegregation of scheduled carrier operations was achieved as the Board used the route award process to minimize direct subsidy payments to air carriers. The result was reduction of monopoly routes and an increase in parallel service by trunks, local service carriers, air taxis, and commuters.

When the 1938 legislation was adopted, government subsidization was viewed as necessary for two reasons. First, the commercial airline industry was in its early stages of development. Secondly, subsidy was seen as a way to insure air service to small communities where service demands were not sufficient to cover the costs of carrier operations.

All types of transport service initially required subsidy. However, administering the subsidy program proved controversial and vexing for the CAB because of political pressures to reduce subsidy levels. Even in the early period of direct regulation, "the subsidy bill was a prime, if not the single most important, concern of the Board and its staff. Much of the energy and resources of the regulators were devoted to the intensive scrutiny of subsidy claims, and the development of regulatory policies to reduce the need of the industry for subsidy support."[4] But the Board was also expected to broaden the availability of air service, including service to small communities. Small community service often proved unprofitable, creating increased subsidy demands. "Community desires and the motive of promoting air transport lead toward expansion of local service; the desire to hold down the amount of subsidy operates as a countervailing force."[5] Board attention to the tension between promotion or expansion of air service and subsidy reduction was a major factor in the politics of regulating interclass competition.

By the mid-1950s, the subsidy question began to receive more intense congressional and presidential attention. Initially, the Board used a need, or individualized, method for calculating carrier's subsidy payment. First, an estimate was made of carrier expenses required to provide a reasonable amount of service and return on investment. All anticipated revenues were then deducted from the estimate to determine a carrier's subsidy needs. This amount was then combined with payments to the carrier for carrying mail, and payment was made by the Post Office Department in a lump sum.[6]

The first major change in the subsidy mechanism occurred in 1951 when the Board began separating subsidy from airmail payments. Separation of the two government payments was permanently adopted when President Eisenhower issued Executive Order No. 10 in October 1953. Separation was intended to clearly identify those funds paid for mail delivery and those necessary to keep a firm financially healthy.

Politically, the reform was significant because it "drew a clear line between the 'have' and 'have-not' airlines"[7] and focused attention on the subsidy question by making subsidy payments more visible. "Buried before in the annual postal appropriation and deficit, [the subsidy bill] was now part of the Board's budget to be justified each year before an inquisitive and not always receptive Congress."[8] The separation of mail pay from subsidy provided a major incentive for the CAB to end subsidy payments to the trunk class and aggressively to seek reductions in the level of subsidy required by the local service carriers.

The Board confronted two significant political pressures in subsequent attempts to eliminate the need for subsidy and achieve a self-sufficient air system. In the words of William Jones, "on the one hand, there is always opposition to lavish disbursements of the taxpayer's money in the form of mail pay subsidy. The Board's staff has traditionally been conservative on this issue. On the other hand, there is a strong desire for the extension of air service to smaller communities, particularly where satisfactory surface transportation is unavailable. These communities have articulate and forceful spokesmen in Congress."[9]

Major developments concerning Board regulation of the relationship between classes of carriers providing scheduled passenger service were a product of CAB attempts to reconcile the two goals of insuring service to unprofitable routes, i.e., small community service, while eliminating or at least minimizing the necessity of subsidizing that service.

Trunk carriers were first targeted for subsidy elimination. The Board adopted three policies aimed at eliminating trunk subsidies: internal subsidization, route strengthening, and airport consolidation.[10] Intially, the Board relied on internal subsidization of a carrier's route system as a means of reducing its subsidy requirements. Revenues from a carrier's more profitable routes were used to subsidize losses on unprofitable routes. The internal subsidy strategy eliminated the possibility of a carrier making an excess profit on one route while requiring government subsidy on another route, a practice which had been a political liability. Excess profits were used to eliminate subsidy requirements.

Board route regulation was used to implement two other policies designed to eliminate trunk subsidies. First, trunk route systems were modified in order to improve the efficiency and profitability of trunk operations. They were allowed to abandon unprofitable routes, transfer routes to other classes of carriers such as locals or commuters, and realign stops on their route system. The Board also liberalized route entry policies granting financially weaker carriers access to the more profitable routes previously monopolized by one trunk carrier. Weaker carriers were also given preference as carriers competed for authority to serve new routes. A major consequence of the Board's route-strengthening efforts on behalf of the trunks was to reduce the number of routes served only by one trunk carrier. Before 1955, nearly 60 percent of the four hundred most-traveled air routes were served or dominated by only one carrier. However, by mid-1958 two or more trunk carriers were operating in 87 percent of the markets.[11]

Finally, route regulation was also used to encourage airport consolidation in order to eliminate trunk subsidies. In an agreement with the Federal Aviation Agency in 1961, the Board announced a route award policy designed to reduce the number of airports served by regulated carriers. It adopted the policy that scheduled air service would be concentrated at one airport if it was determined that airline service to two airports in one area diminished service to each airport and raised the cost of air travel. The policy was intended to improve service and reduce both subsidy and airport development costs for the CAB and the FAA.[12] Airport consolidation in conjunction with internal subsidization and route strengthening combined to help eliminate the need for trunk subsidies. By 1959 all trunks were off subsidy. The only major carrier subsequently requiring assistance was Northeast. It was paid a subsidy from 1963 until 1969.

Though the trunks no longer required subsidy, the Board had not eliminated the basic cause of subsidy need nor had it significantly reduced the subsidy level. Demand for air service to small communities did not abate. In its effort to end trunk carrier subsidies, the Board had transferred the subsidy problem from the trunk to the local service carrier class. To increase trunk profits, unprofitable routes were transferred to local service carriers seeking to expand their route systems. The task of achieving a self-sufficient airline system was transformed from that of eliminating subsidization of the trunks to that of eliminating local carrier dependence on subsidy.

The strategies developed by the Board to take the trunks off subsidy were for the most part applied to the local service carriers. However, there were significant differences in the Board's approach that ultimately had the effect of substantially reducing the operational differences among trunk, local service, and, in some cases, air taxi and commuter services.

When the local service classification was introduced by the CAB in 1947, certificate restrictions placed on each carrier were designed to minimize route competition with the trunks. Locals were made eligible for subsidies, but they were granted only temporary certificates. The intention was to use the threat of nonrenewal as an incentive for the carriers to operate at minimum subsidy levels.[13] Nevertheless, subsidy payments were higher than expected. When the Board announced its intention to deny recertification of a local carrier on the basis of high subsidy needs, Congress intervened. The option of denying certification to a local carrier judged to be too dependent on subsidies was removed when in 1955 Congress directed the CAB to grant permanent certificates.[14]

Congressional action forced the CAB to devise methods for reducing local service subsidies other than that of forcing the errant carrier to terminate its operations. The problems posed by the locals was compounded by the fact that they had purchased equipment identical to that used by many trunk carriers. The larger aircraft were not suitable for short-haul routes, leading the locals to press the Board for routes similar to the type served by the trunks. The large planes used by the locals could not be economically operated on the routes the CAB intended them to use. The dilemma the situation posed for the Board was described in a 1972 study:

The Board had created a separate group of carriers to specialize in providing short haul, low density air service at a lower cost than would trunkline carriers. The dilemma facing the Board was that, as far as the level and quality of service provided was concerned, the local service carriers by the early 1950s differed little from the smaller trunklines. . . . Furthermore, the local carriers appearing to come closest to the Board's goal of financial self-sufficiency were those with routes most like those of the trunklines. The Board decided, therefore, that the routes of the local carriers needed to be "strengthened."[15]

Rather than forcing the locals to limit themselves to small community service (which would have increased subsidy needs), the Board adopted, in order to reduce subsidies, a route-strengthening program similar to that applied to the trunks.

Though some local service operations were indistinguishable from trunk service, the Board adhered to its original policy of segregating local and trunk services as it implemented its route-strengthening program for the locals. For example, a major component of the program was liberalization of certification restrictions. The Board encouraged route adjustments designed to reduce operating costs. However, it continued to discourage direct trunk-local route competition. This was achieved by refusing locals nonstop service between points served by a trunk carrier.[16]

Other components of the Board's route-strengthening program included the transfer of some trunk routes to local carries and a liberalized policy of route abandonments.[17] Some trunk routes were transferred to the local class in an effort to increase local carrier profits. Transfers often benefited both the trunk and local carrier involved. Locals were encouraged to abandon unprofitable routes when the Board adopted a "use-it-or-lose-it" policy. Small communities approved for service by a local carrier were required to provide a minimum level of passenger demand or be by-passed by the carrier.

Despite Board efforts to improve local carrier profits, subsidy payments increased dramatically through the 1950s and into the early 1960s.[18] The subsidy issue received presidential attention when, in a 1962 message to Congress, President Kennedy requested that the CAB make further efforts to reduce subsidy levels. The CAB responded by publicly endorsing subsidy reduction as a major policy goal and submitted to Kennedy in 1963 a four-point plan to achieve it.[19] George Eads comments in his analysis of the plan that it reflected the Board's conclusion that "the policy of strengthening the local carriers' routes while keeping them local carriers had only made the local service subsidy payments higher. . . . The Board was now prepared to embark on another program of 'route strengthening'—but this time with no restrictions."[20]

By 1966, the new route-strengthening strategy for local carriers initially proposed in 1963 was refined and implemented.[21] The Board's "Realignment of System" program retained some components of its earlier efforts to reduce local carrier subsidies. Liberal policies regarding carrier requests for new route authority or route modifications to improve efficiency were continued. The original "use-it-or-lose-it" policy continued to guide Board route-abandonment decisions.[22]

Despite the similarities, the Board's renewed commitment to subsidy reduction made one significant departure from previous policy. It abandoned its earlier policy of minimizing trunk-local competition. In effect, it discarded its original definition of the local carrier's transportation role in the regulatory scheme. The distinction between local and trunk service classifications ended, as the Board largely discarded its original criteria of route length and density as a means for segregating the two carrier classes. Nonstop restrictions on local carriers were lifted. They were granted by-pass authority, which enabled them to provide nonstop service between points also served by trunk carriers.[23]

Another notable shift in Board policy toward the local carriers pointed to the growing significance of third-level carriers. In addition to allowing the locals to abandon or bypass routes that produced little if any passenger traffic, they were also encouraged to eliminate routes that were marginally profitable by transferring them to taxi or commuter airlines.[24] The policy had been used earlier as a means for eliminating trunk subsidies by transferring weak routes from trunks to locals. The rationale was that the weaker routes could be more economically served by third-level carriers, which operated smaller equipment more suited for short-haul, lightly traveled routes. In addition, third-level carriers posed no threat to subsidy levels because they were not eligible for subsidies since they were exempt from CAB economic regulations.

The Board moved cautiously in approving route transfers and terminations, because of adverse congressional reactions to curtailed air service in the states and districts of congressmen. To minimize congressional criticism, the Board adopted a policy of insuring substitute service by another carrier before the local airline was allowed to terminate service. Between October, 1967, and April, 1970, third-level carriers replaced local carriers at thirty-one points.[25] Route transfers from locals to third-level carriers completed the devolution of responsibility for providing air service to small communities from the trunks, to the locals, and finally to third-level carriers.

The deterioration of the boundaries between scheduled passenger carriers was not restricted to the trunk and local service classes. In 1965, restrictions on air taxi and commuter operations were liberalized. The weight limitation was retained, but the original restriction preventing the smaller carriers from providing service on route segments served by certificated carriers was lifted.[26]

By the late 1960s, service distinctions between classes of scheduled passenger carriers had become less significant both as guides to CAB route decisions and as a means of distinguishing among the types of service provided by the different classes of carriers. The policy of carrier segregation was abandoned in an attempt to make the scheduled passenger carriers self-sufficient. As a result, direct competition among trunks, locals, and third-level carriers for passenger traffic was made possible.

Development of CAB policy regarding the relationship between scheduled and non-scheduled carrier classes followed trends similar to those among scheduled carriers. Initially, the Board pursued a policy of strict segregation among scheduled and non-scheduled carriers. A segregationist approach was particularly evident in the Board's treatment of large irregular carriers before they were given an official role in the regulatory framework in 1962 as supplemental carriers. Though the Board never significantly abandoned its attempt to maintain an operational distinction between scheduled and non-scheduled classes of carriers, expanded charter travel in the 1960s increased competition between scheduled and charter airlines.

Early Board policy resulted in tight restrictions on the character and availability of charter and contract services offered by the supplementals. The principal driving force behind the policy was again the Board's goal of reducing subsidies. Although the supplementals were never authorized to receive subsidies, they threatened to increase the subsidy needs of eligible carriers, such as trunk and local service operators, by attracting passengers away from their routes.

The Board responded to growth of the irregular carrier industry after World War II by terminating its initial exemption of some carriers such as local service and all-cargo carriers and incorporating them into the regulatory framework. Letters of registration were required of other noncertificated carriers as a means of monitoring their activities more closely. Eventually, the smaller irregular carriers were allowed to escape the rigors of CAB economic regulation, but only if they complied with equipment and route restrictions mandated by the Board. However, the major problem for the Board was not the smaller carriers in the irregular category, but the large carriers. The source of the problem was the conflict between the large irregular carriers and the trunks.

As Richmond explained, the conflict between the supplemental air "carriers and the certificated carriers (and the Board) was that the latter had consistently opposed 'route-type' operations on the part of noncertificated carriers, while it was apparent that the large airplanes (operated by the large irregular carriers) could be operated economically only under reasonably regular or 'route-type' operations. The other possibility, large scale charter operation, had proven too difficult to develop economically."[27] In effect, large irregular carriers posed a threat to the trunks similar to that of the local service carriers. They were in a position to compete with the trunks for passenger traffic.

A 1958 study characterized Board policy toward the large irregular carriers before their certification in the following manner:

In short, the Board has looked upon the irregular group of carriers as poachers who have frequently skimmed the cream off the top of the air transportation market. The basis for this attitude is that many irregular carriers did not confine themselves to the nonscheduled, strictly limited operations to which their letters of registration and the economic regulations of the Board restricted them. . . . The Board's motive for objecting to the extensive, regular, route-type services being performed by most "irregular" carriers was born of its responsibility to promote and oversee the orderly development of commercial air transportation. This required that the certificated carriers be protected from uneconomic competition, so that they could eventually form the backbone of the optimum national air transportation system, requiring little or no federal subsidy for its operation.[28]

In 1951 the Board was prevented by a court decision from imposing severe restrictions on irregular carrier operations. Two subsequent attempts by the Board to grant irregulars authority to continue their operation were challenged by scheduled carriers and blocked by court action in 1956 and 1959. As a result, the Board appealed for congressional action authorizing it to create a new class of carrier: the supplementals.[29]

Having recognized the large irregulars as a distinct class of carrier, the Board's problem was to define a role for the large irregular carriers that would enable them to satisfy the demand for charter and contract services without causing excessive economic damage to the scheduled carrier system.[30] Its previous policy of segregating supplemental and scheduled carrier operations was incorporated in the 1962 legislation and further developed by CAB regulations. Supplemental carriers were limited to a maximum number of round trips they could offer on the same route in the same month, and a ceiling was placed on their annual gross revenue. Apart from these restrictions, Board control was not extended to specific route authorizations or the mandating of rate levels. Rather, Board regulation was exercised through the enforcement of a social club or affinity charter concept.

The affinity charter concept "presupposed a prior common connection between the passengers on the flight for purposes other than travel."[31] Club groups desiring to take special trips together were defined as affinity organizations by the CAB and authorized to charter either supplemental or other scheduled carriers. In the case of affinity charters, Board regulations applied to the affinity organization and not the carrier per se.

Three criteria were used by the Board to insure that the charter operator fit the affinity charter category. These criteria restricted an organization's ability to engage in charter service.[32] First, the Board required that prior affinity be proven: Passengers on the flight had to prove that they were members of the sponsoring organization at least six months before the flight. This requirement discouraged the formation of a group simply to avoid paying regularly scheduled fares.

A second requirement of an affinity charter was the prorating of traveling costs among the passengers. The effect was to restrict charter trips to large groups. Small groups were discouraged from chartering because individual tickets would exceed the cost of a scheduled passenger fare. Prorating charter expenses among passengers also discouraged participation because of the increased risks to the passenger. Deposits were required and not refunded if the passenger was forced to cancel. Furthermore, ticket prices could not be guaranteed, because they depended upon the number of passengers.

Finally, organizations sponsoring a chartered flight were prohibited from advertising. Affinity group charter operators were not allowed to publicly advertise a planned trip on the grounds that it would draw passengers from scheduled flights and violate the "social club" and prior affinity requirements of the charter concept.

Charter travel throughout the 1960s was of the affinity type for the most part. However, charter services were also available through air travel clubs. An organization achieved Air Travel Club (ATC) status by charging membership fees as well as by prorating travel costs among its members. Unlike affinity charters, ATC charters tended to be more sporadic and were operated on a nonprofit basis. However, ATCs were closely scrutinized by the CAB to insure that their flights did not approach the regularity of certificated carrier services.[33]

Despite continued Board enforcement of the boundary between scheduled and non-scheduled services, developments in the industry during the 1960s had the effect of expanding charter travel with a subsequent increase in competition among scheduled and supplemental carriers. Expansion of the charter industry came in response to a significant change in the character of demand for air services. In the 1960s, recreational travel began to exceed business travel, increasing public demand for low-cost air transportation, especially for charter services.[34] Growth in recreational travel enabled charter carriers to reduce their traditional dependence on defense contracts and led to Board certification of additional carriers to meet the passenger demand, especially in the North Atlantic markets. The Board's traditional emphasis on containment of scheduled operations during the 1960s was moderated as the result of unprecedented growth in passenger demand during the so-called Golden Age of air travel in the mid-1960s.

Intraclass Route Competition

Board regulation of intraclass route competition revolved around the question of how many carriers of the same class were allowed to serve the same route. In the preceding discussion, it was argued that the general trend in CAB regulation of the relationship among different classes of carriers was one of increased competition. This was particularly the case regarding trunk, local service, and third-level carriers. In the case of intraclass route competition, attention is focused on the largest group of carriers, the trunks, which accounted for approximately 90 percent of the passenger service provided in 1970.

Critics of Board route policies contended that the CAB's primary motive was to protect the trunks from competition. However, as previously noted, the Board did approve routes for other classes of carriers which brought them into competition with the trunks. On the other hand, the Board did not grant the carriers official trunk status. Simultaneously, the Board increased route competition among trunks by reducing the number of routes served by only one carrier.

In a 1961 study of trunk competition, Richmond concluded that "since the passage of the Civil Aeronautics Act in 1938, the number of domestic certificated trunkline air carriers has decreased. . . . No new firms have entered this part of the industry. . . . However, the amount of competition in the industry was increased as more and more routes have been certificated for service by more than one carrier."[35] Richmond's conclusion was affirmed in 1972 by another study that found that in the previous thirty years, Board policy regarding route competition had the overall effect of increasing competition among trunks as the result of restructuring air routes.[36]

A cumulative increase in trunk competition was a significant result of CAB route policies. However, the most significant feature of Board regulation of route competition was that it pursued the policy sporadically. In some periods, the Board moved to increase route competition by liberalizing its entry policy, while in other periods it curtailed route expansion by carriers and adopted restrictive entry policies. As early as 1956, Louis Jaffe recognized the cyclical pattern in Board policy when he observed that "the Civil Aeronautics Board in the course of its very short history has shown an almost incredible flexibility in moving toward and away from competition."[37] For the most part, the policy fluctuation stemmed from the Board's responsibility to insure the industry's financial stability and political pressure to minimize the amount of direct subsidy needed to maintain service on some routes.

Variations in Board policy regarding the issue of route competition were often used by some to criticize the CAB. Critics pointed to inconsistencies in CAB implementation of its mandate to promote "competition to the extent necessary to assure the sound development of an air-transportation system."[38] Nevertheless, the Board's "erratic" behavior did have an economic and political rationale.[39]

Price regulation usually was considered the Board's major tool for controlling the financial health of the industry. However, its power to regulate routes also was an effective tool for controlling industry profits, particularly if the goal was to reduce them. In periods when industry profits were judged to be excessive by the Board, it simply increased the number of competitive route awards. As more airlines were permitted to compete for passenger traffic on the same routes, the impact was to drive industry-wide profits down.[40]

Douglas and Miller described the Board's regulatory options in periods of high demand for passenger service.[41] Carriers were affected by rising passenger demand in two ways. First, they experienced equipment shortages which resulted in higher load factors, i.e., the percent of available seats on a flight that are sold. Higher load factors result in lower per-passenger operating costs, leading to increases in carrier profits. There were two possible Board responses to unusually high carrier profits. First, it could raise fares in an effort to curb passenger demand. The effect was to relieve pressure on the airlines without changing the number of carriers on each route. A second approach to reducing industry profits was to increase route competition by allowing other carriers to enter the route and provide parallel service. Passengers would be spread among other carriers with the effect of reducing load factors and airline profits.

The Board relied primarily on competitive route awards to curb industry profits in periods of high passenger demand. However, the strategy was less effective as a means for enhancing industry profits in periods of financial stress. As passenger traffic declined, carriers experienced lower load factors and the problem of over-capacity. Because the CAB was restricted in its ability to terminate route authority once granted, the manipulation of route competition was not an effective means for enhancing industry profits. In other words, in periods of profit stress the Board was not able to raise load factors by reducing the number of carriers on a route. Rather, the Board resorted to other strategies designed to halt the revenue losses of air carriers. A key strategy was a "route moratorium," a term coined in the early 1970s. In periods of industry decline, the

Board adopted an anticompetitive stance toward route awards. Route proceedings that were in progress were delayed and the number of route expansion requests set for hearings was reduced. In cases where new route authority was granted, restrictions were often attached to the new certificate to minimize competition between the new and incumbent carriers on the route.[42] The refusal to continue a procompetitive route policy during periods of financial stress represented a holding action that was maintained until industry profits increased either as a result of increased traffic demand or an increase in passenger fares. Consequently, an anticompetitive route policy was frequently accompanied by Board encouragement of fare increases to offset losses due to passenger traffic decline.[43]

Finally, the Board utilized interchange agreements rather than new route authority as a means of satisfying new service demands. In the early 1970s these were referred to as schedule- or capacity-reduction agreements. Interchange agreements involved the pooling of equipment among two or more carriers enabling them to provide air service which neither could provide acting alone because of facility or certificate restrictions. Agreements required CAB approval because of Board control over intercarrier relations. Furthermore, once the agreement was approved, it was immune from antitrust litigation because of the CAB's exemption authority. An interchange agreement enabled the Board to adjust route patterns of existing carriers to accommodate alterations in passenger service. When new service demands developed on a route segment, Board-approved agreements could be used as a substitute for new carrier entry, thereby minimizing route competition. In periods of declining passenger traffic, intercarrier agreements compensated for the Board's lack of authority to directly mandate a reduction in service frequency in an effort to increase carrier profits by increasing load factors. Carrier agreements to reduce the frequency of flights served the same purpose.

Interchange agreements were generally approved by the Board if it concluded that there was adequate service demand and that the agreement would not result in a carrier monopoly on the route.[44] Initially, interchange agreements were not used by the Board as a substitute for increased route competition. In the Southern Service to the West Case (1951), however, the Board for the first time used the interchange agreement as a substitute for new carrier entry in order to satisfy a service need. It denied the request of several carriers to provide nonstop service from the southern United States to the West Coast and approved an interchange agreement that enabled three carriers already serving the market to provide the service.[45]

The first major period of industry decline and Board implementation of an anticompetitive route strategy occurred between 1946 and 1955. This followed a period beginning with passage of the Civil Aeronautics Act in 1938 during which the Board developed its "presumption doctrine." In the initial years of regulation, the industry prospered and the Board pursued a policy of increasing route competition. Under its presumption doctrine, emphasis was placed on the promotion of competitive service in city-pair markets where traffic demand was considered to be great enough to support existing and additional air service. On routes deemed to have sufficient traffic, there was considered to be a strong presumption in favor of competition.[46]

By the mid-1940s, however, industry finances began to suffer from the effects of recession. Industry conditions were attributed by many to the Board's presumption doctrine. The CAB was accused of promoting "competition for competition's sake," resulting in adverse effects on the industry. Critics argued that the magnitude of new route awards was not justified by the amount of passenger demand. New carriers were granted entry on the assumption that passenger traffic was very elastic and the new service would generate new demand. However, in many cases the new traffic never developed, and the resulting low load factors depressed carrier profits. Declining carrier profits were also blamed on Board efforts to reduce carrier rates which included a 1949 show cause order forcing fare reductions. Growing criticism of Board competitive policies was a major factor in President Truman's refusal to reappoint James Landis to the CAB chairmanship.

The CAB responded to its critics and deteriorating economic conditions by abandoning the presumption doctrine and adopting anticompetitive measures. The Southern Service to the West Case and the use of interchange agreements as a substitute for competitive route awards were the hallmarks of the subsequent anticompetitive period of CAB regulation, which extended from the mid-1940s until the mid-1950s. Gellman observed that beginning with the Southern Service to the West Case in 1951 and extending through 1954, "the Board continued to approve and encourage interchange agreements rather than grant route extensions or permit entry through the issuance of new certificates where traffic and public convenience were found to merit additional service."[47]

By the mid-1950s, industry conditions began to improve, and the Board returned to a procompetitive policy under its new chairman, Ross Rizley. In a series of route decisions beginning in 1955, the Board significantly expanded the route system of domestic trunk carriers as "the result of a conscious and expressed policy of the Board that assumed that it is not necessary to support monopoly in order to protect existing carriers and that competition between carriers where the traffic is adequate to support the competing carriers is in the public interest."[48] In effect, the Board returned to its earlier presumption doctrine, which it continued to pursue until 1960. From 1955 until 1960, the Board's procompetitive stance resulted in a decline in monopoly routes from 44 to 27.8 percent.[49]

The anticompetitive phase in the cycle was repeated from 1961 until 1965. In 1961, airline costs exceeded profits for the first time since 1947. In an effort to bolster their financial situation, carriers petitioned the CAB for rate increases and the authority to execute mergers. Again, excessive competition was blamed.

Regulatory promotion of carrier competition was readopted in the mid-1960s. Passenger demand increased dramatically as the recreational travel industry developed, and jet equipment provided more efficient and economical operations. From 1966 until the latter part of 1969, the commercial aviation industry experienced its so-called Golden Age.[50]

By late 1969, however, persistent inflation and other adverse economic trends were signaling another period of industry decline and abandonment of competitive regulatory policies. The Board's resumption of anticompetitive policies in conjunction with other developments in the early 1970s was a major catalyst for the movement to deregulate the industry.

Rate Competition

Two overall policy trends were dominant in CAB responses to the issue of intercarrier price competition. Beginning in the late 1940s, "a high degree of rate differentiation [was] built into the rate structure, providing for a wide variety of discounts from basic rates. . . ."[51] The growth of discount fares offered by carriers reflected the growing variety of services offered by the industry. Special discount fares such as the popular "Discover America" plan joined with variations in coach service to provide a greater variety of travel and price options than was the case in the early years of commercial passenger travel. In addition to greater service differentiation, "the main thrust of passenger rate regulation [was] in the direction of maintaining a ceiling on passenger fares."[52] The use of discount pricing strategies in conjunction with the Board's downward pressure on fares represented, in the long term, a trend toward the reduction of fare levels.

Greater service differentiation and reduced fare levels, however, represent overall trends and consequently mask the variability in Board treatment of the two issues of fare structure and fare level. A cyclical pattern characteristic of the regulation of route competition was also evident in rate regulation. Depending upon the financial condition of carriers, the Board was more or less willing to encourage discount pricing strategies. During periods of high carrier profits, the Board pressured the carriers to reduce rate levels, while in times of financial stress it was sympathetic to carrier requests for rate increases. As in Board regulation of route competition, variability in Board policies regarding rate structure and level were linked to the financial condition of the industry.

The distinction between rate level and rate structure is useful both in assessing trends in Board rate regulation and in describing the process by which the Board influenced passenger fares. The question of fare structure concerned pricing differentials among types of service offered by a carrier. For example, the pricing relationship between first-class and coach service or flights on short as opposed to long routes were problems related to the fare structure issue.

On the other hand, fare level referred to the average revenue earned by a carrier for all its service. Rate level was described in terms of average yield per mile, which was the ratio of total passenger revenues to total revenue passenger miles. For example, a carrier's fare level would be the average of both first- and coach-class service, whereas fare structure emphasized service and pricing differentials between the two classes.

In evaluating the structural dimension of rate requests, the Board traditionally, though not exclusively, used the criteria of "discrimination," "preference," and "prejudice." A fare was judged to be discriminatory if the fare differentials among different passenger groups could not be justified in terms of differential costs in service. For example, lower fares for coach service in relation to first-class service had to be related to lower service costs for coach due to the absence of the on-board amenities—free meals, more spacious seating configurations, etc.—characteristic of first-class service. "Preference" and "prejudice" referred to the relationship between fares and a given characteristic of the route in question. For example, the Board might find a rate proposed for a short-haul route "unduly preferential" on the grounds that it did not reflect the higher costs of operating on short as opposed to long route segments.[53]

Rate levels were evaluated as to whether or not they were "reasonable" or "just." A rate was judged unreasonable or unjust if it was "too high," leading to an excessive return on the carrier's investment, or if it was "too low," financially damaging the carrier proposing the rate or adversely affecting other carriers.[54]

Formally, the price a carrier could charge for passenger service between two cities was determined in the following manner. A carrier setting its fare in a new market or seeking to change one in a market it was already serving notified the Board of its intended action. The Board then had the option of letting the fare change become effective after a 30-day period or suspending the tariff change and delaying its implementation for at least 180 days. The decision to suspend a tariff was generally followed by a hearing on the proposed change. The Board had several options after the suspension period and/or the hearing was over. It could deny or approve the change, or it might prescribe a tariff or set a maximum and/or minimum level for rates in a market.[55]

In the great majority of rate cases, the Board's role was one of reacting to initiatives taken by the carriers. Redford notes that "the powers granted to the Civil Aeronautics Board by the regulatory act are primarily enabling (granting or withholding consent), rather than directive (by order) on its own initiative. It normally acts on petition."[56] The CAB chose to implement its considerable authority to determine carrier rates by approving or disapproving rates requested by the carriers rather than by exercising its direct powers to prescribe rates.[57] Aberrations in the Board's reluctance to formalize rate policies occurred in the 1950s when it conducted the General Passenger Fare Investigation. Then, in 1970, the Board renewed its efforts to develop rate-making policies when it initiated a series of investigations collectively referred to as the Domestic Passenger Fare Investigation.[58]

The formal rate-making procedure was supplemented by an informal negotiation process between the CAB and carriers seeking rate changes. Fruhan concluded in his analysis that most changes in carrier rate structures or levels approved since 1952 followed a similar pattern.[59] Before the CAB would consider the possibility of a rate increase, the carriers' return on investment would have had to decline to very low levels. Carriers expecting a downturn in profits began making public statements about their need for additional revenues. The CAB responded by suggesting that the carriers seek alternatives to rate hikes, such as reductions in flight schedules or other economizing measures, in order to improve their profits. More formal action was then taken by the carriers, who directed their trade association, the Air Transport Association (ATA), to point out their financial problems in a formal presentation to Board members and staff. After the carriers met individually with Board personnel to gauge their reaction to the carriers' position, they filed for tariff changes. The CAB then suspended the tariff filings and initiated closed discussions with carrier management under its authority to grant antitrust immunity to such meetings. At the conclusion of its discussion with the carriers, the Board issued a public statement indicating the type of rate proposals it would find acceptable. Carriers then reformulated their rate proposals accordingly and resubmitted them for Board approval.

During the rate-negotiating process, the CAB was sensitive to possible violations of antitrust laws. Even though it was authorized to grant antitrust immunity to joint actions or agreements among carriers, it was traditionally conservative in invoking it, especially if the agreements concerned carrier pricing policies. For example, an attempt to depart from the above procedure was initiated by the major carriers through the ATA in the mid-1950s, when carrier profits were declining. The ATA requested CAB permission and extension of antitrust immunity for meetings among certificated carriers to discuss methods to increase revenues. The CAB rejected the petition stating that

in view of the fact that such discussions contravene the underlying philosophy of the antitrust laws and may well be considered contrary to
the declaration of policy in our Act, we believe that such permission
should be granted only upon a convincing showing: 1. Of an immediate need for basic changes in fare or rate structure levels. 2. That such
changes can practically be accomplished only through the requested discussions. In our opinion the industry has failed to make a convincing
showing that rate or fare changes are needed at this time.[60]

The Board decision indicated "that as long as the industry remained
reasonably prosperous, joint action [anticompetitive measures and
policies] with respect to rates and fares was precluded."[61]

Through the 1950s and 1960s, a high degree of rate differentiation was built into the rate structure, resulting in the availability of a
wide variety of discount fares. By 1970, two basic categories of fares
had evolved.[62] First were general fares, which were those available
to all passengers with little or no restrictions. They included first-
class and coach services, and variations of each such as night coach
or economy coach.

Promotional fares were classified as "identity," "excursion," or
"tour-based" fares, according to the types of restrictions placed on
travelers. Identity fares were available only to passengers having
one of a set of previously approved characteristics and included
discount fares for military personnel, youth, elderly, and families.
Under excursion fares, a discount was available only on a specific
route for a specific period of time. Finally, a passenger participating
in a tour-based fare would agree to purchase a package of related
services such as hotel accommodations or meals in order to receive
the flight discount.[63]

Prior to 1948, the first-class fare was dominant in the commercial
passenger industry.[64] However, in 1948 the Board set in motion a
major trend in the implementation of its rate-making authority. In
that year, the CAB allowed carriers to adopt several pricing innovations. Capital Airlines was permitted to offer a discounted coach
service that provided no meals and late night flights. The "Family
Plan" discount fare was approved to encourage travel in off-peak
periods of traffic demand. Other carriers were allowed to offer
off-season excursion fares at a discount on routes to Florida.[65]

The Board's rationale for approving these early discounts was
based on "the fact that the traffic stimulated by innovation would be

largely of a sort that would not otherwise have moved by air, and would, therefore, not represent any substantial diversion from regular fare services. The fact that more efficient and full utilization of equipment would be achieved as a result of these promotional fares was also recognized."[66] In other words, the Board did not view discounting or price differentiation in terms of its potential for allowing intercarrier price competition. In fact, it initiated policies regarding carrier discount proposals in an attempt to minimize the use of discounting as a competitive pricing strategy.

Through the 1950s, the CAB adopted a "discrimination approach" to carrier price competition.[67] Pricing innovations that could not be emulated by a carrier's competitors were denied on the grounds that they were discriminatory. A 1958 study concluded that as a result of the policy "there have been few instances of intercarrier price competition between certificated airlines since passage of the Civil Aeronautics Act in 1938."[68] The Board's policy was described in the following manner:

Intercarrier price competition in air transportation would be discouraged; if any carrier was permitted to introduce rates differing from those previously prevailing, all carriers competitive to the first carrier would be permitted to offer identical rates upon filing for them. With this sort of policy, there is little wonder that there has been so little intercarrier price competition. Pricing innovations are much less attractive, of course, where the innovator cannot reasonably expect to enjoy the beneficial differential effects of his innovation.[69]

The Board's assumption of industry-wide emulation in ruling on carrier fare innovations did not prevent the implementation of new types of fares. Through the 1950s and into the 1960s a wide variety of discount fares were introduced. However, Board policy did restrict the use of pricing differentials as a means for carriers to compete for passengers.

In the mid-1960s, there were indications that the Board's restrictive policy toward discount pricing was beginning to change. The Board's assumption of industry-wide emulation and its heavy reliance on a discrimination approach to the issue of differential pricing strategies began to waver. Again, Board policy change was associated with the industry's economic condition. Douglas and Miller observed that in the mid-1960s when "industry profits sprinted upward and the Board applied pressure for lower fares, the carriers responded with a variety of discount tariffs directed toward limited, allegedly more price elastic markets. The Board approved these initiatives . . . and actively encouraged their use."[70]

Discount fares became very popular with the recreation passenger market, which grew rapidly in the 1960s. The Board liberalized its policy in ruling on carrier discount proposals in response to the popularity of discount fares and growing passenger demand. It began skirting the issue of discrimination and approving proposals on the basis of experimentation. Fares were given temporary approval on the grounds that they were experiments designed to induce new customers to enter the market. Carriers embarked on a period of intense pricing competition through the use of discount pricing strategies as a consequence of the Board's more liberal policy. The so-called discount fare wars spanned roughly the same time period as the "Golden Age" of air travel (1965–69). However, by late 1969 the CAB was being lobbied by some carriers to adopt a more conservative approach to discount pricing because of declining carrier profits.[71]

Board policies regarding the issue of rate levels were not developed in isolation from the question of fare structure. In fact, decisions about rate differentiation influenced fare levels. Fare levels were directly affected by changes in the fare structure that added or deleted types of passenger service. Fare levels were also altered when a carrier was restricted in the number of passengers it could serve on a discount basis. These two methods used to manipulate fare levels by altering rate structure illustrate the close relationship between the level and structure of fares. However, the most direct and obvious method for altering fare levels was through Board orders for an increase or decrease in fares.

When the CAB was requested to approve a rate change, the appropriate rate level was determined, i.e., how much revenue was needed for a carrier to cover operating expenses and realize a predetermined return on investment? Then the structural issue was addressed by specifying how the increase or decrease in rate level was to be distributed across classes of service, i.e., would a rate increase be absorbed totally by hikes in first-class service or be spread between first-class and coach service? Changes in rate level might be restricted to one or several markets, or they might be applied industry-wide. For example, between 1946 and 1965, the

CAB approved nineteen fare changes. Only eight, however, were general fare changes that applied to all classes of service.[72]

Board receptiveness to carrier requests for rate increases varied during the 1938–70 period. The question of rate levels did not create much controversy prior to 1948: "Virtually all the fare changes until 1948 were permitted to go into effect without Board action."[73] However, the following pattern began to emerge in the early 1950s.

As previously discussed, the Board used competitive route awards as a means to moderate carrier profits when they were judged to be "excessive." This approach to reducing carrier profits was more commonly adopted than that of mandating general fare reductions. An exception was in 1949 when the CAB, embarrassed by unusually high airline profits, issued a show cause order for a general fare reduction.

Route manipulation, however, was not an effective method for bolstering carrier profits when they were in a period of decline. Imposition of a "route moratorium" was simply a holding action that froze the level of route competition until either passenger demand or airline rates increased. The freeze on route awards was reinforced by the more direct action of approving rate increases in an effort to increase carrier profits.

Domestic trunk profits showed a decline in 1967, and the carriers began petitioning the CAB for rate increases. Two general fare increases were eventually approved by the Board. The methods used to increase fares in both cases illustrate the dilemma facing the CAB when it used rate increases as a strategy for maintaining industry health. On the one hand, fare increases were politically unpopular. Consequently, when carriers began petitioning the Board for a rate increase, the CAB's response was to suggest that the carriers find alternative methods for improving their profits. For example, the Board would criticize the carriers for failing to curtail their scheduled stops to keep costs in line with passenger demand or for overestimating their equipment needs and incurring unnecessary debt. On the other hand, political criticism was directed at the Board if it failed to act promptly in order to moderate carrier losses. As a result, route award freezes were joined with rate increases in periods of financial stress.

Two controversial fare increases were approved by the Board in

1967, and each was designed to moderate the Board's rate-making dilemma. Each rate change provided carriers with increased revenues, but they were designed to offer "low public visibility to the increase out of deference to the CAB's potential exposure to criticism for allowing an increase."[74] The first proposal submitted by the carriers was designed to increase carrier revenues by restricting the use of discount fares. By restricting discount traffic, more passengers would pay full rates. The second increase came as a result of Board approval of a fare-rounding formula. Fares would be rounded up or down to the nearest dollar, depending on route length. The carriers justified the proposal in terms of cost savings that would result from more simplified tariffs and procedures for writing tickets. However, the effect was to boost industry revenues by 10 million dollars in 1968.[75] Board receptivity to carrier requests for rate increases as the solution to declining profits continued through 1969 and into the 1970s, sparking criticism of Board rate policies and increasing support for deregulation.

Service Competition

While the Board was directly and aggressively involved in regulating inter- and intraclass route and rate competition, it refrained from direct intervention in the area of carrier service competition. One reason for the lower level of activism can be attributed to restrictions on its authority to regulate carrier managemenet decisions regarding service issues, such as type of equipment used and frequency of service provided on a route. On the other hand, the Board's grant of authority in other areas, such as route and rate regulation, provided ample opportunity to influence carrier decisions affecting service quality. Nevertheless, the Board's policy toward service competition was largely laissez-faire until the early 1970s.

There was "a marked trend towards product differentiation"[76] in the 1950s and 1960s, while at the same time the Board encouraged route competition among the carriers. Carrier service competition involved differentiating airline services by altering flight frequencies, equipment, seating configurations, or in-flight or ground services available to customers. Service competition was encouraged by the lack of pricing flexibility available to regulated carriers, as well as by conservative CAB policies regarding pricing innovations proposed by carriers. Gellman offered the following explanation for the trend:

From the very nature of the air transportation industry, it is to be expected that there will be powerful drives toward product improvement and differentiation as a general method of competition. With price largely unavailable to certificated carriers as a means of competition, since rate differentials disappear quickly, the motivation is particularly strong for an airline management otherwise to differentiate its identically priced services from those of a competitive carrier.[77]

Though "the Board's attitude toward service competition [was] largely . . . a laissez-faire one,"[78] there were exceptions. The Board exercised significant indirect influence over service competition in its rate actions. Service differentials and their corresponding costs figured heavily in rate proceedings, indicating that "price competition and service competition was inseparably intertwined."[79] Furthermore, the CAB was authorized to initiate an investigation if it suspected a form of service competition to be discriminatory, deceptive, or unfair. Finally, the Board had the opportunity during the certification process to define adequate service and was authorized to insure that carriers fulfilled the "duty to serve" requirements of their certificates.

Despite the CAB's authority to tightly control service competition, it infrequently chose to invoke it. Instead, it more consistently looked to other provisions in its statute limiting intervention and regulation of major forms of service competition, especially scheduling and flight equipment. Treatment of the service-competition issue during the 1938–70 period reflected "a belief by the Board that the selection of equipment, like the scheduling of aircraft, was also an inviolate management prerogative and that the use of new and more modern aircraft was a legitimate method for management to use in attempting to differentiate its product from that of its competitors."[80] In the early 1970s, the Board's laissez-faire attitude changed.

SUMMARY

The characterization of regulatory politics presented here is not entirely consistent with an interpretation that views the primary function of Board regulation as being that of protecting the industry. It was such an interpretation that guided efforts to discredit airline regulation during the move to deregulate the industry in the 1970s. Its protection or "capture" thesis holds that CAB actions were primarily designed to promote the interests of the larger regulated carriers at the expense of smaller carriers and other groups affected by regulatory actions. The anticompetitive phase of airline regulation is most compatible with an industry protection or capture interpretation of airline regulatory politics. However, the interpretation is not in accord with procompetitive phases of CAB regulation. During some periods, regulatory initiatives were designed to enhance competition among carriers and remove regulatory barriers that protected a carrier from the threat of competition. Furthermore, CAB policies in the long term had the effect of increasing carrier route competition because of the deterioration of carrier class boundaries and elimination of monopoly routes. In sum, a protectionist interpretation of regulatory politics is not entirely valid in the airline case.

Finally, the cyclical dynamic of regulatory policy had a significant impact on the politics of deregulation, a point developed more fully in the next chapter. In the 1970s, the CAB resumed an anticompetitive posture toward airline regulation. Inflation and fuel shortages, conditions absent in previous periods of industry stress, led the Board to take traditional anticompetitive policies to new extremes. The coincidence of anticompetitive regulation with other conditions in the regulatory environment provided the opponents of regulation an opportunity to discredit the regulatory regime and to accuse it of serving a protectionist function. In this sense, the character of regulatory politics and the dynamics of the regulator's response to its political circumstances are crucial to the politics of airline deregulation.

5 | The Adoption of Airline Deregulation

INTRODUCTION

The return by the Board in 1969 to the anticompetitive phase of the regulatory policy cycle did not represent a significant substantive departure from the historical dynamics of CAB regulation. With the exception of aggressive regulation of service competition, the Board resurrected its traditional anticompetitive policies employed when the major domestic carriers were experiencing declining passenger traffic and shrinking profits. Record high inflation and fuel shortages placed additional burdens on the depressed airline industry, encouraging more vigorous pursuit of restrictive policies by the CAB. Rate hikes, coupled with restrictive route award and discount fare policies, renewed enforcement of service segregation among carriers, especially between chartered and scheduled operations, and the use of intercarrier service agreements to restrict service availability in order to increase passenger loads were aggressively pursued in the early 1970s.

Nor was the political reaction to the Board's resumption of an anticompetitive posture significantly different from previous periods. Consumers of airline services, such as recreational travelers and shippers, voiced their traditional objections to CAB rate hikes and curtailment of airline service and discount fares. Opposition from recreational travelers was perhaps more vigorous than in previous periods because of the tremendous growth in the 1960s of that segment of the airline industry and the growth of consumer advocacy organizations. Large carriers experiencing economic stress, airport operators who depended on a stable industry for revenue, and financial institutions carrying the equipment loans of air carriers were supportive of CAB efforts to buffer major carriers from the adverse impact of the business cycle.

Why, then, in 1978 did Congress statutorily direct the CAB to adopt a more competitive approach to regulation, reduce its regulatory authority, and provide for its eventual termination? In previous episodes of heightened political criticism of CAB regulatory policies, Congress had responded statutorily, if it responded at all, in an incremental fashion by increasing the authority of the agency and expanding its regulatory jurisdiction. Why, in this instance, did Congress respond by deregulating the industry if both the CAB's reaction to a decline in the economic fortunes of major carriers and the subsequent political reaction to the resumption of the anticompetitive phase of the policy cycle in the 1970s were not substantially different from previous periods?

Another important question raised by airline deregulation is how the reform process progressed from a proposal to curtail regulatory control to one mandating its termination. In the airline case, the policy process progressed from relatively modest reform proposals to adoption of a much more radical break with traditional policy. Initially, legislative proposals only advocated relaxing the application of regulatory controls by limiting the Board's authority to regulate airline routes and rates. Termination of regulation and abolition of the CAB were not proposed. Deregulation was not included in legislative proposals until very late in the reform process. Provisions in the final bill concerning CAB termination came much closer to mandating deregulation than many thought possible in 1975. As discussed in chapter 1, policy studies frequently assert that policy innovators achieve a degree of change but, because of the incremental nature of the policy process, not as much as they originally sought. The airline case contradicts this assertion.

Several explanations for airline deregulation are presented in the literature. One group of studies emphasizes the importance of the efforts of bureaucratic entrepreneurs at the CAB who favored deregulation. The determinants of regulatory reform are presented in terms of agency characteristics thought to influence administrative

behavior. Factors such as organizational structure and legal authority of the agency, policy preferences and other characteristics of
agency personnel, and agency resources are used to explain why
airline deregulation was eventually approved by Congress.[1]

In contrast, another group of studies stresses factors external to
the regulatory agency. Deregulation is attributed to legislative responsiveness to political interest groups,[2] attacks on the regulatory
policy subsystem by political entrepreneurs,[3] or alterations in economic, technological, or ideological circumstances.[4]

Policy entrepreneurs, advocacy by the regulatory agent, presidential support, changes in public opinion, and alterations in
interest-group structure all played roles in the reform process.
Current explanations for airline deregulation, however, fail to give
adequate attention to the traditional pattern of CAB policy behavior
and its relationship to the deregulation movement. In this chapter
we will argue that a factor crucial to the adoption of airline deregulation was the coincidence of the regulatory policy cycle with
particular stages in the reform process. Board resumption of its
traditional anticompetitive posture in the early 1970s made the
regulatory framework vulnerable to attack by supporters of the
traditional competitive approach to regulation as well as by opponents of industry regulation. As economic conditions improved in
the mid-1970s, the CAB, under the chairmanship of John Robson,
reinstated policies typical of the competitive phase of the policy
cycle. Growing industry prosperity was attributed to the less restrictive policies of the CAB, and this lent credibility to arguments for
industry deregulation.

PHASES IN THE REFORM PROCESS

The critical junctures in the reform process occurred in three
phases.[5] The first was characterized by growing criticism of the CAB's
return to the anticompetitive phase of the regulatory policy cycle.
The early 1970s were marked by widespread dissatisfaction with
CAB regulation. In late 1969, the airline industry began experiencing
financial difficulties which were exacerbated in the early 1970s by
double-digit inflation, a recession that depressed passenger demand, and rising fuel prices. The CAB responded in its traditional

manner by retrenching and returning to an anticompetitive stance that discouraged rate and route competition and used fare increases to offset declining carrier profits.

As industry conditions continued to deteriorate during the early 1970s, the Board went to new extremes of anticompetitive regulation. It became more aggressive in restricting service competition, abandoning its traditional reluctance to intervene directly in this area. It also moved to severely restrict charter operations, going so far as to propose rate regulation for the supplemental carriers. Finally, it liberalized its use of antitrust exemptions by approving a large number of anticompetitive route agreements among carriers. Accelerated enforcement of charter regulations, the attempt to impose restrictions on previously unregulated charter fares, and reliance on schedule reduction agreements were more extreme versions of Board policies typically adopted during periods of industry financial stress.

The second phase of the reform process commenced in late 1974 with Senator Edward Kennedy's announcement that his Subcommittee on Administrative Practices and Procedure would hold investigative hearings on CAB regulation. The period was marked by debates over the relative merits of a decremental as opposed to an incremental approach to reform. CAB policies were widely criticized, and, at the Kennedy hearings in 1975, the necessity of some degree of reform was clearly registered. The reform issue became a question of whether to refine the existing regulatory framework or diminish it. The Ford administration's linking of inflation and overregulation, the Kennedy investigation and attack on airline regulation, and the CAB's position on reform contributed to support for decremental reform. Senator Howard Cannon's conversion to the cause resulted in passage of a Senate reform bill in April 1978 that was based on the assumption that the problem with airline regulation was regulation itself. Consequently, the solution seemed to be a reduction in regulatory intervention and not more regulation.

The endorsement of decremental reform by the Senate in April 1978 set the stage for the third phase in the reform process, which ended in October of that year when President Carter signed the deregulation bill. Under John Robson, the CAB returned to a procompetitive stance typical of earlier periods of industry prosperity. Alfred Kahn continued the liberalization trend initiated by Robson but took the procompetitive policies to new extremes after the

Senate passed reform legislation in April 1978. Support for deregulation grew as the dire predictions about the supposed ill effects of nonintervention failed to be confirmed. Events in the few months preceding passage of the legislation dissipated opposition to deregulation, paving the way for a conference committee compromise that included a strong mandate for policy termination.

ANTICOMPETITIVE REGULATION AND POLITICAL BACKLASH

As noted in the preceding chapter, the airline industry experienced very favorable economic conditions from the mid-1960s until 1969. In response to unprecedented traffic demand, the Board adopted a procompetition stance and liberalized route and rate regulation. To accommodate passenger traffic, route entry was relaxed, allowing more carriers to serve the same route and increasing carrier competition for customers. Rate competition among carriers also increased. Increased airline profits encouraged the CAB to relax restrictions on discount pricing, and discount fares spread through the industry. By 1969, however, the Golden Age of passenger travel was showing signs of decline. In an effort to curb mounting financial losses of the major airlines, the CAB initiated a return to anticompetitive policies that was to prove highly unpopular.[6]

More restrictive and extensive regulatory controls were adopted to improve the industry's financial condition. A reversal of the Board's procompetitive policies of the 1960s was reluctantly initiated under Board chairman Secor Browne in 1969. Beginning in 1973, the policies were aggressively pursued by his successor, Robert Timm. As in earlier episodes of industry stress, excessive rate and service competition were blamed for declining airline profits. The Board responded with anticompetitive rate and route allocation policies and moved to expand its control over airline operations through closer regulation of service competition.

Airline profits were adversely affected by a severe over-capacity problem in the industry, brought on by declining passenger traffic. The Board adopted two strategies to ameliorate the problem. Hearings to consider new route applications were severely curtailed. A so-called route moratorium was imposed in an effort to discourage airlines from expanding their operations. A second strategy was to encourage airlines to negotiate flight schedule reductions on mutual routes. Legally prohibited from directly regulating flight frequencies, the Board resorted to its authority to grant antitrust immunity for intercarrier agreements. Carriers were thereby enabled to dictate service levels without fear of antitrust prosecution for collusion in restraint of competition.[7]

Rate policies were also adopted to bolster airline profits. A succession of rate hikes and restrictions on discount pricing were approved as a result of a major investigation of rate policies. In 1969, an industry fare increase was challenged in court by Rep. John E. Moss and several other congressmen. The Board initiated a series of rule-making proceedings to address the issues raised in the Moss case. These began in 1970, concluded in 1974, and were collectively referred to as the Domestic Passenger Fare Investigation (DPFI).[8] The primary purpose of the proceedings was to establish standards and a formula for future rate decisions.

As a result of the DPFI, the Board concluded that carriers were entitled to a 12 percent return on investment. In an attempt to achieve this figure, rate hikes were approved in 1974 that resulted in a 20 percent increase in the average industry fare. The Board also ruled that certain discount fares were "unduly discriminatory" and ordered their termination. Other regulations were approved that discouraged airlines from using discount fares.

The Board also sought to improve airline profits by making changes in charter regulations.[9] Charter carriers were authorized to provide service only on demand, with no direct regulation of their fares by the CAB. Pricing flexibility and demand service enabled them to offer passenger fares substantially lower than scheduled fares. The scheduled airlines viewed charter carriers as economic competitors capable of diverting passengers from their markets. As scheduled industry profits began to decline in the late 1960s, the carriers attributed part of their losses to charter operations, just as they had in previous periods of financial stress. In response to scheduled carrier charges of "cream skimming," the CAB stepped up enforcement of charter restrictions. Court action was taken against several private travel clubs for failure to abide by charter regulations. Efforts were also made to prevent participation in scheduled operations through stricter regulations. Furthermore, the Board took the unprecedented step of proposing minimum charter rates in order to restrain their competitive advantage over the scheduled carriers.

Finally, the Board sought to improve profits by mandating airline performance and efficiency standards. The CAB became increasingly concerned with service competition in its efforts to curb airline operating expenses. Rate regulation was used to discourage passenger amenities such as free movies and beverages, and to force more efficient seating configurations.[10] This represented a significant departure from the CAB's traditional laissez-faire policy toward service competition.

Opposition to Board policies was widespread by late 1974. Smaller and less financially depressed carriers were critical of the Board's curtailment of route extensions. The departments of Transportation and Justice initially acquiesced in Board approval of schedule reduction agreements. However, the incidence of capacity agreements accelerated during the Timm chairmanship. The agreements were challenged by the Antitrust Division on grounds that the Board was abusing its antitrust exemption authority. Airline management accused the CAB of illegally extending its regulatory authority by dictating airline performance and efficiency standards and restricting ancillary services. Consumer groups were highly critical of rate hikes, reductions in flight frequencies, and the termination of very popular youth and family discount fares. In response to CAB charter policies, supplemental carriers and charter groups complained of harassment and charged that the Board was moving to eliminate low-cost air transportation.

To make matters worse, Chairman Timm became involved in political scandal. In late 1974, it was revealed that he had accepted airline hospitality on junkets to Florida, Bermuda, and several European countries. His credibility also suffered because of his ties with the Nixon administration. The Watergate investigations revealed that two major airline firms had made illegal contributions to Nixon's reelection campaign. Timm was later accused of thwarting a Board investigation into the matter.[11]

The accumulation of unpopular regulatory actions and political scandal damaged the credibility of the agency. Complaints quickened congressional interest in airline regulation, prompting several investigations. Senator Edward Kennedy, chairman of the Senate Judiciary Subcommittee on Administrative Practices and Procedure, announced in June 1974 his intention to hold an oversight investigation into CAB policies in early 1975. In August 1974 Gerald Ford succeeded Nixon to the presidency. The new administration's twin problems of attempting to develop a domestic policy and coping with the political liability of the Timm chairmanship set the stage for presidential intervention in the controversy over airline regulation.

THE ENDORSEMENT OF DECREMENTAL REFORM

On April 19, 1978, the Air Transportation Regulatory Reform Act was passed by the Senate. Though it did not endorse deregulation and termination of the CAB, the bill did include decremental reforms relaxing Board regulation of airline rates and routes. Between August 1974 and passage of the legislation, an influential political alliance supporting reductions in CAB authority was forged. It included both the Ford and Carter administrations, Senators Edward Kennedy and Howard Cannon, consumer groups, some regulated carriers, and the CAB itself.

Proponents and Opponents

A diverse coalition of individuals and interest groups eventually joined forces to support the Senate reform legislation and the final version of the deregulation bill. Early and leading proponents of deregulation were professional economists both in and outside government.[12] During the 1950s and 1960s, academic economists had developed an impressive body of literature critical of economic regulation. These studies were used extensively during the reform process to further the case for deregulation. Derthick and Quirk conclude from their analysis of deregulation that "except for the development of this academic critique of policy, the reforms we are trying to explain [airline, trucking, and telecommunication deregulation] would never have occurred."[13] Furthermore, academic economists provided a readily available pool of influential and credible witnesses who were frequently called upon to testify before congressional committees during the reform debate.

A variety of government agencies proved to be influential supporters of deregulation. The Antitrust Division of the Department of Justice, the Federal Trade Commission, Department of Transportation, and the Council on Wage and Price Stability were inclined to support deregulation because their agency missions were predicated on the assumed benefits of competition. These and other agencies were also influenced by professional economists who were well represented on agency staffs. Derthick and Quirk note that in the 1960s and early 1970s, "economists entered public service in large enough numbers, and in offices sufficiently influential and strategically placed to constitute an important force for advocacy within government."[14] Economists on the Council of Economic Advisers, at the Office of Management and Budget, and at the CAB proved to be influential advocates of deregulation. Congress' own nonpartisan staff agencies, the General Accounting Office and Congressional Budget Office, eventually joined in support of deregulation.

Regulatory reform was a top priority for both the Ford and Carter administrations. White House task forces such as the Domestic Council Review Group for Regulatory Reform, created during the Ford administration, assisted in the organization of reform advocates and the drafting of reform proposals. President Carter became personally involved in lobbying Congress for passage of the legislation and in supporting key legislative leaders such as Senators Edward Kennedy and Howard Cannon.

The Carter White House was instrumental in organizing an ad hoc coalition of interest groups in support of deregulation. Included in the coalition were Nader's Aviation Consumer Action Project, the American Conservative Union, National Association of Manufacturers, American Farm Bureau Federation, and the National Federation of Independent Business. Individual firms with large shipping operations—such as Sears Roebuck—also joined in support of deregulation.[15] Generally, consumers of airline service lent their support to deregulation in the belief that better service and lower rates would result from airline competition.

A final group supporting deregulation included individual firms and segments of the air carrier industry itself. Some carriers supported deregulation because they considered themselves exceptionally disadvantaged by regulation. Pan American, for example, had sought authority to serve domestic routes but continued to be restricted to international passenger service by the CAB. For several years, the Board had prevented United Airlines from expanding its route system. Intrastate carriers such as Pacific Southwest saw in deregulation the opportunity to expand their systems into an inter-state network. All cargo carriers had been deregulated in 1977, but they hoped passenger carrier deregulation would bring them the opportunity to expand into the scheduled passenger market. Char-ter and commuter carriers desired freer access to the denser and more lucrative routes served predominantly by the larger certifi-cated carriers.

The principal opponents of deregulation were the larger sched-uled carriers and their employees.[16] The trunk carriers were repre-sented by their trade organization, the Air Transport Association, and the Association of Local Transport Carriers spoke on behalf of the regional airlines. Initially, the carriers were united in their opposition to removal of entry, exit, and rate authority of the CAB. Regulated carriers feared that deregulation would lead to "cut-throat competition" among carriers. In an effort to keep costs as low as possible, carriers would reduce maintenance costs jeopardiz-ing the safety of airline operations. Without the stability and protec-tion provided airline operations, carrier revenues would be less predictable, thereby undercutting their ability to finance new air-craft purchases on attractive terms. Beginning with United Air-lines, some carriers began to qualify or abandon their opposition to deregulation later in the reform process, for reasons examined later in this and the next chapter.

Several employee unions joined airline management in opposing diminished CAB regulation. The Airline Pilots Association, Interna-tional Brotherhood of Teamsters, Transport Workers Union of America, Association of Machinists and Aerospace Workers, Brotherhood of Railway and Airline Clerks, and Flight Engineers International Association opposed deregulation because of the threat it posed to organized labor and to the job security of their members. Deregulation promised greater competition between the certificated carriers, which were heavily unionized, and nonunion-ized carriers, which included existing commuter airlines and new carriers that would be organized after deregulation. Lower labor costs would give a competitive advantage to nonunionized carriers by enabling them to offer lower fares. Airline employees feared that the established carriers would be forced to restructure their operations or renegotiate labor contracts resulting in loss of jobs and lower wages and benefits. Union opposition to deregulation did not diminish until labor protection provisions were included in the reform bill.

Two other groups were also influential opponents of deregulation. They included a variety of state and local organizations that represented the interests of airport operators and small communities. Airport operators were split on the issue of deregulation. Operators of the major hub airports feared that route deregulation would reduce the number of major carriers serving their airports. In previous anticompetitive phases of the CAB regulatory policy cycle, the Board sought to consolidate scheduled service at fewer airports in an effort to improve the efficiency of airline operations. Smaller airports such as Dallas Love Field and Chicago Midway experienced an exodus of carriers under CAB regulation. Operators of regional airports supported deregulation because they saw the potential for new business. Established carriers would be free to reinstitute service at abandoned airports, and it was expected that new carriers organized after deregulation would be attracted to the uncrowded facilities and underserved markets of the regional airports. On the other hand, operators of the major hub airports, many of which were not as conveniently located to major urban centers as were the regional airports, feared loss of service to the smaller airports.

Rural states and small communities opposed deregulation for fear that airline service would be severely curtailed or ended by it. If the duty-to-serve obligation enforced by the CAB under regulation was ended, carriers would be attracted to the more profitable routes and abandon the less heavily traveled routes serving rural areas. Opposition to deregulation from rural interests was not overcome until provisions restricting service abandonment and a new subsidy program for airline service to small cities were included in the reform bill.

The coalition supporting statutory reduction of CAB authority influenced the resolution of two critical issues in the reform debate. First, widespread support for some type of reform was crystallized in 1975 by the Kennedy oversight hearings. The hearings discredited CAB policies of the previous six years and publicized opposition to the anticompetitive phase of the regulatory policy cycle. Second, the question of whether reforms should be incremental or decremental in nature was resolved in 1976 when Cannon, chairman of the key Commerce Subcommittee on Aviation, endorsed legislative reductions in Board authority.

President Ford, Inflation, and Deregulation

In the early months of the Ford administration, regulatory reduction was adopted as a major component of Ford's anti-inflation program. Shortly after taking office, the Ford White House targeted double-digit inflation as the centerpiece for the new administration's domestic program. A series of inflation conferences was held in September 1974 to solicit views from government officials, academics, congressmen, and interest groups regarding methods for curbing inflation. Administration and academic economists were well represented and united in their view that direct economic regulation was costly and anticompetitive. Their efficiency argument for deregulation was very compatible with the administration's goal of reducing costs and curbing inflationary pressures. Their position was also ideologically compatible with Ford's "small government" philosophy.[17]

Ford endorsed a decremental approach to regulatory reform shortly after the inflation conferences. In a message to Congress on the economy, delivered October 8, 1974, he echoed an earlier Nixon linkage between inflation and excessive regulation, stating that "the Federal government imposes too many hidden and too many inflationary costs on our economy." He asked Congress to establish a National Commission on Regulatory Reform that would "identify and eliminate existing Federal rules and regulations that increase costs to the consumer [and pledged] to return to vigorous enforcement of antitrust laws."[18]

The commission proposal was not enthusiastically endorsed by Congress. While it delayed and finally suspended action on Ford's request, deregulation proponents lobbied the White House for more direct reform initiatives by the president. Ford was persuaded to endorse legislation pending in Congress that sought the repeal of anticompetitive laws. The White House was also convinced that CAB chairman Robert Timm was a political liability to Ford's anti-inflation program. Timm's support for rate hikes, his strong endorsement of Board restraints on airline competition, and his involvement in political scandal were politically embarrassing for the new administration. Refusing to yield to White House pressure for his resignation, Timm was stripped of his chairmanship by Ford on December 10, 1974. Board member Richard O'Melia was appointed to replace Timm until a new chairman more receptive to White House policy could be found.

The Kennedy Hearings

By late 1974, the Ford administration had yet to develop a specific position on airline reform. However, a deadline was imposed on the development of an administration policy by Kennedy's oversight hearings scheduled in early 1975. In the months preceding the Kennedy hearings, deregulation supporters in the administration were consulted by Kennedy's aide, Stephen Breyer, as he designed the hearings and prepared materials for the subcommittee members. The hearings were organized so as to favor the opponents of airline regulation. The critics of regulation were given the initiative in that they were asked to present their case first. Furthermore, testimony scheduled by the staff was designed to discredit the major arguments for continued regulation of the industry. The subcommittee staff under Breyer's direction also took steps to insure that testimony given at the hearings by various agencies would be prepared and delivered by deregulation advocates.[19]

On February 6, 1975, the first day of the hearings, the strong adversarial and proreform thrust of the subcommittee investigation was revealed. In his opening remarks, Kennedy noted that "regulators all too often encourage or approve unreasonably high prices, inadequate service, and anticompetitive behavior. The cost of this regulation is also passed on to the consumer. And that cost is astronomical."[20]

On the first day, the Ford administration publicly stated its position on aviation reform. John W. Barnum, acting Secretary of Transportation, announced that the administration was preparing a legislative proposal that represented "a major departure from the regulatory regime we have relied upon in the past [and] will fundamentally redirect our air transportation regulatory policy." Barnum went on to endorse the economists' position that the current regulatory system "misplaces incentive and disincentive, distorts competitive advantage, protects inefficient carriers from effective competition, over-restricts market entry, artificially inflates rates, and misallocates our Nation's resources."[21]

During the next eight days of hearings, it became clear that there was widespread dissatisfaction with CAB regulation, even among the regulated carriers. There was disagreement, however, on the type of reform necessary to correct the problems. Officials from the Council of Economic Advisers and the Department of Justice joined with academic economists in supporting the decrementalist position that economic regulation of the industry was inherently inefficient and costly. Consequently, dissatisfaction with CAB regulation would continue unless statutory reductions in, and preferably removal of, CAB rate and route controls were legislated.

Regulated carriers were the principal spokesmen for an incremental approach to reform. They blamed regulatory problems on the Board's misuse of its discretion and not on the regulatory structure. As one airline spokesman put it, "the kinds of changes we feel are worthy of consideration are those which would tend to improve the present system, and not destroy it."[22] Substantive amendments to the regulatory statute were generally opposed by this group. Carriers were particularly adamant against reductions in the Board's route certification authority. If substantive amendments were to be made, the airlines urged the committee not to disturb the sections of the act dealing with route entry and exit. They were more favorably disposed toward changes that would increase carrier pricing freedom. However, deregulation advocates were just as adamantly opposed to decontrolling rates without relaxing route regulation. The threat of market entry by a competing carrier was viewed as an essential restraint on monopoly pricing by carriers.

The free market analysis of the benefits of deregulation was dismissed by opponents as mere academic theorizing. They maintained that deregulation would have several adverse consequences. Two major objections to deregulation were raised. First, critics predicted disruptions resulting from the transition to a deregulated environment. Since the industry had no experience operating in the absence of rate and route regulation, the potential for chaos was great. Employee unions, loan institutions, and airport management objected to deregulation because of potential financial disruptions if airline rates and scheduled service became unstable.

A second set of objections was based on the predicted consequences of rate and route competition. The most volatile issue concerned passenger service to small communities. Opponents of deregulation argued that CAB regulation maintained a fragile and highly interdependent route system than enabled carriers to serve routes which it would be economically impossible for them to serve under unregulated circumstances. The argument was premised on the assumption that regulation forced carriers to serve unprofitable routes by requiring them to subsidize their operations with profits from more lucrative routes. Deregulation would free the carriers to teminate service in their attempt to gain a bigger market share on more profitable routes.

Opponents of rate deregulation predicted it would result in a more concentrated industry as the larger airlines monopolized routes through predatory pricing strategies. Lastly, it was predicted that, in an attempt to remain competitive, companies would reduce their airline maintenance expenditures, thereby jeopardizing the safety of their operations.

Deregulation supporters did not advance arguments that completely removed these concerns. The 1978 legislation included provisions such as phased deregulation, limits on route entry and exit, a guarantee of continued service to small communities, and airline employee compensation for reform-related layoffs. However, the Kennedy hearings and the subsequent subcommittee report did challenge the assumptions on which the critics' arguments were based.

For example, the validity of an Air Transport Association study purporting to prove that deregulation would result in substantial service reduction was discredited. A major assumption in the ATA study was that service on some routes was possible because of cross-subsidization, a practice not likely to continue under deregulation. A study commissioned by the subcommittee, however, concluded that little if any cross-subsidized service actually existed in the route system. The argument that predatory pricing and monopolization would result from deregulaton was refuted by witnesses who observed that such practices were illegal under existing antitrust laws. Finally, deregulation advocates pointed out in their testimony before the subcommittee that regulatory and certification requirements of the Federal Aviation Administration would prevent airlines from reducing the safety of their operations in an effort to cut costs.

In addition to discrediting some of the strongest arguments against deregulation, the Kennedy investigation successfully polarized the reform issue and discredited CAB anticompetitive policies of the previous six years. In subsequent debates, the need for reform was no longer questioned. Rather, the question was, what type of reform? Would a redirection of CAB discretionary authority and the reversal of specific policies such as the route moratorium suffice? Or would substantive reductions in Board authority be the more effective approach? In 1976, following the first substantive Senate committee hearings on aviation reform since the Kennedy hearings, the question was decided in favor of decremental reform.

Senator Cannon's Endorsement

Reform of whatever type would have little chance without the endorsement of Senator Howard Cannon, chairman of the Senate Commerce Subcommittee on Aviation. A known supporter of regulation, Cannon was displeased with Kennedy's meddling in his committee's jurisdiction, and the prospects for his support of decremental reform were not optimistic. However, since Timm's demotion in 1974 and Ford's proposal for a study commission, both the CAB and the administration had embarked on courses of action that were influential in gaining Cannon's support for decremental reform legislation.

Beginning in late 1974, Congress had become the focal point of the reform debate as the result of Ford's request for legislative action on his study commission proposal and Kennedy's oversight initiative. The lull in presidential activism ended shortly after the Kennedy hearings in the spring of 1975. In the closing months of 1975, Ford became personally involved in pushing for decremental reform on both the legislative and administrative fronts.

Ford officially resumed his push for decremental reform on April 18, 1975. At a White House conference in New Hampshire, he called for relaxation of direct rate and entry regulation and application of antitrust laws to regulated industries. Ten days later, in a speech before the national meeting of the Chamber of Commerce, he announced plans to submit to Congress "a comprehensive transportation program designed to achieve maximum reform of Federal regulations governing our railroad, airline, and trucking firms."[23] He also announced plans to hold conferences with the heads of regulatory agencies and congressional leaders regarding regulatory reform.

In the same speech, Ford outlined the character of future administration reform efforts. He distinguished between social and economic regulation and prescribed different reform approaches for each. Decrementalism would guide reform in economic regulation where "regulations [are] designed to deal with the competitive performance of such industries as railroads, trucking, airlines, utilities, and banking. . . . Elimination of obsolete and unnecessary regulations" would be the goal of reform. However, incrementalism would guide reform of social regulation. "The central issue here is the need for a proper assessment or evaluation of costs and benefits."[24]

Shortly after the April speech, the Ford White House began preparations for legislative initiatives. Administration officials who had worked on an ad hoc basis to promote deregulation were organized into the Domestic Council Review Group for Regulatory Reform (DCRG). Chaired by Roderick M. Hills, Ford's newly appointed special counsel, the DCRG began drafting legislation relaxing railroad, airline, and trucking regulation.

On May 19, 1975, Ford transmitted the first of three reform bills drafted by the DCRG. It proposed relaxing regulation of the railroad industry and was subsequently passed in 1976 as the Railroad Revitalization and Regulatory Reform Act. On October 8, Ford transmitted a second DCRG bill, the Aviation Reform Act of 1975. The Ford bill and legislation subsequently introduced by Kennedy were the subject of hearings before Cannon's subcommittee in early 1976.

Ford cultivated bipartisan legislative support for his reform program at a meeting with twenty-four congressional leaders on June 25, 1975. Following the conference, the twelve Democratic congressmen in attendance released a policy statement agreeing in principle to the need for regulatory reform. The June meeting with legislators was followed by a conference with the heads of ten independent regulatory commissions on July 10. Ford pressed them to initiate internal reforms designed to promote competition and reduce the costs of regulation. John Robson, appointed chairman of the CAB by Ford in April 1975, was in attendance. At the meeting, he announced his intention to seek Board approval of a plan experimentally deregulating airline rates and routes.[25] The proposal was indicative of significant developments at the CAB since Timm's demotion as chairman.

The CAB reversed most of its policies criticized during the Kennedy investigation between Richard O'Melia's appointment as acting chairman in December 1974 and the opening of the Cannon subcommittee hearings in April 1976. The Board's return to the competitive phase of the policy cycle coincided with a general improvement in the economy and the airline industry. There were also indications of growing staff support for deregulation. In January 1975 an internal review of CAB policies was initiated that would later influence the Board's position on reform. An internal task force headed by Roy Pulsifer, assistant director of the Bureau of Operating Rights, was directed to conduct an independent appraisal of Board regulation. During the Kennedy hearings, the Board proposed a liberalization of its charter policies, eventually adopting rules in August 1975 that lifted restrictions on charter operations.

John Robson lent his support to policy liberalization after assuming his post in June 1975. His proposed deregulation experiment was not adopted; however, it indicated the new chairman's willingness to consider deregulation. In July 1975 the Board cancelled the remaining schedule reduction agreements. In the same month, the Pulsifer Committee released its report recommending "that protective entry, exit, and public-utility type price control in air transportation be eliminated within three to five years by statutory amendment to the Federal Aviation Act."[26] A second committee was appointed by Robson to study CAB procedures. It was headed by Elroy Wolff, a past Robson associate, and included consumer, airline employee, and other representatives. This committee also strongly criticized CAB regulation.

The Ford and Kennedy bills were the subject of the Cannon hearings, which convened in April 1976.[27] Neither advocated total deregulation of the industry nor termination of the CAB, provisions which later became a part of the Airline Deregulation Act. Both bills, however, included most of the provisions eventually passed by

Congress. Both bills proposed a two-stage process to reduce CAB control over the industry. First, policies and procedures were outlined for the Board to follow during a specified period of transition to a more relaxed regulatory regime. Second, the substantive boundaries of CAB authority that would become a permanent feature of the regulatory regime after the transition period were specified. Rather than route deregulation, carriers were granted more freedom, under certain conditions, to enter and exit markets without CAB interference. A guarantee of continued service to small communities was included to alleviate concern that exit freedom would result in loss of service. Instead of rate deregulation, a "zone of reasonableness" would grant carriers fare flexibility without CAB interference if rate reductions or increases did not extend above or below the zone.

The specifics of the Ford and Kennedy bills framed much of the debate during the Cannon hearings. The critical issue Cannon had to resolve was the question of how reform should be accomplished. Opponents of decremental reform restated their arguments made during the Kennedy hearings. They were dissatisfied with Board administration of the statute, not with the statute itself. Furthermore, they argued that recent CAB policy changes supported their contention that the existing statute adequately provided for effective regulation. Senator Kennedy and the Ford administration repeated their argument that reform would be ineffective unless statutory reductions in the Board's authority were adopted. If Cannon accepted the incremental solution, the chances for eventual deregulation would be delayed indefinitely.

Arguments presented on the first day of the hearings by the CAB persuaded Cannon to support the decremental approach. Speaking for a unanimous Board, Robson announced that there would be "significant risks and uncertainties, and fewer potential benefits, if the present regulatory regime is continued."[28] The Board rejected the alternative of a "progressively stricter utility-type scheme" and supported a system "which moves in the direction of relying fundamentally on competition and the operation of natural market forces—a system which minimizes government interference to the greatest extent possible and emphasizes greater management freedoms in entry, exit, and pricing."[29]

Cannon was visibly shocked by Robson's statement. Up to this point, Cannon had not been receptive to the argument that regulation itself was the root cause of the industry's economic problems. Endorsement of the position by the regulators themselves, however, provided the credibility necessary to insure his support.

Furthermore, the CAB's justification of its decision recast the argument for deregulation. During the Kennedy hearings, the argument was presented within an efficiency framework. Deregulation was proposed on the grounds that regulation contributed to inflation, increased costs to consumers, and caused economic inefficiencies. The CAB's rationale for deregulation, however, emphasized the adverse impact of the regulatory framework on the regulated industry itself. Robson argued that decremental reform was necessary primarily because continuation of the system would destroy the financial health of the industry. The prospect of the airline industry going the way of the railroads was not insignificant in winning Cannon's support.

Cannon endorsed the Board's position in a speech before airline industry leaders shortly after the 1976 hearings. Careful to make a distinction between deregulation and regulatory reform, he rejected the former as an unrealistic alternative proposed by "zealous economists." However, he agreed that reform was necessary to "revitalize the airline industry with new competition" and announced plans to introduce legislation reducing the Board's authority.[30]

Cannon's subcommittee began a second round of hearings in March 1977 to consider two bills. One was jointly sponsored by Senators Cannon and Kennedy. The second bill was endorsed by the CAB and sponsored by Senators James B. Pearson, ranking minority party member on the Cannon subcommittee, and Howard Baker, Senate minority leader. Deregulation was still generally unacceptable. As Cannon noted in opening the hearings, "neither [bill] deregulates the airlines or puts the CAB out of business. Both redirect regulation while preserving it."[31]

The Pearson-Baker bill reserved more discretion for the CAB in implementing the reforms. Its introduction as S.3536 followed the introduction of the Ford bill (S.2551) and the Kennedy bill (S.3364) in 1976. These were the first three legislative proposals for CAB reform. The Pearson-Baker bill was later reintroduced as S.292 and titled the Commercial Aviation Regulatory Reform Act of 1977. A compromised version of the initial Ford and Kennedy proposals was sponsored jointly by Cannon and Kennedy. Commonly referred to as the Cannon-Kennedy bill, S.689 was titled the Air Transportation Regulatory Reform Act of 1977. It included the major provisions of the earlier Ford and Kennedy bills with the addition of an airline employee compensation program designed to weaken labor opposition to reform.

The most significant event during the hearings was the endorsement of decremental reform by United Airlines, a major scheduled carrier. United's president Richard Ferris announced that "the regulatory status quo is unacceptable. Significant changes are necessary in the regulatory environment."[32] United's support of relaxed rate and route regulation was the first break in the unified opposition of major carriers to statutory reductions in CAB authority.

Following a lengthy Senate Commerce Committee markup of the Cannon-Kennedy bill, the Air Transportation Regulatory Reform Act of 1978 was reported to the Senate. During the markup, the Carter White House heavily lobbied committee members for a favorable report. Shortly after taking office in January 1977, Carter had endorsed the Cannon-Kennedy bill, and the White House had spearheaded the organization of interest groups in support of the legislation. Carter was also successful in enlisting the reluctant cooperation of Secretary of Transportation Brock Adams, who gave his influential support to the bill.

Presidential endorsement, compromise to compensate potential victims of the policy shift, and the influential Cannon-Kennedy-CAB alliance all contributed to passage of the Reform Act by an overwhelming Senate majority on April 19, 1978.

LEGISLATIVE ENDORSEMENT OF DEREGULATION

Developments during House consideration of companion legislation and policy initiatives by the CAB combined to reduce opposition to deregulation, especially among the regulated carriers. The result was final agreement on a bill that was better designed to terminate the regime of direct regulation and its agent, the CAB.

Administrative Deregulation

In June 1977, Alfred Kahn, Carter's first appointment to the CAB, assumed the chairmanship after Robson's resignation. Kahn, the first economist to serve on the Board, endorsed reforms that would remove restraints on carrier competition. Under his leadership, the CAB eventually abandoned Robson's cautious approach to reform and implemented policies approximating rate and route deregulation.[33]

Kahn's first initiatives concerned the staffing and organization of the agency. Personnel changes were made that increased support for deregulation at the CAB. Key staff positions were filled with individuals such as Michael Levine, Reuben Robertson, and Phillip Bakes, who were well known supporters of deregulation. A strong management team was appointed by Kahn, and it proceeded to scramble the CAB's organization. The reorganization was designed to strengthen staff support for deregulation. Rate and route responsibilities were redistributed in an effort to wrest control from staff members committed to the public-utility type regulation adopted in the DPFI. Administrators supporting implementation of the Pulsifer study recommendations were moved to influential positions within the organization. Kahn's position was further strengthened when Carter appointed Elizabeth Bailey to the Board in July 1977. She, like Kahn, was an economist who supported airline deregulation.

On the policy front, Kahn initially worked to continue the reform trend begun in 1975. Robson, a lawyer by training, had been reluctant to go beyond a conservative interpretation of the Board's legal authority in reforming regulatory procedures. Since 1975, the Board had opposed deregulation. Reforms primarily were aimed at reinstating policies that had characterized Board regulation in the mid-1960s. These reforms had been popular because they encouraged discount fares, low-cost charter travel, and more frequent scheduled service. Furthermore, the industry had recovered from its economic slump of the early 1970s, which many attributed to the Board's procompetitive policies.

Kahn and other staff members were convinced that further reductions in regulatory restrictions were needed. Kahn was also convinced that this would not be possible unless Robson's conservative approach was abandoned. He encouraged his staff to explore ways to further reduce CAB interference in carrier rate and route decisions. The most significant procedural and policy changes that resulted violated regulatory precedents and were of questionable legality. As one informant remarked, "Robson was too much the lawyer and Kahn too little." Nevertheless, the Airline Deregulation Act was passed before the policies could be overruled by the courts. They also proved to be very popular, influencing two of the three remaining Board members to join Bailey in supporting Kahn.

During Kahn's chairmanship, more restrictions on carrier pricing policies were lifted and price competition encouraged. Low-cost air service and pricing competition between charter and scheduled airlines was promoted by the Board. The trend toward minimizing restrictions on charter travel was continued with the effect of reducing the distinction between supplemental and scheduled operations. Discount pricing regulations were also relaxed. This combined with competitive threats from charter carriers and other scheduled carriers as a result of competitive route awards to spread discount fares throughout the industry.

Two other major policies were adopted to encourage carriers to use competitive pricing strategies. First, the Board adopted a Pulsifer study recommendation that fare levels be used as a major criterion in route decisions. Preferential treatment would be given to carriers in route cases who proposed to introduce low fares on a route. Route cases involving low-fare proposals were also given expedited hearings. Second, the Board adopted a zone of downward fare flexibility that approximated the rate zone provision in the Senate reform bill. Carrier price reductions as much as 50 percent below the standard industry fare level would in most cases be approved automatically by the Board.

The most significant and controversial changes occurred in Board route policies. Procedural innovations such as non-oral hearings and show-cause orders were used to speed up the route award process and bypass lengthy evidentiary hearings. The Board also adopted decision criteria designed to minimize obstacles to carrier route expansion. A new applicant was no longer required to prove that its proposed service would be profitable, a policy adopted in the DPFI. Carriers seeking to block another carrier in its bid for a new route could no longer do so on the grounds that the route award would divert traffic from its own operations.

Adoption of a multiple permissive entry route policy came very close to de facto route deregulation. In order to increase carrier route discretion, the Board initially adopted the policy of granting permissive entry authority to a carrier when service on a new route was approved. The carrier was not required to maintain a minimum level of service and could initiate or terminate service at its own discretion.

A major obstacle in applying the new policy to all carriers was the traditional Board interpretation of the Administrative Procedure Act. In the past, the act was read as requiring full evidentiary hearings in route cases and the comparative selection of only one applicant seeking the new route authority. The process was time-consuming and meant that permissive entry could only be granted on a carrier-by-carrier, route-by-route basis.

In order to bypass the procedural obstacles to widespread and expedited application of its permissive entry and exit policy, the Board adopted a multiple permissive entry concept and im-plemented it through a show-cause order. Rather than selecting only one carrier in a route proceeding and conferring permissive authority, all applicants were granted the right of entry as well as entry and exit freedom if they could prove they were "fit, willing, and able" to serve the route. The show-cause order gave the pro-cedural advantage to new entrants by shifting the burden of proof to opponents of the proposed route awards.

Board aggressiveness in the spring of 1978 significantly increased the prospects for favorable action on the reform bill pending in the House. By the end of the summer, the CAB on its own initiative had implemented most of the bill's provisions. The adverse conse-quences of deregulation predicted by opponents of the legislation had not materialized. On the contrary, airline profits significantly increased in 1977 and 1978, diminishing airline opposition to dereg-ulation.

As early as March 1978, two other major carriers, Western and Braniff, joined United in supporting CAB decontrol. In April 1978, United revised its support for relaxing regulations to the more extreme position of total and immediate deregulation of the indus-try. Opposition by the Air Transport Association ended in June 1978, when its member firms in the scheduled passenger industry endorsed a policy statement calling for reductions in Board control.[34]

Major opposition from the airlines did not end just because of rising profits in the wake of administrative deregulation. The new Board policies and the uncertain legislative future of the reform bill created an unstable regulatory environment that both the major airlines and other traditional opponents of statutory reform found disconcerting.[35] Uncertainty about the industry's regulatory future adversely affected the carriers' ability to plan future marketing strategies and equipment purchases. Furthermore, loan institutions were hesitant to extend financial aid on favorable terms. Continuation of the new Board policies was contingent on pending court decisions regarding their legality. However, court litigation would take months, and legislative action presented the most expeditious route to stabilizing conditions in the industry.

The Board had yet to totally decontrol route and rate regulation, but there was the possibility that it would go even further toward deregulating the industry on its own. Some congressmen as well as airline companies were aggravated with the Board's boldness in pursuing deregulation without waiting for a legislative mandate. For them, the pending legislation was significant not because of the substantive reforms it proposed but because it provided the means for stopping "the madmen at the CAB."

House and Conference Action

Up until the final months of legislative action, deregulation or CAB termination was considered too volatile an issue for inclusion in a reform bill. However, CAB actions in late 1978 and differences in the Senate and House versions of reform legislation paved the way for adoption of "sunset" provisions that enhanced the possibility of eventual abolition of the Board by specifying the date on which the CAB's regulatory duties would cease.

Glenn Anderson's House Public Works Subcommittee on Aviation had delayed action on a reform bill in order to deal with House legislation concerning aircraft noise abatement. Subcommittee markup of a House bill did not begin until March 1978. In the following months, relaxed route regulation proved to be the most controversial issue. Committee action was delayed in order to work out a compromise which eventually included a sunset proposal.

A bill similar to the Senate proposal was initially used as the markup vehicle. However, on March 8, the first day of subcommittee markup, Elliott Levitas introduced and the subcommittee approved an amendment striking the automatic entry provisions. Later in the month, Allen Ertel successfully reinstated the provisions setting the stage for a complete breakdown in the markup process.

Levitas responded to the Ertel action by proposing a new bill to be used as the markup vehicle. It was substantially weaker than the Anderson proposal, deleting almost all provisions that relaxed airline rate and route regulation. However, the Levitas proposal formally recommended CAB termination for the first time in the reform debate. Levitas, a strong advocate of sunset review, proposed that the Board be scheduled for termination on December 31, 1983, and its functions transferred to other agencies unless reauthorized by Congress. The subcommittee approved the substitute bill in a thirteen to eleven vote. Anderson quickly adjourned the markup session to prevent a vote that would send the weaker bill to the full Public Works and Transportation Committee.[36]

During the next seven weeks, Anderson attempted to work out a compromise that would salvage the deregulation provisions in his original bill. The stalemate was finally broken on May 9, 1978, when the subcommittee approved a compromise bill that was subsequently approved by the full House Public Works and Transportation Committee in a thirty-seven to five vote. Restrictions on CAB regulation were less severe than in the Senate bill, but Anderson succeeded in retaining a modest automatic entry program. Also included in the House bill was Levitas' original sunset proposal, with the CAB reauthorization date rescheduled for 1982. The House approved the subcommittee proposal on September 21, 1978, in a lopsided vote of 363 to 8.

The sunset provision had been presented as a major concession to deregulation proponents in exchange for reductions in regulatory authority less dramatic than those proposed by the Senate. However, most supporters of the stronger Senate bill were not impressed. Many considered the sunset provisions meaningless, and few predicted that Congress would not reauthorize the CAB. Mimi Cutler, director of the Consumer Aviation Project, described the proposal as a "farce."[37] However, the House proposal later provided the opportunity during conference committee action to strengthen provisions aimed at terminating the CAB and ending rate and route regulation.

Conference committee work began on October 2, 1978. A key compromise involved House and Senate differences on automatic route entry and the House sunset proposal. Both Senate and House versions of the reform bill contained provisions designed to encourage route competition. In the Senate version, conditions were specified under which the Board was required to honor the request of a carrier to serve a route not originally authorized in its certificate. Intrastate and ceticated carriers were authorized to initiate nonstop service on one route without CAB approval in 1979 and again in 1980. In 1981 and each subsequent year, a carrier could enter two new routes without fear of CAB interference. At the same time, a carrier was authorized some degree of protection from new competition by being granted the right to exempt some of its routes from the automatic entry program. A carrier could block entry by another carrier by annually designating three of its routes as ineligible for entry in the years 1979, 1980, and 1981. In 1982, the number of routes a carrier could protect from competition would diminish to two, to one in 1983, and thereafter all a carrier's routes would be eligible for automatic entry by other carriers. There were some special protections from route competition provided for subsidized and small carriers, but, generally, the Senate provisions represented a substantial reduction in Board control over route entry.

In House action, the Senate's automatic entry program was significantly weakened. First, the House limited the entire program to one year rather than subscribing to a pattern of progressive liberalization of a carrier's right to initiate new service without Board approval. Second, carriers were only allowed to enter one new route during the life of the program, while the number would eventually increase to two under the Senate plan.

Third, the House version rejected the Senate recommendation to terminate after 1983 a carrier's right to block entry into some of its routes. Finally, the House proposed to retain the Board's authority to reject a carrier's request for new route authority. Under the Senate plan, Board approval was required unless the route requested had been withdrawn from the program by another carrier.

The conference committee's substitute version of the Senate and House automatic entry proposals allowed carriers to request entry into two routes in 1979, 1980, and 1981, respectively. In each of these years, a carrier could protect one of its routes from entry. The conference version of the route program was more conservative than the Senate's in that it limited the program to a specific time frame, limited the carriers to one new route for each year of the program, and did not provide for termination of the route-protection provision. On these points, the conference substitute more closely resembled the limited plan proposed by the House conferees.

The Senate yielded to the more conservative automatic entry program because of changes in other provisions in the reform package. Specifically, the amended version was not opposed because House conferees agreed to modifications in the sunset proposal first introduced by the House. Essentially, the sunset proposal was strengthened, thereby accomplishing to an even greater extent the goal guiding the Senate's version of the automatic entry program—the termination of the CAB's authority over carrier route decisions. At the same time, the changes in the sunset provision, purchased by deregulation proponents with a more conservative route-entry program, enhanced the prospects for terminating Board regulatory authority in other areas.

The House sunset proposal represented the traditional "dropping the gauntlet" approach in that it only specified a future date for review and reauthorization of the entire spectrum of Board operations. Senate conferees proposed a phased sunset approach that created intermediate steps to Board termination. Dates were specified for the sunset of individual blocks of CAB authority before the issue of agency termination was considered.

Using functional termination as a transition to structural termination was a strategy characterized by one architect of the proposal as "pulling the teeth of the tiger." Separating out the Board's key functions of rate, route, and antitrust regulation and assigning each a termination date was expected to facilitate abolition of the CAB itself. Phased and piecemeal termination was expected to present fewer political obstacles than cataclysmic and comprehensive termination. Furthermore, if the Board's major regulatory functions were successfully terminated, there would be little justification for reauthorizing the agency.

The conference committee compromise was easily passed by both the House and Senate and signed by President Carter on October 14, 1978. Adoption of a more conservative route-reform proposal and inclusion of phased sunset provisions insured support from both opponents and supporters of deregulation. Immediate reforms in regulation were not as deregulation-oriented as reform activists wished. However, specific dates for terminating the Board's authority convinced them that the final bill was actually stronger than any of the earlier proposals. Furthermore, the idea of deregulating the industry apparently had become more acceptable as the result of administrative deregulation by the CAB. The conference committee titled the bill the Airline Deregulation Act of 1978, the first time the term deregulation had been included in an airline reform proposal.

THE AIRLINE DEREGULATION ACT OF 1978

The legislation signed by President Carter in October 1978 was designed first to relax, and then to terminate, direct economic control of the domestic airline industry. In other words, phased deregulation of the industry was mandated. The CAB was scheduled for termination in 1985, following a transition period during which its key regulatory functions would be terminated.

During the transition period, the Board was directed to prevent anticompetitive airline practices and to "place maximum reliance on competitive market forces."[38] Its authority to regulate market entry, exit, and fares was curtailed and procedures implemented to expedite Board decisions and promote relaxed rate and route regulation.

Restrictions on entry of new airline firms into scheduled passenger service and controls over certificated carrier entry into new routes were substantially reduced. Though still required to obtain a certificate, a carrier must only prove that it was "fit, willing, and able" to provide the service and not that it was "required by the public convenience and necessity." The Board was also required to allow carriers previously restricted to charter or cargo service to provide scheduled passenger service. Non-oral and show-cause proceedings authorized by the bill enhanced the ability of carriers to receive new route authority and speeded up the certification process. The less stringent fitness standard, a shift in the burden of proof to opponents of new entry, and expedited procedures—all significantly opened the air transport route system.

Relaxed entry requirements were supplemented with dormant authority and automatic entry programs that provided virtually a guarantee that carriers could enter new routes without CAB interference. Under the dormant authority provisions, carriers were permitted to provide nonstop flights on routes where another carrier was certified but not providing service. The automatic entry program required the CAB to grant intrastate and certificated carriers at least one new route during each of the 1979, 1980, and 1981 calendar years.

Carriers were also granted more freedom to exit markets. They were only required to give advance notice and were not bound by the requirement of full evidentiary hearings before terminating service. The major restriction placed on exit freedom was the requirement that "essential air service" be maintained at cities receiving scheduled passenger service before the bill was passed. The small-community service program was included to preclude abrupt termination of service on less profitable routes. The Board was directed to define essential service to small communities, and the service was then guaranteed for ten years and maintained by a new subsidy program. It was directed to block exit until a replacement carrier could be found if exit reduced service below the required minimum.

Pricing freedom was also granted. However, an upper and lower limit on pricing flexibility was set. The Board was ordered to determine, and semiannually to revise, a standard industry fare level (SIFL). Carrier rate increases or reductions not greater than 5 percent above or 50 percent below the SIFL could not be suspended by the Board unless it found them to be predatory. As in route proceedings, the burden of proof was placed on opponents of the fare change. Furthermore, the CAB was authorized to revise the lower limits of the zone. Restrictions on differential or discount pricing were also relaxed.

Finally, the Board's antitrust exemption authority was changed. It was the first step toward eventual transfer of the industry to market regulation under antitrust. Under the old law, Board approval was required for all intercarrier agreements regarding proposed mergers, pooling arrangements, and interlocking relationships. Board approval exempted carriers from prosecution under the antitrust laws. Intercarrier agreements still required Board approval under the new law. However, the law limited

Board discretion by directing it to apply the procompetitive thrust of antitrust statutes in immunity decisions. A carrier was required to prove that the exemption was necessary, and the Board was prohibited from approving an agreement which substantially reduced or eliminated competition, unless the carrier could prove a serious transportation need or an important public benefit. Furthermore, the Board could not approve an agreement that limited capacity among air carriers or that fixed rates, fares, or charges.

During the transition period, the major components of the classical regulatory framework would be terminated. Regulation of carrier routes was scheduled to end on December 31, 1981. On January 1, 1983, regulation of carrier fares, mergers, and intercarrier agreements would terminate. By January 1, 1984, the CAB was required to present a detailed opinion to Congress "as to whether the public interest requires continuation of the Board and its functions beyond January 1, 1985."[39]

After its termination on January 1, 1985, the CAB's residual responsibilities would be transferred to the Departments of Justice, Transportation, and State, and the Postal Service. Transportation would assume administration of the small-community service program and would work with the State Department on air service agreements with foreign countries. Finally, the Justice Department would inherit the Board's residual antitrust authority and the Postal Service its responsibilities regarding mail transport. The CAB's consumer protection responsibilities, such as the regulation of baggage handling and booking practices, were not allocated by the bill. The oversight subsequently led to a jurisdictional struggle between the Department of Transportation and Federal Trade Commission, which was resolved by the CAB Sunset Act of 1984.

The CAB authority over carrier routes and domestic fares expired as provided for in the 1978 legislation on December 31, 1981, and January 1, 1983, respectively. As the January 1, 1985, termination date for the CAB approached, House members became convinced of the need for legislation clarifying the disposition of the CAB's remaining authority. On June 5, 1984, the House passed HR 5297, a bill whose primary purpose was to resolve the issue of CAB authority in the consumer protection area. The Reagan administration favored transfer of the authority to the Federal Trade Commission upon CAB termination. The House bill, however, transferred the authority to the Department of Transportation.[40]

Another major provision in the House legislation concerned the antitrust authority retained by the CAB. The 1978 Deregulation Act provided for transfer of the CAB's authority over carrier mergers, interlocking relationships, intercarrier agreements, and antitrust immunity to the Department of Justice upon CAB termination, a provision supported by the Reagan administration. House members, however, argued that antitrust authority over the airline industry should be transferred to the Department of Transportation since most of the other residual responsibilities of the CAB would also be given to the DOT. On August 8, 1984, the Senate passed legislation which approved the transfer of CAB consumer-protection and antitrust authority to the DOT. A conference version of the House and Senate bills was approved by both chambers in September 1984 as the CAB Sunset Act.[41] The CAB was terminated as scheduled on January 1, 1985.

CONCLUSION

The regulatory policy cycle and its impact on efforts to secure statutory deregulation of the airline industry suggest that the politics of deregulation were in large part a continuation of the politics of regulation. The Board's typical resumption of restrictive policies during the economically depressed period of the early 1970s provided the opportunity for traditional supporters of competitive regulation to discredit the regulatory regime. The opportunity was also seized by advocates of the more extreme deregulation alternative.

A return to competitive policies in the mid-1970s was associated with industry recovery. The confluence of industry prosperity and competitive regulation increased support for legislation that would initially restrict and eventually terminate the CAB's ability to reimpose restrictive policies. Essentially, the reform bill represented the statutory endorsement of the competitive approach, thereby precluding, short of legislative action, the reassumption of the traditional restrictive approach by the CAB.

Analysts attribute legislative passage of the airline deregulation bill to several factors. Policy entrepreneurs, advocacy by the regulatory agent, presidential support, changes in public opinion, and alterations in interest group structure are credited with having played roles in the reform process. An explanation for airline deregulation must incorporate these aspects of the reform process. The regulatory policy cycle, however, suggests political continuities and patterned economic-political relationships that are perhaps more fundamental in determining the success or failure of regulatory reform initiatives.

The regulatory policy cycle contributed to the conditions that facilitated passage of the deregulation bill. Conditions and opportunities, however, must be exploited or they must coincide with the activities and efforts of participants in the reform process in order for them to be considered politically significant in their impact on the success or failure of reform. Reference to general trends and conditions alone cannot fully explain why statutory changes in the CAB's authority were adopted nor why the more radical deregulation provisions eventually implemented in 1985 were included in the legislation. The significance of conditions associated with a political event is a function of their relationship to political behavior. Conditions associated with airline deregulation must be evaluated in terms of their relationship to the behavior and to the strategies of deregulation proponents, a task reserved for chapter 6.

6 | Deregulation Strategies

INTRODUCTION

An argument developed in chapter 1 was that predictions based on much of the policy process and regulatory politics literature as well as on historical trends in aviation regulatory reform would prescribe failure for deregulation proponents. However, the chronology of events presented in the preceding chapter indicates there can be exceptions to the presumption of policy perpetuation and regulatory expansion. Furthermore, the political history of the deregulation bill illustrates how the proposal developed from a relatively modest to a more radical reversal of established policy. Initially, decremental reform was proposed, in that legislative proposals advocated merely relaxing the application of direct regulation by limiting the Board's authority to control airline routes and rates. Termination of regulatory controls and abolition of the CAB were not at first formally proposed. Deregulation, the scheduled termination of specific regulatory functions, was not included in legislative proposals until very late in the reform process. Provisions in the final bill concerning structural and functional termination came much closer to mandating deregulation than many thought possible when Ford proposed the first reform bill in 1975.

An important condition facilitating deregulation was the cyclical character of CAB regulatory policy. Major airlines were enjoying benefits of an improved economy in 1978 when the CAB took its traditional competitive policies to their logical extreme. A variety of other conditions such as the popular anxiety over inflation and "big government" contributed to the passage of deregulation. Policy reform, however, is not caused by conditions. It is the result of political actors who either identify and expolit conditions to their advantage or who benefit from the coincidence of their reform initiatives with favorable circumstances. In either case, analyzing, not the conditions alone, but the *behavior* of political actors in relation to conditions is important to an understanding of policy reform.

The concept of strategy was discussed in chapter 2 as a useful approach in analyzing how advocates of airline deregulation overcame the obstacles to policy termination. In this chapter, the adoption of airline deregulation and the synergistic character of the termination process are explained in terms of the effective use of strategies in conjunction with conditions that enhanced their effectiveness. The strategies are referred to as deregulation strategies because they are types of political behavior aimed at building support for the termination of regulatory functions.

The analysis goes beyond describing coalitions that supported or opposed deregulation and detailing the rationales for their various positions. The key question is how the proponents of deregulation sought to develop support for their position and how they overcame obstacles to policy termination. Attention is directed to the political behavior and conditions associated with a successful effort to marshal support for a radical policy change.

Analysis of the airline case suggests that at least six deregulation strategies were at work. They are (1) the articulation of a policy alternative, (2) policy evaluation, (3) political packaging, (4) strategic compromise, (5) strategic staffing, and (6) administrative deregulation.

ARTICULATION OF A POLICY ALTERNATIVE

The articulation strategy involves the specification of a policy to be substituted for the incumbent policy. The importance of a clearly articulated alternative to the success of a termination proposal is suggested by Peter deLeon when he notes that "many critics would only move to terminate a program if they could offer alternative programs to rectify the problem; the inherent complexity of some policy issues might well insulate organizations and programs from termination actions because attractive alternatives are not available."[1]

Comparison of the incumbent policy and its substitute—which is implied, if not specified, in the termination proposal—reveals the ideological dimensions of a particular termination act. In a more practical vein, delegitimizing of the status quo and acceptance of the termination proposal are affected by the degree to which the process of articulating the alternative serves to polarize the issue, clarify the consequences of termination, and legitimize the critiques of the incumbent policy.

Eugene Bardach argues that ideological conflict contributes to the unique and significant character of termination politics. He comments that there is "much more to the understanding of termination processes than predicting the composition of the opposing coalitions. The most interesting theoretical aspect of termination politics is the interrelationship between the political order and the moral order."[2] It is in the articulation of a policy alternative that the ideological dimensions of the deregulation process are most clearly illustrated.

In chapter 2 it was noted that the airline deregulation proposal essentially meant the transfer of the industry from control under a classical regulatory regime to control through antitrust enforcement. Direct regulation of the airlines represented resource-allocation planning, which "is the governmental substitute for marketplace decisions in the private sector."[3] The point is elaborated by Louis Jaffe in his description of the "public philosophy" during the 1930s when the Civil Aeronautics Act was passed:

Much of the thinking of the thirties was based on the notion that the industrial system was "mature" or even senescent. . . . Administration was a branch of geriatrics. This thinking was a not unnatural reaction to the terror of the depression. In 1933 we could see that our resources and our already developed plant were immensely productive, capable of providing an unprecedented standard of living. On every hand it was said that our problem was not one of production but distribution. . . . To deal with distribution problems we assumed a given level of output and a given organization of resources for producing it. This, at least, was the implicit psychology of the planning thesis. To a shattered nation the gospel of salvation by competition was a devilish irony.[4]

From this perspective, the adoption of airline deregulation represents one case in which the "psychology of the planning thesis" gave way to "the gospel of salvation by competition." The debate over airline deregulation involved the classic ideological conflict between government planning (direct regulation) and marketplace competition policed by antitrust enforcement.

Articulation of the competition-antitrust alternative to airline regulation was accomplished principally by economists. They presented a united front to President Ford during his 1974 inflation summit, arguing that economic deregulation would reduce inflationary price increases. Shortly thereafter, the deregulation alternative was seized upon by Senator Kennedy and his staff. His subcommittee provided the forum for the economists' position on airline regulation. Lucille Keyes later commented on the significant impact of economists in the deregulation process:

In the airline field, the framers of reform legislation both in the Administration and in Congress drew on the work of professional economists, and the Civil Aeronautics Board justified its reform program largely on the basis of academic economic analysis. As a leading cargo airline executive has remarked, "The push for deregulation started not in the business community, but in the universities. The movement spread from academia to the executive and legislative branches of the government and finally found acceptance among the public at large."[5]

Articulation of an alternative to the incumbent policy furthers the goal of delegitimizing the status quo and facilitating termination in four principal ways. First, the question of reform becomes polarized when proponents of policy change articulate an alternative, and this polarization aids in the decision-making process because it clarifies and simplifies policy options. Decisions are rarely made unless the issue is sufficiently polarized to allow for identification of the opposing positions. During the Kennedy hearings, it became clear that there was general support for some type of reform due to widespread dissatisfaction with CAB policies. More significantly, the adversarial and proderegulation design of the hearings as well as the Ford administration's endorsement of the economists' argument clarified the policy positions. The incremental versus decremental reform positions framed subsequent debates.

Second, the articulation strategy serves to clarify the consequences of temination in that an alternative policy is specified. This function of the strategy is the most problematic for those seeking policy change because clarifying the policy alternative may also be somewhat dysfunctional in that it can stimulate conflict and opposition. Support for a termination proposal may be diminished not from lack of dissatisfaction with the incumbent policy, but because the alternative implied in the proposal is even less satisfactory. For example, the notion of substituting antitrust enforcement for direct regulation was not without its critics. William Herman contended that "those who want to maximize price competition expend most of their efforts on the tangle of issues associated with regulations, but they obviously want to go beyond deregulation. Some, therefore, almost casually bring up antitrust policy. . . . Surely the antitrust policies are as ineffective as regulation in promoting (or at least not preventing) price competition."[6]

In the debate over airline deregulation, however, much more attention was given to the consequences of current regulation than the deficiencies of the proposed alternative. This can be explained in part by the fact that it was easier to catalogue the undesirable consequences of an existing policy than convince others of the yet-to-be-proven benefits of a new policy. Also, disagreements among termination proponents may be created because of disagreements over a replacement policy. Consequently, there may be an incentive to keep the debate focused on the deficiencies of the existing policy with much less energy given to the articulation and promotion of an alternative. In sum, the extent to which the alternative policy implied in a termination proposal is developed and clarified will vary with the expected impact clarification will have on support for the termination proposal.

A third major advantage of presenting a clearly articulated policy alternative is that it lends legitimacy and credibility to the request for policy termination. A preoccupation with the deficiencies of the existing policy casts the reformer in a negative role. An alternative policy enables termination advocates the opportunity to argue that termination should occur both because the current policy is ineffective and because the proposed change is more effective in addressing the problem.

Finally, having a clearly defined policy alternative also helps termination proponents by providing a framework useful in the development of two other strategies to be discussed later—policy evaluation and political packaging. The policy alternative provides a common reference point and language for those dissatisfied with existing policy. Furthermore, it is possible to publicize the benefits of termination in terms other than the deficiencies of current policy. A more positive approach is made available by offering a policy alternative whose benefits to specific groups can be identified and illustrated.

POLICY EVALUATION

An important feature of the airline deregulation process was the significance of policy studies. The debate was marked by extensive analysis of CAB regulatory policies and proposed reforms. For some, the proposal for decremental reform was studied to the point of absurdity. In testimony before the House Aviation Subcommittee in March 1978 Chairman Kahn noted that "since November of 1974, there have been eight sets of hearings by five separate congressional committees, over a period of 60 days. . . . There have been dozens of studies and reports by the Board, the Department of Transportation, the General Accounting Office, and several congressional committees—an accumulation of evidence totaling nearly 20,000 pages. . . . There is certainly no point in still further study."[7] The tendency to study a radical policy proposal "to death" is well illustrated in the airline case. Nevertheless, even though the demand for more study can be used to delay action, policy evaluation can be used as an effective tool by termination proponents.

As a deregulation strategy, policy evaluation refers to the use of policy analysis as a means to discredit the existing policy framework and the arguments made against termination. A major function of "the empirical effort [is] to determine who is actually being helped or hurt by the program in order to evaluate arguments made in its favor."[8] In other words, policy analysis goes beyond simply assessing the effectiveness or efficiency of the incumbent policy. It can be used to clarify the policy's impact in terms of its equity, which in turn facilitates the task of building support for the termination proposal.

Empirical studies germane to the airline deregulation process were of two general types. Theodore Keeler refers to them as "academic studies versus policy studies."[9] The two types also can be differentiated according to when they were completed. Senator

Kennedy's staff director noted that by 1974 the airline industry was already a natural candidate for reform because of the large volume of academic studies critical of the anticompetitive effects of airline regulation.[10] However, during and after the Kennedy hearings, policy evaluations assumed a narrower and more strategic focus in that they examined either specific arguments made against reform proposals or the expected consequences of the proposals.

A large amount of literature criticizing CAB policies toward the airlines developed in the years after World War II. One of the first major studies arguing for deregulation of the industry was completed by Lucille S. Keyes in 1951. She argued that Board policies were designed to protect the revenues of carriers holding route authority. The anticompetitive and protectionist thrust of CAB policies led her to conclude that carrier certification requirements should not be retained. Furthermore, she felt there was "no apparent reason for the retention of the specific rate powers now possessed by the Board."[11] In another influential study published in 1962, Richard Caves argued that "the major standing policies of the Civil Aeronautics Board do not coincide with the economist's usual criteria of efficiency," resulting in unnecessarily high costs of air service.[12] He concluded that "the root of the problem is the notion of a certificate of public convenience and necessity" because it created an incentive for the Board to protect and be more responsive to carriers already holding a certificate.[13] Caves joined Keyes in endorsing deregulation, noting that "the air transport industry has characteristics of market structure that would bring market performance of reasonable quality without any economic regulation."[14]

In the period when the Caves' and Keyes' studies were published, a major weakness in the argument for deregulation was the fact that the industry had always been regulated. Emmette Redford, in an evaluation of Caves' position, noted that "there is no history of unregulated air transport under similar conditions to those of 1938 to the present by which tests can be made of the findings from economic logic."[15] This problem was remedied when, in the mid-1960s, economists began comparing the operations of CAB-regulated interstate carriers to intrastate carriers in California and Texas that were not regulated by the CAB.[16] The studies concluded that CAB-regulated carriers experienced higher operating costs and subsequently higher fares than a non-regulated carrier serving the same route. Comparative studies of CAB regulated and non-regulated carrier operations provided strong evidence to support the view that regulation caused inefficiencies and made industry operations more costly. More importantly, the intrastate carrier experiences provided deregulation proponents concrete examples of the consequences of their policy alternative.

For the most part, academic studies of CAB regulation completed prior to the Kennedy investigation supported a "producer protection" explanation of regulatory behavior. Douglas Anderson succinctly describes the hypothesis.

> It is now a commonly held view that regulation by its very design protects only producers. If regulators in their own self-interest do not assure a capture-type result, large private groups, acting to cartelize their industry to enhance their economic status, will. The strongest evidence in support of the producer protection hypothesis comes from the regulation of three oligpolistic or competitive industries: interstate airlines, railroads, and freight motor carriers.[17]

As noted earlier, Board policies and political scandal associated with the CAB in the early 1970s contributed to reform agitation. Both reinforced a protectionist interpretation of Board regulation. One informant contended that "deregulation would not have been well accepted if the CAB had not gone so far under Timm in limiting competition. . . . The horribles of the Timm administration preceded Ford, and the defenders of the status quo had no record on which to oppose change."[18]

Board opposition to carrier requests to enter new routes and proposals for low fare operations "played into the hands of the deregulators. It proved the points made by the critics of regulation [i.e., that the Board's top priority was to protect the large scheduled carriers from competition]."[19] Chairman Robert Timm's unabashed support for the large scheduled carriers and his close ties with the Nixon administration provided additional support for the protectionist thesis. In sum, Board actions in the early 1970s lent credibility to policy evaluations critical of regulation.

In addition to academic studies that were used to structure the Kennedy investigation, other policy evaluations contributed to deregulation support. In the legislative phase of the reform process during and subsequent to the Kennedy hearings, a variety of studies, most at the request of congressional committees, were commissioned to examine specific reform proposals, narrow aspects of airline regulation, or questions raised by deregulation opponents. For example, in April 1974 the Air Transport Association released a study critical of deregulation.[20] Senator Kennedy and his staff initiated an extensive review of the study, soliciting the views of numerous economists and government agencies that would discredit the report. A study sponsored by the Department of Transportation and released in February 1976 concluded that President Ford's reform bill would increase passenger traffic and lower air fares.[21] The General Accounting Office released a study one year later contending that rate deregulation would result in substantial savings to the traveling public.[22] Finally, the CAB itself sponsored two major studies providing support for deregulation. The Wolff Committee was created by Chairman Robson in the summer of 1975. Though the committee had been directed to eliminate the "great tangle of procedural spaghetti" at the CAB, its report was more preoccupied with the virtues of deregulation.[23] The Pulsifer Committee argued strongly for deregulation in its report released in July 1975.[24]

The credibility of the narrower type of policy evaluation was enhanced because the studies appeared to be objective as well as comprehensive in addressing the myriad issues raised by airline deregulation. Most of the evaluations were conducted during the course of the Kennedy investigation. In assessing the hearings, Breyer suggests that "there may be an advantage in placing initial responsibility for reforming a particular program in the hands of a committee that does not ordinarily supervise the agency concerned."[25] The fact that the Kennedy subcommittee was investigating a regulatory program that it did not also supervise contributed to the credibility of the subcommittee's report. As an "outsider," the subcommittee was not constrained or tainted by direct political ties with the regulated industry. However, the most important feature of the evaluation strategy was its comprehensiveness. It addressed all major objections to deregulation and in the process actively sought input from the various groups concerned. Consequently, the recommendations of the Kennedy subcommittee were difficult to attack, and its report was praised for its thoroughness. Even President Ford wrote a personal letter to Senator Kennedy praising his subcommittee's work.[26]

POLITICAL PACKAGING OF THE POLICY ALTERNATIVE

The strategy of political packaging of the termination proposal differs from the strategies of articulation and evaluation in that it takes into account the political context in which policy termination is pursued. This strategy serves to make the proposal politically relevant by promoting the development and clarification of linkages between the proposal and the political interests represented in the policy area.

Effectiveness of the strategy in building support for the termination proposal is contingent on the ability of those who employ the strategy to assess accurately the interests affected by the proposal and subsequently to present the proposal in terms that are relevant to those interests. This assessment process resembles what Eugene Bardach refers to as "the problem of mapping the attentive public."[27] An understanding of the political context—"what groups oppose or favor a specific policy termination and why"[28]—is a prerequisite to the next step in the process—translation of the proposal into the "language" of the affected interests.

The essence of political packaging is the presentation of the termination proposal in a manner that maximizes its serviceability to various individuals and interest groups. This process frequently involves lobbying efforts that isolate one feature of the termination proposal, locate a group that will benefit from it, and consequently acquire their support for the termination effort.[29] Rather than promoting the benefits of termination, the strategy may be used to clarify and present the political and economic costs of the incumbent policy to specific groups. Regardless of the approach, political packaging is based on the assumption that different groups will have different views regarding the instrumental value of the termination proposal.

One informant cautioned in regard to the airline case: "An important point to remember is that the reasons for deregulation varied with the types of groups joining the drive."[30] The implication for strategists is that they must proceed on the assumption that their proposal is a means to multiple ends.[31] Translation of the proposal in terms of those multiple ends requires a particularistic rather than a general approach in presenting and arguing for the proposal. In other words, the goal of the political packaging strategy is not harmony among the affected interests but independent assent to the same proposal.[32]

The airline deregulation debate underwent a shift in emphasis that highlights the significance of political packaging as a deregulation strategy. Up to and including the Kennedy investigation, economic and operational efficiency arguments dominated the debate. However, once it was clear that there was a consensus for some type of reform, a point well publicized by the Kennedy hearings, the debate turned to equity issues raised by subsequent reform proposals. As one informant noted, "During the Kennedy hearings the arguments were cast in an efficiency framework. During the Senate and House hearings, they were cast in terms of equity."[33]

The disparity between equity and efficiency arguments was emphasized by Col. John J. O'Donnel, president of the Airline Pilots Association, in testimony during the first round of hearings before Senator Cannon's subcommittee in 1976:

> Up to this point, the debate has centered around the more theoretical issues of airline economics and public service requirements. But for the men and women who earn their living in the airline industry, the deregulation debate has a more personal meaning: the outcome could very well have an adverse effect on their careers. . . . There is widespread agreement that the chances are good that one or more airlines will fail in a deregulated environment.[34]

Implied in his statement is the preeminence of equity considerations in the reform process. A political packaging strategy is required because of the problem of equity in termination politics. It provides a means for coping with the problem as well as a method for turning equity issues to the advantage of termination proponents.

Reactions to the first legislative reform proposals revealed formidable opposition even to decremental reforms that did not go so far as to completely terminate the CAB and its authority to control airline routes and rates. In April 1976, when Cannon held hearings on the first set of reform bills, those opposed to major legislative reductions in CAB authority proposed in the Ford and especially the Kennedy bill were well represented. Most scheduled and local service carriers, airline labor groups, aircraft manufacturers, investors and creditors of the industry, and airport operators generally agreed with the position taken by the scheduled carrier industry: "the airlines are reluctant to see sweeping changes in the way regulation is carried out. They don't believe basic changes are necessary."[35]

Despite such opposition, there were other conditions that enhanced the attractiveness of deregulation. The proposal for curtailing airline regulation coincided with a general political reaction against regulation and a record peacetime inflation rate. In explaining the airline reform initiative, Herbert Kelleher noted that "there has been a growing public reaction against regulation of all kinds, manifested by sunset legislation, hostility against such agencies as the FDA and OSHA, and disgust at the debacle which the ICC has made of the railroads."[36]

The antiregulation mood can be attributed in part to the unique economic conditions of the 1970s. One commentator observed that

there undeniably is a growing political and popular disenchantment with many old government regulatory and promotional programs. There is a feeling that the programs have not ensured adequate supplies of goods and services at reasonable prices. The programs as they exist today essentially grew out of New Deal times of oversupply and depression. That regulatory pattern does not necessarily fit the new economic order of shortages and inflation.[37]

Disenchantment with regulation coincided with the record-setting pace of inflation in the mid-1970s. Inflationary increases resulted in mounting public pressure on the White House and Congress to do something.[38]

The most significant example of the political packaging strategy at work in the airline case involved the presentation of deregulation as a solution to inflation and, more obviously, as a solution to excessive regulation. Inflation and economic regulation were linked by both academic economists and officials in the Ford administration. Major proponents of the argument that economic regulation created higher prices were located in the Justice Department's Antitrust Division, Council on Wage and Price Stability, Council of Economic Advisers, the Department of Transportation, and the Civil Aeronautics Board. Consumer groups affiliated with the Ad Hoc Committee on Aviation Reform were also major advocates.

An early and leading advocate of the position that anticompetitive behavior was a major contributor to inflation was the Antitrust Division. In the summer of 1974, one commentator observed that the Division, "by increasingly intervening in proceedings before regulatory agencies, has become the major force advocating that regulated industries be required to engage in a greater measure of economic competition."[39] One official characterized the Division's attack on economic regulatory agencies as "institutional Naderism."[40] Antitrust officials also took their case directly to congressmen by appealing to their concern over rising inflation. For example, in August 1974 Assistant Attorney General Thomas E. Kauper, in a speech before the House Republican Task Force on Anticompetitive Practices and Monopolistic Powers, estimated that anticompetitive conduct cost consumers 80 billion dollars annually.[41] Other congressional observers detected "a growing mood for tougher enforcement of the antitrust laws, motivated partially by a desire to protect the consumer from high prices resulting from lack of competition."[42]

In the fall of 1974, the inflation-regulation linkage received presidential endorsement. The promise of lower prices and reductions in regulatory intervention made airline deregulation attractive to both consumer advocates and more conservative elements. One informant attributed the proposal's success to its bipartisan appeal. "The most significant reason for passage of the act was its bipartisan support. Pro-consumer Democrats joined with free enterprise Republicans."[43]

STRATEGIC COMPROMISE

Eugene Bardach suggests that policy advocates have two major options: to design their proposal to fit an existing consensus or to articulate their proposal and then proceed to build a consensus around it.[44] Political acceptability is emphasized in the first approach, whereas the integrity of the original proposal is paramount in the latter. The consensus-building approach more closely relates to the political packaging, evaluation, and articulation strategies previously discussed. Each emphasizes the importance of efforts to persuade others of the advantages of the termination proposal without modifying the proposal itself. However, any policy proposal calling for major changes is unlikely to be adopted in its original form. In most cases, some features of the initial proposal must be sacrificed because persuasive strategies which stop short of modifying the proposal frequently fail to secure its adoption. Consequently, substantive changes, i.e., compromises, in the original proposal are needed to attract the necessary support. Changes made in the reform proposal that serve to build support for the termination option are referred to as strategic compromises.

Three types of strategic compromise are suggested by the airline case: (1) design compromises, (2) equity compromises, and (3) targeted benefit compromises. A precondition for both design and equity compromises is general agreement on the need for, or at least belief in the inevitability of, some degree of policy change. The key issue is not whether change is necessary but rather how it will be implemented. Such a situation in the airline reform process existed in the period following the Kennedy hearings. One commentator, reviewing the airline debate in 1977, observed that "even the critics of the pending proposals agree that the airline industry no longer needs much federal support. Where people part company is on how quickly the goal of greater competition can be attained and what protections the federal government should give during the transition period."[45]

The issue of "how quickly" is the focus of design compromises, whereas the issue of "protections . . . during the transition period" is the subject of equity compromises. In contrast, targeted benefit compromises are relatively peripheral to the central issue of terminating regulatory functions, but nonetheless serve to generate support for the deregulation proposal.

Design Compromises

Design compromises are those made in connection with the issues of timing and approach in the implementation of the termination proposal. Essentially, they address the questions of how and when the particulars of the termination proposal are to be implemented. The significance of implementation design is noted by Peter deLeon when he cautions termination proponents to have "a termination plan for the ineffective policy and an implementation plan for the new one."[46] Obviously, equity considerations and the uncertain consequences of policy change will influence design decisions. In this sense, design compromises affect the degree of political support given to a termination proposal. How the transition to a new policy framework is to be made is often as important as the substance of the new policy itself in terms of gaining political support. However, design compromises are significant for another reason. Legislative enactment of a termination proposal is only the beginning of its implementation. Design compromises made in an effort to diminish opposition have a future impact in that they can facilitate or hinder implementation of the new policy.

Two critical issues were the subject of design consideration in the airline case. They were the timing of and approach to the termination of airline economic regulation. An early and continuing conflict was over the question of approach. Mitnick identifies two types of deregulation: formal and informal. The distinction is based on the degree to which deregulation is formally structured or planned as opposed to being unplanned or evolutionary.[47] Another distinction in approaches to deregulation similar to Mitnick's formal-informal dichotomy is statutory versus administrative deregulation. It was this distinction that dominated much of the debate over airline deregulation.

As previously noted, the CAB under Robson's chairmanship joined with those advocating a reduction in Board regulatory control over airline route and rate decisions. However, in his testimony before Cannon's subcommittee in 1976, after explaining the Board's position, Robson went on to advocate an administrative approach to the implementation of decremental reform. In comparing the CAB's position on implementation with that in Ford's bill, Robson concluded that:

Both call for a redirection of public policy toward reliance essentially on competitive market forces rather than governmental decisions. Neither the Board nor the administration advocate a program for the total elimination of regulatory powers, either at once or on a day certain in the future. But there the similarity of approach ceases and the difference begin. The administration approach is premised on the notion that transition toward a freer system can only be achieved if Congress spells out in the statute, and sets dates for, the precise substantive and procedural steps along the road, and removes or hedges any Board supervision or discretion over critical areas of decision. . . . Fixed dates and fixed actions which leave no administrative flexibility. That, essentially, is the administration bill's proposal, which we see as being excessively rigid.[48]

Like the CAB, many of the regulated airlines supported an administrative as opposed to a statutory approach to reform. As one airline executive stated, "Basically, there is nothing wrong with the statute; the problem has been its administration. Most of the objectives—the encouragement of competition in certain areas of the system, and fare experimentation—can be achieved without . . . drastic legislative surgery. . . ."[49]

In his testimony before Cannon's subcommittee in 1976, Robson also referred to the second major issue associated with design compromise—timing. "What should be the process of change? The Board believes that there are two basic alternatives: one, gradual or phased loosening of entry, exit and price controls; and two, abrupt elimination of such controls after some period of notice. . . ."[50] The two alternatives concern the timing of implementation. Shall the termination proposal be implemented catastrophically, i.e., "the program or agency ceases on a certain date without appreciable wind-down . . ."[51] or, shall the termination be phased, i.e., "all functions are at least nominally retained, but at continually lower levels of activity."[52]

In the airline case, phased deregulation was adopted. Enactment of the 1978 legislation marked the beginning of a statutorily guided transition period culminating in the termination of the CAB's principal regulatory functions, the transfer of some programs to other agencies, and finally structural termination of the organization itself. Functional termination in this case is equivalent to what Mitnick refers to as "stripping," which occurs when "functions, activities, and/or subprograms are dropped, one by one." Structural termination is equivalent to what Mitnick calls "disintegration with transfer of programs," which occurs when "the program or agency is disintegrated, with parts transferred to a new or different agency."[53]

During the transition period, the CAB would retain its regulatory functions. However, the manner and conditions under which they could be exercised were severely restricted. Also, CAB intervention was limited by the directive to place "maximum reliance on competitive market forces" in the exercise of its regulatory authority.[54] Specific programs designed to phase in rate and route decontrol were also legislated, including a "zone of reasonableness" for rates and automatic entry and dormant authority programs for routes.

One decision faced by termination proponents is whether the

termination will be a gradual, decremental process or an immediate and total action. Peter deLeon contends that phased is preferable to catastrophic termination.[55] He concludes that the decremental approach will be more successful because it provides an opportunity for those affected to adjust gradually. In contrast, the catastrophic approach will meet with greater resistance because of its abruptness and the greater preparation required for adjustment.

Phased deregulation, however, is not without its problems. For one thing, it provides deregulation opponents opportunities to intervene and delay or even preclude completion of the transition to deregulation. This is the second horn of a dilemma in the deregulation process: although phased deregulation may be the most politically acceptable approach, it enhances the potential for deregulation opponents to stymie the process. Furthermore, partial deregulation practiced during the transition period may create problems precisely because it is partial. Two months before the Airline Deregulation Act became law, CAB chairman Alfred Kahn related his experiences with CAB initiatives to deregulate. He concluded that "what has been genuinely illuminating to me . . . is how rich a comprehension I have acquired of the distortions of the transition, and how thoroughly I have as a result been converted to the conclusion that the only way to move is fast. The way to minimize the distortions of the transition, I am now thoroughly convinced, is to make the transition as short as possible."[56] Fast transitions, however, are usually not popular or politically feasible.

Equity Compromises

Equity compromises are provisions in the termination proposal designed to prevent or anticipate a possible consequence that is unacceptable to some group. They constitute what Eugene Bardach refers to as the strategy of "cushioning the blow."[57] It involves including provisions in a policy termination proposal that will ameliorate injuries to those interests adversely affected by policy change.

This form of strategic compromise is necessary because issues revolving around equity become major obstacles to deregulation.[58] The equity problem arises simply because there are vested interests in the existing regulatory framework. The problem is exacerbated by the uncertain consequences of termination. Equity problems in the airline case were graphically illustrated by Chairman Kahn:

> People who profess to be in favor of freer competition nevertheless demand from the advocates of deregulation guarantees that no town will lose service, even temporarily; that no carrier will be subject to unequal competitive pressures because it may have inherited a less favorable route structure than its rivals; that there will, furthermore, be no wastage of fuel, no excessive entry into any market, no injurious discrimination, no bankruptcies, no loss of seniority rights anywhere, no danger of increased concentration, and no impairment of scheduled service. Or they will oppose free entry unless and until the advocates can predict in complete detail how the new pattern of operations will look, while professing to be content to leave the fashioning of the future air system, in its every detail, to the very same Civil Aeronautics Board that stoutly asserts its inability to make these predictions.[59]

In sum, termination attempts generate predictions of adverse consequences for particular segments of the regulated community as well as demands that those consequences be forestalled.

Equity compromises result in programs that are intended to prevent the undesirable consequences of termination from developing, or they provide mechanisms to deal with a predicted consequence in the event the prediction proves correct. In other words, they are responses to the "what if" question posed by termination opponents because of the uncertainty associated with major policy change.

Two major equity compromises were included in the airline deregulation bill. They were the labor protection provisions and the small-community service program. One of the strongest opponents of the Cannon-Kennedy bill, which was eventually revised and passed by the Senate, was airline labor led by the Airline Pilots Association (APA). On February 25, 1977, the executive council of the AFL-CIO released a statement endorsing the APA's position. The statement charged that the proposal "would emasculate the nation's scheduled airline network provided in the Federal Aviation Act of 1958 and substitute a mistaken reliance on so-called free market competition for the development of a public air transportation system."[60]

A major factor in organized labor's opposition was that the proposed bill threatened labor's position in the industry and employee job security. The legislation would grant broader operating authority to and encourage the expansion of the commuter airline industry. Historically, organized labor had difficulty in unionizing commuter airline employees. In part, this was because the commuter industry was not subject to provisions in the National Labor Relations Act that applied to the certificated carriers. Regulated airline employees would also lose CAB protection from loss of seniority and benefits in the event of airline acquisitions or mergers. Under regulation, the CAB required carriers who were parties to a merger or acquisition to include labor protection provisions in their agreements. Furthermore, deregulation opened the industry to new airlines who could compete with established carriers without the burden of high labor costs. These concerns of organized labor led to the incorporation of labor protection measures into the legislation.

During the Senate Commerce Committee markup of a revised version of the Cannon-Kennedy proposal, Senator John C. Danforth (D-Mo.) proposed the original labor protection amendment to the reform proposal.[61] Trans World Airways was headquartered in Missouri and was the state's second largest employer. Danforth expressed concern that route decontrol would have an adverse impact on the airline, which was already experiencing financial problems. As the Senator's legislative aide put it, "Sen. Danforth has campaigned against the heavy hand of government regulation, but he was not sent here to deal in abstract exercises. There are 14,000 people in Missouri who work for TWA, and he wants to make sure they and their families are treated fairly."[62] Citing airline employee fears that the reforms would cause massive layoffs, Danforth proposed that the government offer them some financial assurances because "no one can show that their anxieties are groundless."[63]

With some minor revisions, Danforth's proposal passed the Senate, survived House and conference action, and was included in the final bill.[64] It directed the Secretary of Labor to develop rules and regulations for the administration of monthly assistance payments to airline employees who are dismissed or forced to relocate because of reform-related disruptions in the industry. Furthermore, airline firms were required to give hiring preference to dislocated or terminated airline employees.

A second major equity compromise concerned airline service to small communities. Opponents of relaxed route regulation argued that the existing regulatory system insured service to cities that generated little passenger traffic. Service was available because the CAB enforced a system of cross subsidy in the industry, which meant that service to less profitable city-pairs was made possible by revenues derived from more profitable route segments. Given exit freedom, it was expected that airlines would terminate these unprofitable route segments in order to shift their equipment to more lucrative routes. Despite extensive efforts during the Kennedy investigation to refute this argument, fear of service terminations forced deregulation supporters in the Ford administration to offer a compromise.

Shortly after President Ford and Senator Kennedy submitted their reform bills to the Senate and just prior to the first round of Cannon's subcommittee hearings in the spring of 1976, the Department of Transportation released a recommended program designed to dispel concerns about service loss. Both Ford and Kennedy adopted the proposal as an amendment to their own bills. It was also endorsed by the CAB and subsequently incorporated into the Pearson-Baker reform bill. Essentially, the program was designed to establish a minimum service level for small communities,[65] require replacement service before a carrier could reduce flights below the minimum level, and provide a subsidy program to maintain minimum service for at least ten years.

Though the small-community program guaranteed "essential" service, it did not guarantee existing service levels. Fear of service reductions was also a major reason for opposition to the automatic entry and relaxed exit provisions in the reform bills. Both were highly controversial during the Senate Commerce Committee's markup of the bill in the fall of 1977. Twelve of the eighteen senators on the committee were from western states and only four from densely populated states. Western states are characterized by small and widely separated communities, prime targets for service terminations because of low traffic demand. Senator John Melcher expressed the concern of many other congressmen from rural states: "I have real misgivings about what may happen. We have real good service now, but Northwest might switch some of its flights and not leave us high and dry but with less service."[66]

The service issue reemerged during the House committee markup session. However, a weakened version of the Senate proposal was included in the House bill. An acceptable resolution of the issue was worked out in conference committee action. A Senate Commerce Committee staff member who participated in the conference deliberations explained how the problem was resolved.

A key compromise concerned the automatic entry provision. In order to satisfy the House, the Senate agreed to compromise the automatic entry provisions in their bill. From our perspective, we did not see this as a big issue. The CAB had already significantly opened up route entry. What was important was the sunset provision.[67]

In return for a more restricted automatic entry program—one which gave the carriers more protection from other carriers wanting to enter their route system—Senate conferees recommended a more elaborate and stronger version of the House proposed sunset provision. Consequently, the functional or "pulling the teeth of the tiger" approach to CAB termination was included in the final bill as a conference substitute for the House sunset proposal.

Targeted Benefit Compromises

Targeted benefits represent the third type of strategic compromise used in the airline deregulation process. It is similar to what Eugene Bardach refers to as a "special benefit tactic."[68] It involves including a benefit in the termination proposal targeted toward a specific group that one wishes to have as a supporter. Provisions of this type appear to, but may not necessarily, be unrelated to the termination provisions themselves. Consequently, they can be characterized as "riders" on the termination proposal. In sum, targeted benefit compromises are those provisions in a termination proposal that confer benefits to specific groups but that do not directly alter their proposal's termination provisions.

Several examples of targeted benefit compromises were evident in the airline case. Most concerned specific classes of carriers. Several concerned the commuter carrier industry. In 1977, the Commuter Airline Association, the trade association representing small air carriers operating under an exemption from CAB economic regulations, announced its position on regulatory reform.[69] Commuters were almost exclusively concerned with changing CAB policies and legislative provisions that were limited to the commuter industry. Major policies that were opposed by the carriers included their ineligibility for operating subsidies, exclusion from the federal loan guaranty program for aircraft purchases, and restrictions on the size of aircraft commuters could operate.

When the local service carrier class was created by the Board in 1945, no restrictions on equipment size were imposed. Consequently, the CAB was unable to prevent the carriers from purchasing large aircraft that could be economically operated only on long-haul routes with high passenger demand. The use of large aircraft contributed to regulatory problems and conflicts betwen the local service and trunk carriers. In an effort to avoid a repetition of the trend in the small irregular carrier industry, the CAB renewed its exemption of commuter carriers in 1952 but under the condition that they not operate planes that weighed more than 12,500 pounds. The intent was to prevent competition between commuter and local service carriers. However, in 1965, commuters were authorized to serve route segments in competition with certificated carriers. This policy, in conjunction with new aircraft technology, led the CAB, upon request by the commuters, to revise the aircraft weight restriction. In 1972, the Board adopted a revision which abandoned the total weight criterion by limiting commuter carriers to a maximum of thirty passenger seats and a 7,500 pound payload capacity.[70]

After 1972, the commuter industry continued to pressure the CAB for further liberalization of the aircraft restriction. In 1976, the industry requested legislative exemption from CAB regulations that included increasing aircraft limitations from thirty to fifty-five seats and from a 7,500-pound to a 16,000-pound payload capacity.[71] The proposed change would enable the carriers to compete more effectively with other carriers by allowing them to fly larger planes while simultaneously avoiding the rigors of economic regulation. Also, the proposal would prevent the CAB from imposing more restrictive aircraft requirements in the future without going through Congress. The 1978 act adopted the 55-seat maximum and provided an 18,000-pound payload capacity, which was more liberal than the industry-requested figure.

In addition to liberalized exemption limitations, the commuters also sought eligibility for the CAB's subsidy program and the government's loan guaranty program. In both cases, commuter participation was precluded under the current statute because only certificated carriers were eligible. Unlike certificated carriers, commuters would not be compensated for serving routes that proved unprofitable. However, the small-community service program outlined in the 1978 legislation was based on the assumption that the commuter industry, because it used smaller aircraft, would be the principal replacement carriers in the event the larger local service and trunk carriers decided to exit small-community routes. In recognition of the commuters' significant role during the transition period, the House amended the reform proposal making them eligible to receive subsidies provided under the small-community service program.[72]

Eligibility for federal loan guarantees on equipment purchases was also extended to the industry. In an attempt to ameliorate airline industry financial problems in the 1950s, Congress enacted the Government Guaranty of Equipment Loan Act of 1957. However, only certificated carriers were eligible for the loan guarantees. The act was set to expire in September 1977. The 1978 bill extended the program for five years and was revised to accommodate the commuter carriers by making them eligible.[73]

Like the commuters, the charter or supplemental carriers were primarily interested in receiving specific concessions from a reform bill. In testimony before Senator Cannon's subcommittee in 1976, Edward J. Drischoll, president of the National Air Carrier Association representing the supplemental carrier group, summarized the charter industry's position on reform:

I would like to discuss only three features of the bill which are of vital importance to both the supplemental carriers and the traveling public. These are: the specific statutory authorization for advance booking charters; two, the provision authorizing common control air carriers and charter tour operators; and three, the removal of the language currently in section 401 (d) (3) of the act, which, at least as interpreted by the CAB, prevents the supplemental carrier from obtaining a certificate to perform scheduled service.[74]

Of the three, the requests for statutory liberalization of charter operating restrictions and opportunity for certification of scheduled operations were granted in the 1978 legislation.

Criticism of Board policies toward charter carriers had intensified in the early 1970s as the CAB moved to severely restrict supplemental operations in an effort to minimize competition with scheduled carriers.[75] Several congressional committee investigations were held in response to growing discontent with CAB policies. One product of the investigations was a bill sponsored jointly by Senators Kennedy and Cannon. Entitled the Low Cost Air Transportation Act, its provisions had been worked out in 1974 and then introduced in the Senate in 1975.[76] It directed the CAB to adopt an advanced booking charter (ABC) concept in regulating the supplementals. It was considered less restrictive in that it required that passengers only purchase tickets in advance of a charter flight. In contrast, the affinity-group concept had guided CAB regulation since the 1960s. It was more restrictive in that it limited charter travel to individuals who had maintained membership in a non-travel organization for at last six months prior to the charter trip.

In response to the Cannon-Kennedy initiative, and pressure from the Ford White House, the CAB embarked upon a program of charter liberalization during the chairmanship of John Robson. In October 1976 it adopted the ABC concept, and further liberalization occurred under Kahn's chairmanship.[77] In 1978, the Airline Deregulation Act specified that "no rule, regulation, or order issued by the Board shall restrict the marketability, flexibility, accessibility, or variety of charter trips provided under a [charter] certificate." Furthermore, any CAB regulation in the future affecting charter carriers "shall in no event be more restrictive than those regulations regarding charter air transportation in effect on October 1, 1978."[78]

Finally, the supplementals were also granted dual certification rights. For many years the charter airlines had sought authority to engage in scheduled carrier service, but to no avail. The CAB position, supported by the scheduled carriers and the courts,[79] was that the statute did not pemit certification of the same carrier for both chartered and scheduled operations. This situation was changed by the 1978 bill, which directed the CAB to consider all applicants for a certificate during the transition period.[80]

STRATEGIC STAFFING

Strategic staffing occurs when the principal criteria for appointment decisions are the policy attitudes of candidates for the position. As a deregulation strategy, it involves the recruitment of individuals for government positions who are committed, or at least not actively opposed to, the termination of the existing regulatory framework. In Eugene Bardach's discussion of the opportunity a change in administration provides those seeking to terminate a policy, he notes the importance of staffing decisions. Staffing vacancies that occur when a new administration takes office permit the appointment of officials who are known opponents of or who at least have no vested interest in continuing the incumbent policy.[81]

Strategic staffing as illustrated in the airline case went beyond the appointment of individuals who were simply not committed to existing policies. The appointment process involved the selection of candidates who were already opposed to the existing policy and in favor of its termination.

Attempts to influence an agency's development and administration of policy through staffing decisions are not unusual.[82] Attention to agency appointments may be due, as Charles Perrow suggests, to the belief that one of the best ways to control an organization is to surround oneself with loyal people.[83] Appointments to independent regulatory commissions such as the CAB take on added importance because of the latitude of discretion granted the commissions by Congress. Commissioners occupy influential positions because of their policy discretion. The post of chairman is in most cases particularly important because of its strategic position in the agency's administrative process.[84] Staff members may also occupy positions that enable them to signficantly influence commission actions.

The signficance of staffing decisions for airline deregulation was suggested by one informant who argued that "there were two brilliant strokes during the move to deregulate the airlines. They were the appointments of Robson and Kahn. . . . The President may want something but he needs to have people in the right places who agree with his perspective because it is these people—experts—who will be listened to. Having people in the right places who can lend credibility to the executive viewpoint is crucial."[85]

During President Ford's term, members of his administration proved as effective in shaping his perspective as they did in agreeing with it. Deregulation advocates were located in such key executive branch agencies as the Council on Wage and Price Stability, the Office of Management and Budget, the Department of Transportation, the Council of Economic Advisers, and the Antitrust Division of the Justice Department. Economists were particularly well represented and played a critical role in persuading Ford to adopt economic deregulation as a major component of his anti-inflation program during his economic summit conference in the summer of 1974.[86] However, neither Ford nor John Robson, his appointed successor to Robert Timm as chairman of the CAB, used strategic staffing as consistently as did President Carter and his appointee, Alfred Kahn.

Paul Quirk argues that the appointment of Robson illustrates the Ford administration's "lack of attention to policy attitudes . . . obtained even in appointments by President Ford to positions heading agencies high on the list of those his administration was seeking to reform."[87] Prior to his appointment, Robson had not been a deregulation activist nor did he have a clear cut position on the issue of airline deregulation. Consequently, his staff appointments while chairman included both supporters and opponents of deregulation.[88] Despite Robson's initial indecisiveness, one informant contended that he "created the willingness to look at the problem of airline regulation." Though cautious in his approach to reform, "his instinct was to undo what Timm had done."[89] Under his administration, the Board hastened the swing back to the more procompetitive posture which had characterized Board regulation prior to the administrations of Secor Browne and Robert Timm.

Appointment policies during the Carter administration and at the CAB during Alfred Kahn's tenure reflected a more consistent use of strategic staffing as a means to influence regulatory reform.[90] During his campaign, Carter had allied himself with public interest and consumer groups, promising to emphasize regulatory reform in his legislative program and appointment policies.[91] The result was the appointment of individuals such as Michael Pertschuk as chairman of the Federal Trade Commission, Joan Claybrook to the National Highway and Traffic Safety Administration, Daniel O'Neil to the chairmanship of the Interstate Commerce Commission (later succeeded by Darius Gaskins), and Alfred Kahn, Marvin Cohen, and Elizabeth Bailey to the CAB. In these and other cases, the appointees were known to support the administration's position on regulatory policy.

Alfred Kahn endorsed the Senate version of the deregulation bill during his confirmation hearings in 1977 and indicated a preference for airline deregulation in testimony before the Kennedy subcommittee in 1975.[92] Once at the CAB, Kahn implemented staffing and organizational changes that had the effect of insuring organizational commitment to a policy of deregulation. One informant characterized the process in the following manner: When Kahn came to the CAB, there was still a very strong interventionist sentiment among the staff. Many staff members were strongly dedicated to policies adopted as the result of the Domestic Passenger Fare Investigation conducted in the 1970s. In part, the DPFI codified policies typically used by the CAB in the anticompetitive phase of the regulatory policy cycle. Kahn had to overcome staff dedication to the DPFI policy approach and commitment to regulatory intervention. To do this, he brought in some key staff people.[93]

A reorganization of the CAB staff occurred which was orchestrated by Dennis A. Rapp, who served first as the chairman's special assistant and later as managing director of the CAB. Rapp had a reputation for effectively using reorganization for policy purposes.[94] The reorganization enabled Kahn to move proderegulation staff members into key positions. A new Office of Economic Analysis was created, and Darius Gaskins, a former economics professor and director of the Federal Trade Commission's Bureau of Economics, was hired as its director. Michael Levine, an outspoken advocate of deregulation, was appointed to direct a new Bureau of Pricing and Domestic Aviation. Reuben Robertson, formerly with Nader's Consumer Aviation Action Project, assumed directorship of the CAB's new Bureau of Consumer Protection. Finally, Phillip Bakes, a lawyer from the Antitrust Division, was appointed as legal counsel.[95] In sum, staffing and organization changes in 1978 made before House passage of the deregulation bill were in accord with the Board's officially stated intention to "produce an industry more promptly responsive to the workings of the marketplace, less tethered to regulations, and hence more responsive to the real needs of the public."[96]

ADMINISTRATIVE DEREGULATION

Administrative deregulation refers to the use of agency discretion to implement the termination proposal before it receives statutory sanction. The initiatives of the CAB in the months preceding House passage of the legislation went even further toward deregulating the industry than did provisions in the bill. The latitude of administrative discretion exercised by the CAB led some critics to argue that legislation was not necessary to realize the reforms deregulation proponents had been seeking. However, as the agency moved more aggressively to curtail regulatory controls, the traditional opponents of statutory reform became advocates, not because the CAB could not go far enough toward deregulating the industry under the current statute, but because it had gone too far.

Administrative deregulation by the Board transformed statutory reform from a proposal for policy termination to a device for preventing the CAB from deregulating even more than was proposed in the legislation. For example, the CAB's policy of permissive entry enabled carriers, once licensed to serve a route, to intitate or terminate service virtually at will. However, under the automatic entry program in the legislation, carriers were limited in the number of new routes they could add to their system. Furthermore, they could declare certain routes ineligible for entry by a competing carrier.

The significance of administrative deregulation was proven in subsequent deregulation initiatives. Reform of trucking, railroad, and communications regulation, following airline deregulation, support the conclusion that the regulatory agencies themselves have historically played a pivotal role in bringing about reform. Instances of significant reforms in the 1970s lead some to conclude that "urging the agencies to proceed with initiatives within the range of their permissible discretion under existing legislation might be a more effective way of eventually getting desirable changes in the statutes."[97] Another writer was more emphatic about the use of administrative deregulation to expedite statutory reform. Christopher DeMuth concluded in a review of the deregulation movement "that major administrative reform is a necessary prerequisite to statutory reform."[98]

The amount of discretion available to agency personnel, political support for agency initiatives, and the timing of the initiatives influence the effectiveness of administrative deregulation. Regulatory discretion delegated to an agency in its enabling statute is frequently criticized as an abbrogation of legislative responsibility that contributes to capture by regulated groups.[99] However, CAB actions illustrate that agency discretion is not always used to serve the interest of the regulated as they define it; nor is its use limited to protecting the agency's authority or blocking policies and programs opposed by agency personnel.

Administrative discretion depends largely on how agency personnel define statutory provisions regarding agency authority. Agency actions based on these interpretations are then subject to judicial

review if they are challenged. Under Robson's chairmanship, reform efforts were limited by a conservative interpretation of the
CAB's statutory authority. However, under Kahn's chairmanship,
strategic staffing was used to bring in staff members "who were
willing to interpret the 1958 act broadly." Furthermore, the new
chairman's management style encouraged the staff to break with
precedent and to search for opportunities to implement policies
that diminished the CAB's regulatory role. As one staff member
observed: "Kahn quickly began to question all the standard policies
and procedures. Instead of going ahead as usual, he would get his
staff to do a review."[100] Consequently, administrative discretion was
used to diminish rather than expand regulatory intervention.

The effectivenes of administrative deregulation is not solely dependent on the parameters of administrative discretion. "How far
one can go unilaterally is as much a question of politics and timing as
of statutory language."[101] Agency policy innovations will not be
successful and are usually not attempted unless they are assured of
political support from groups outside the agency.[102] A corollary is
that the agency will depend on its political allies for protection when
attempts are made to curtail its authority. James Landis pointed out
the importance of political support to agencies, declaring that "the
agency must have friends, friends who can give it substantial political assistance with which to fend off measures aimed at circumvent-
ing its program or curbing its powers."[103] However, political assistance is equally important to an agency that is seeking to curtail its
authority. Overwhelming Senate support for reductions in airline
regulation was registered in April 1978 when the Senate passed its
bill. President Carter had personally lobbied for the bill, pressing
for quick action by the Senate Commerce Committee, and continued his activism on the House side. With White House encouragement, a variety of consumer and business organizations
spanning the political spectrum later joined to form the Ad Hoc
Committee on Aviation Reform. United Airlines, a major trunk
carrier, supported the bill, causing opposition from regulated carriers to begin to unravel. Such support lowered the political costs of
CAB activism.

Finally, the timing of deregulation initiatives by the agency is
critical. Administrative deregulation will likely be challenged in the
courts by parties adversely affected by deregulation policies, and

the agency risks reversal of its actions by the courts. Consequently, one reason for statutory reform is to provide protection for policies already adopted by the agency. Chairman Kahn made the point in an interview during House action on the bill. "The main value of the legislation to me is its declaration of policy, which wil increase the likelihood of our being sustained in the courts."[104] The question of CAB authority to deregulate never reached the courts. As one informant explained, "There was no time for a test case to be filed to challenge the Kahn policies on the basis of inadequate legislative authority. The new bill passed before the courts had the chance to hear or rule on a case."[105]

Timing administrative deregulation also involves taking into account the possibility of legislative backlash. Aggressiveness in the exercise of its policy discretion places the agency in a vulnerable position. If the industry experiences financial decline or other problems occur subsequent to agency initiatives, the agency and its policies are easily blamed, diminishing the prospects for statutory reform. Fortunately for deregulation proponents, CAB initiatives coincided with rising industry profits and declining fares. It was not clear whether improved financial conditions were due to the pro-competitive policies of the CAB or simply the general upturn in the national economy during 1978. Regardless of the primary cause, deregulation opponents took advantage of the situation and pointed to it as proof of the wisdom of deregulating the industry. The association of CAB deregulation efforts with financial improvements in the industry was clearly stated in the committee report on the House version of the deregulation bill.[106]

The effectiveness of administrative deregulation by the CAB is best indicated by its impact on the reform debate itself. For some, Board actions and their association with improvements in the domestic aviation industry simply confirmed arguments for deregulation. However, for others, statutory reform was valued more as an instrument for checking administrative deregulation than because of substantive policy changes it would mandate. As one informant commented, "Kahn moved so fast he angered both the airlines and Congress. . . . Actually, the bill was passed in part to slow down the CAB."[107] The intention of statutory reform to regain congressional control of the CAB was clearly stated in the conference report on the final bill:

In adopting this new, comprehensive legislation, which entirely over-hauls the aviation regulatory system, Congress was mindful of recent activities of the CAB. This new charter is intended as a legislative man-date to the CAB both as to the direction and policy of aviation regula-tion and also, it should be noted, the limits of such a policy. In short, Congress expects the deregulation of the aviation industry to move in accordance with this legislation and not in accordance with the, per-haps, differing concepts of some members of the CAB.[108]

SUMMARY

In the preceding analysis, airline deregulation was treated as a termination policy. As noted in chapter 2, those seeking termina-tion of an existing policy confront prodigious obstacles. The pur-pose of this chapter was to suggest how, in the case of airline deregulation, the opposition to policy termination was counter-acted.

An analysis of the airline case suggested six strategies that in-fluenced the course of the deregulation process. Antitrust enforce-ment was presented as an alternative to classical regulation of the airline industry. Articulation of the alternative served to polarize the reform debate, clarify the consequences of deregulation, and legitimize the critiques of airline regulation. Deregulation propo-nents effectively used policy evaluation as a tool to discredit the regulatory framework and enhance their proposal. Deregulation was politically attractive for a variety of reasons and was easily "packaged" to serve the needs of a variety of groups. It was various-ly presented as a means to fight inflation, to end a government-supported cartel, and to improve the financial health of the indus-try. Compromises and staffing decisions were also used to increase support for deregulation. Finally, that airline deregulation was proposed by the regulator contributed to the ease with which it obtained legislative endorsement.

Characterizing the deregulation process in terms of strategic behavior is useful in accounting for a case in which policy perpetua-tion and regulatory expansion was reversed. The approach is also useful in describing how the reform process proceeded from a moderate to a radical departure from established policy. Finally, the analysis suggests that significant policy change is possible, and more probable, if attention is given to the design and implementation of identifiable strategies. However, the implications of the airline case go beyond the importance of strategic considerations in the policy process. The study began with the contention that the airline case has theoretical implications for the analysis of the regulatory process. These are examined in the concluding chapter.

7 | Economic Deregulation and the Regulatory Process

INTRODUCTION

The central question addressed in the preceding chapters was how a realignment in aviation regulatory policy was effected. Attention now turns to the implications of the airline case for the theory and analysis of the regulatory process. Illustrations in the following analysis are limited to the case of airline deregulation. However, deregulation initiatives in the areas of telecommunication and transportation are very similar to the airline case. The Federal Communications Commission and the Interstate Commerce Commission became aggressive deregulation proponents in the 1970s and, like the CAB, played a major role in the reform process in each regulated sector.[1]

Richard Posner notes that "a major challenge to social theory is to explain the pattern of government intervention in the market."[2] In efforts to meet this challenge social scientists have evolved two principal theories about economic regulation in the United States—theories that address the origins of regulation, the behavior of regulators, and the effects of regulatory intervention. Initially, explanations were based on a public interest concept that assumed that regulation was a government response to public demands for the rectification of inefficient or inequitable practices by individuals and organizations, that government intervention was effective, and that government regulation benefited a large segment of the general public.[3]

However, observations of regulatory practices that did not in fact promote the public interest led to the development of a revisionist literature pointing to the dark side of regulation.[4] Revisionist scholars concluded that government regulation was more frequently the product of interest group efforts to acquire government benefits or protection from the vicissitudes of the marketplace. Furthermore, they found that economic regulation was usually ineffective and costly to the public.

Revisionist explanations of economic regulation were widely accepted by the 1970s. At the same time, with the advent of economic deregulation in national politics, revisionist theories of the regulatory process were being discredited. Ironically, revisionist studies of the regulatory process were used to develop and promote deregulation. Yet, the theories and assumptions supporting the revisionist literature were unable to explain deregulation.

A reevaluation of revisionist assumptions is needed, and in fact has begun, because of the airline case and other instances of deregulation in the 1970s and 1980s. The preceding analysis of deregulation and the politics of policy realignment suggests that revisionist theories of economic regulation are not adequate. A major weakness of revisionist theory is that it reveals very little about the process by which policy alternatives are communicated and promoted.

PUBLIC INTEREST THEORY OF REGULATION

Significant reductions in the scope of economic regulation were adopted in the 1970s and 1980s in response to critiques of long-standing government regulatory policies. Deregulation initiatives commencing in the 1970s were the result of both legislative and executive action. Some of the significant legislative acts in addition to the Airline Deregulation Act of 1978 were the Staggers Rail Act of 1980, the Motor Carrier Act of 1980, and the Depository Institutions Deregulation and Monetary Control Act of 1980. Some of the significant executive initiatives included the Federal Communications Commission's deregulation of satellite earth stations, cable television, and radio in 1979, 1980, and 1981, respectively.[5]

Much of the literature that provided the intellectual foundation for arguments to deregulate or curtail regulatory intervention represented a critique and revision of the public interest theory of regulation.[6] The theory is associated with early defenders of industry regulation by independent commission who viewed government supervision as an effective method to prevent or remedy market-induced inequities or economic dislocations typical of the depression era.

Richard Posner argues that two assumptions typify public interest explanations of economic regulation.[7] First is an assumption that the operation of private markets can result in inefficiencies and inequities in the absence of public control and supervision. A second assumption is that government regulation operates effectively and that its benefits to the public at large outweigh its costs. To this list can be added the asumption that economic problems can be managed effectively through government intervention, and that the administrative process is an appropriate tool for solving complex industrial problems.

Assumptions underlying the public interest perspective were used to justify broad grants of discretion to administrative agencies by Congress. As Thomas McCraw observed, the "'public interest' served as an ideological glue binding together the quasi-legislative, quasi-executive, quasi-judicial duties of regulators."[8]

The public interest theory of regulation reached its zenith in the New Deal reform era of the 1930s. It also was closely associated with the regulatory commission movement, which commenced at the national level with the creation of the Interstate Commerce Commission in 1887. The public interest would be realized through investigation, deliberation, and the expert analysis of industrial problems by a collegial body of regulators protected from the emotionalism of the legislative process and undue political influence by the executive.

REVISION OF PUBLIC INTEREST THEORY

Observed deficiencies and exceptions to the public interest theory stimulated the development of a countervailing literature that grew rapidly in the 1950s and 1960s. Researchers pointed to the operations and consequences of economic regulation that contradicted the assumptions of public interest theory. Revisionist scholars concluded that economic regulation served the interests of powerful economic groups and not the public at large, was an expensive and often ineffective remedy for economic problems, denied consumers the benefits of market competition, and retarded the economic growth and technological development of the regulated industrial sector.[9]

Most initial revisions of the public interest theory did not reject the theory's basic assumption of the appropriateness of government intervention and the presumption of government efficacy.[10] Critics did, however, point out the deficiencies of the public interest perspective. For example, some observers noted that the regulatory process could be corrupted by regulators who used their position to serve their personal interests. Others noted that public interest characterizations of the regulatory process broke down when incompetent regulators were appointed or elected. Another perspective on regulation developed by revisionists was the "capture" view which "holds that the regulatory mechanism is basically workable and desirable but is somehow 'captured' by the regulated parties so that it serves their interest rather than the public interest."[11]

A common thread running through much of the literature critical of the public interest theory is the assumption that "the disappointing performance of the regulatory process is the result not of any unsoundness in the basic goals or nature of the process but of particular weaknesses in personnel or procedures that can and will be remedied (at low cost) as the society gains experience in the mechanics of public administration."[12] As pointed out in chapter 2, this assumption underlies an incremental approach to regulatory reform. The approach is reflected in proposals expected to improve the performance of regulatory agencies by attracting qualified personnel, developing effective management techniques, adopting realistic legislative mandates, providing adequate resources, and insuring effective legislative oversight of the agency.

Another genre of revisionism, however, was more germane to the deregulation movement. A more extreme version of the revisionist critique of the regulatory process was used to articulate and promote economic deregulation as a policy alternative in the 1970s. Some studies concluded "that the socially undesirable results of regulation are frequently desired by groups influential in the enactment of the legislation setting up the regulatory scheme" and "that the typical regulatory agency operates with reasonable efficiency to attain deliberately inefficient or inequitable goals set by the legislature that created it."[13] This assumption underlies the deregulation approach to regulatory reform discussed in chapter 2. From this perspective, the inefficient and inequitable consequences of regulation can be remedied only by terminating regulatory intervention. Regulation per se and not its design or maladministration is the problem.

The more radical revisionist assumption is closely associated with what Richard Posner labels the "economic theory of regulation."[14] This theory is based on two assumptions. First, economic regulation is viewed as a benefit that is allocated on a supply-and-demand basis by government. Second, the demand for regulation comes from industries who are unable to form a cartel because firms in the industry lack the resources to enforce a cartel agreement. Firms seek protective regulation from the government because it is an attractive and feasible substitute for private cartelization.[15]

The economic theory of regulation closely resembles interest group theories of capture developed by political scientists.[16] Like them, economic theory accepts the assumption that economic regulation serves the private interests of politically effective groups. The economic theory, however, refines the interest group theory of capture by replacing the capture metaphor with the more neutral "supply and demand" formulation and allowing for the capture of regulatory agencies by groups other than the regulated. The economic theory also goes further than interest group theory in rejecting the public interest motivations of regulators and legislators because it adopts the economic assumption that individuals seek to fulfill their self-interests rationally.[17]

The revisionist interpretations developed by historians, economists, and political scientists in the 1950s and 1960s had become widely accepted by the 1970s. As Thomas McCraw observed: "By the 1970s, the 'public interest' as a credible standard for interpreting regulatory behavior had few defenders. In its place reigned the 'capture' thesis, which was rapidly nearing the status of a truism, a cliché of both scholarship and popular perceptions."[18]

REVISIONISM AND DEREGULATION

A paradigm problem developed in the wake of successful deregulation initiatives of the 1970s and early 1980s. Overwhelming support for statutory deregulation and aggressive administrative deregulation, despite strong opposition from the regulated industries, were at odds with revisionist theories about regulatory dynamics. Michael Levine, in a review of dominant theories of regulation, concluded that "the problem with these theories is that they cannot accommodate, or can accommodate only with extreme difficulty, moves by regulators or Congress away from regulation and toward efficiency and reduction in bureaucratic discretionary power."[19] Ironically, having provided plausible explanations for the failure of regulation to achieve intended objectives, the revisionist version of the regulatory process was unable to explain how the regulatory policies it attacked came to be reformed or terminated.

Cases of regulatory reduction or termination such as airline deregulation illustrate James March's observation that many case studies of the decision process are "horror stories" in that they demonstrate some unexplained variance in received theories.[20] The received theories are those presented in the revisionist literature on economic regulation. The unexplained variance concerns the behavior of regulators and the dynamics of the regulatory process typified in the airline case and similar deregulation initiatives of the 1970s and 1980s.

Goals of Regulators

In the revisionist literature, most explanations for regulatory behavior are based on two assumptions about the goals of regulators. As previously discussed, the more traditional is the capture thesis which assumes that the regulator is motivated by the desire to promote the interests of the regulated group. The second goal assumed to guide the behavior of regulators is bureaucratic survival. Neither assumption about regulatory behavior is supported by the airline case.

Douglas Anderson divides explanations for agency capture into two categories.[21] The first is the "natural life cycle" school, which relies on the biological metaphor of aging to explain why an agency becomes industry-minded: Over time the agency loses its vigor and is unable to successfully oppose the policy preferences of the regulated.[22] A second explanation for capture is based on an economic model of regulatory behavior that uses the metaphor of the marketplace. Capture is viewed as a predictable consequence of rational responses by the regulators to incentives in their environment.[23] Industry-serving behavior occurs because it furthers the self-interest of the regulators. They may support industry policy preferences in order to insure favorable budgetary action for their agency by the legislature or to open future career opportunities for themselves in the regulated industry, or regulators may support the industry position simply because they did so before being appointed to the agency.[24]

A second assumption about regulatory behavior dominating the revisionist literature is that the primary motivator is bureaucratic survival. "The regulatory agency is hypothesized to act so as to perpetuate its own existence."[25] Organizational maintenance, risk aversion, or bureaucratic imperialism become the "simplifying assumption of unitary motivation."[26] It is assumed that regulators will oppose any significant reduction in their regulatory jurisdiction. If retrenchment occurs, it is viewed as a temporary strategy subsumed under the broader goal of expanding the agency's domain.[27] For regulators to advocate permanent reductions in their agency's authority and jurisdiction is viewed as irrational.

The survival hypothesis also dominates assumptions about the role of regulators in the politics of deregulation. It is assumed that in the adoption process, "the bureaucrats who administer the existing regulation . . . will almost always oppose deregulation." Furthermore, "during implementation of deregulation . . . individuals in regulatory agencies (or any other agencies) subject to cutting down will take every opportunity to delay, divert, or avoid the reduction entirely."[28]

The CAB performance during the chairmanship of Alfred Kahn from 1977 to 1978 violated both the capture and survival propositions about the behavior of regulators. First, the CAB promoted deregulation despite objections from the majority of its regulated clientele, contradicting the presumption that agency resources are used to support the position of the regulated. Furthermore, Board support for deregulation presented the unusual case of administrative officials advocating reductions in their agency's authority. The CAB pursued policies under Kahn that were antithetical to its traditional mission. De facto deregulation undermined the very reason for the agency's existence. The proposition that bureaucratic behavior is motivated by organizational survival was discarded as the CAB became more committed to the policy of deregulation.

A common characteristic of many studies of the regulatory process is "the imputation of a superordinate goal"[29] or motivation to explain the behavior of regulators. As previously discussed, the two most common goals attributed to regulators in the revisionist tradition are the survival and capture hypotheses. A basic requirement of an approach which imputes a superordinate goal to explain and predict regulatory behavior is that the goal is stable.[30] Therefore, when the goals of actors deviate from those assumed in the theory, the theory is not useful. In a case such as airline deregulation, which involved a significant deviation in preferences from those assumed in the revisionist literature, conventional wisdom cannot account for the aberrant behavior.

Furthermore, to assign a superordinate motivation or goal to regulators fails to give insights into how the motivations and preferences of regulators and other political actors are changed. Cases of policy realignment such as occurred in commercial airline regulation suggest that the more important task of analysis is to determine the dynamics of the preference-formation process rather than to search for universal motivations of political actors. This would provide a better understanding of how and under what conditions the goals of political actors change.

Regulatory Policy Development

A second incongruity between revisionist descriptions of the regulatory process and the actual history of the airline case concerns the character of regulatory policy development. Deregulation is an example of nonincremental policy development, whereas the revisionist literature emphasizes the importance of incrementalism. In chapter 1, it was argued that historical and theoretical treatments of regulatory politics and policy development yield a hypothesis that states that proposals to curtail regulatory controls will generate substantial political opposition. According to this hypothesis, the benefactors of regulation command superior political resources to those seeking to terminate regulatory intervention. Consequently, alterations in a regulatory framework adopted to remediate problems associated with regulation result in the consolidation or expansion of established regulatory arrangements. Regulatory reform is incremental and not conducive to policy realignment because of the character of regulatory politics.

The revisionist literature chooses to focus on the continuation, stability, or at most the incremental elaboration of established policies and patterns of behavior. While cases of deregulation illustrate reductions in the scope of government intervention, revisionists stress the importance of growth and expansion of government policies and programs. Furthermore, revisionist studies stress the perpetuation of existing programs, policies, and agencies. Consequently, the revisionist literature concludes that policy realignment is a deviant case rather than a source of analytical insights into the policy process.

Airline deregulation, as a case in point, is not compatible with an incremental model of the policy process in two respects. First—in violation of what an incrementalist assumption would predict—the adoption process was not characterized by a tapering of demands for policy reform from the optimal to the acceptable in order to achieve majority support for change.[31] Second, and most obvious, is the fact that deregulation is a nonincremental policy in that it represents a major policy realignment that cannot be explained away as a simple elaboration or extension of an existing policy framework. Policy realignments affecting economic regulation in recent years are a reminder that not all policy phenomena conform to the assumptions of the incremental model. Such cases illustrate the nonincremental aspects of policy development.

Deregulation initiatives of the past decade indicate the need for a better understanding of the process of nonincremental change in regulatory policy. The nonincremental policy process is significant despite its presumed uniqueness or infrequent occurrence. Policy realignments set the parameters for political debate and decision options for years to come. One need only examine the longevity of New Deal policies such as economic regulation to appreciate the impact of policy realignments. Furthermore, a preoccupation with the incremental features of the policy process masks the contribution of political leadership to the functioning of the political system. Innovative or "reconstructive leadership" that responds to a new alignment of preferences or interests is perhaps more essential to the survival of the system than leadership which limits itself to the compromise of existing preferences.[32]

An incremental bias in the conceptualization of the policy process is not limited to analyses of economic regulation. Paul Schulman cautions the analyst "to recognize the extent to which incremental and equilibrating outlooks dominate political science. Policy analysis repeatedly stresses the degree to which marginal balances are struck between bureaucrat and client, between policy goals and public pressure, and between bureaucratic decisions of the present and organizational routines of the past. . . . Yet there is a real danger . . . that such outlooks will command a disproportionate amount of both analytical attention and political support at the expense of important nonincremental and indivisible policy objectives. . . ."[33] The revisionist literature too easily leads to the conclusion that incrementalism, the most common form of political decision making discussed by Lindblom, is the only form.[34]

Schulman suggests that "entirely new models must be fashioned to account for deviance-amplifying processes . . . [because] decision-making models, as well as most models of the political system itself, describe deviance-minimizing, self-stabilizing, and equilibrating operations exclusively. . . ."[35] The observation is especially germane to regulatory policy making because of recent nonincremental policy developments. Airline deregulation, in particular, is an example of a deviance-amplifying process in that the reform movement escalated from calls for moderate reform of established policy to statutory policy termination.

An insistence on the validity of a nonincremental model of policy development, however, also can be carried to extremes. The incremental character attributed to the regulatory process in the revisionist literature and the nonincremental nature of the deregulation case highlight different features of the same process. Exclusive reliance on either model is inadequate to an understanding of regulatory policy development. Incrementalism may be useful in identifying and explaining the longevity and immutability of economic regulatory policies. However, its utility is limited in periods of policy realignment where nonincremental models are needed to explain the policy process.

Determinants of Regulatory Policy Making

A distinction is often made in analyses of regulatory policy making between two sets of factors thought to influence regulatory decisions. One set of influences includes the characteristics of the regulatory agency and its personnel. A second set of factors thought to influence regulatory policy making are to be found in the environment in which the agency operates. For example, the dichotomy is reflected in Weingast and Moran's[36] discussion of the bureaucratic and congressional dominance models of regulatory behavior. Douglas Anderson[37] presents the distinction in terms of bureaucratic imperatives and external pressures.

Complex classification schemes have been developed based on the analytical bifurcation of internal and external determinants of regulatory policy making and behavior.[38] Schemes using the endogenous approach stress the important influence of the regulatory agent in policy development. Regulatory policy is explained in terms of the exercise of agency discretion. Consequently, the most important determinants of policy development are considered to be agency characteristics such as organizational structure and legal authority, personnel characteristics and policy preferences, and agency resources. The exogenous approach minimizes the impact of agency discretion on policy development and focuses on external determinants of regulatory policy such as technological and economic conditions, interest groups, and other government institutions.

Much of the revisionist literature, especially the contributions by economists, relies extensively on an exogenous explanation of regulatory behavior. As Michael Levine notes,

the revisionist theories of regulation do not posit the character of the bureaucrats as a variable. Rather, they posit basic forces, acting on agencies and on the Congress, which will produce the results they predict *regardless* of who is running the agency or, alternatively, which will operate to *select* regulators who are comfortable "delivering the goods" in accordance with revisionist theories. In a sense, the character of bureaucrats is for the revisionists a dependent, rather than independent, variable.[39]

In the airline case, however, the regulators' preference for deregulation had consequences as great, if not greater, for the direction of policy development than the preferences of the regulated industry or the agency's congressional overseers.

Some analysts treat the approaches in an exclusive fashion in that their analyses emphasize either external or internal factors as the primary determinants of policy development. For example, Bailey[40] and Behrman[41] stress endogenous factors and credit much of the success for airline deregulation to the bureaucratic entrepreneurs at the CAB who supported deregulation during the chairmanship of John Robson and Alfred Kahn. Several other studies focus on exogenous determinants. These studies attribute airline deregulation and other cases of policy realignment to external conditions such as mass political movements,[42] legislative responsiveness to a new set of political interests,[43] attacks on the regulatory subsystem by political entrepreneurs,[44] or alterations in economic, technological, or ideological circumstances.[45]

Though there is disagreement as to the relative importance of exogenous and endogenous factors in understanding policy making, most agree that both agency characteristics and environmental conditions must be considered for adequate analysis of regulatory policy development. For example, Wilson views regulatory policy as the product of both endogenous and exogenous conditions when he explains regulatory policy making in terms of political coalitions in the agency and the technological, economic, ideological, and institutional features of the regulatory environment.[46]

Analyses of regulatory policy making, however, should do more than simply catalogue the variables associated with policy outputs. It should direct attention to the process by which exogenous and endogenous factors are integrated into policy making. Theories of policy making are theories of decision making, and the factors are relevant to the extent they are accorded relevance by policy makers as they justify and explain their decisional behavior.

Altering Policy Preferences

Failure of the revisionist literature to account for deregulation is primarily due to its neglect of the preference-formation process and the assumption of static policy preferences. Revisionist explanations tend to ignore the possibility that, though the composition of interest groups in a policy area may be stable, the policy preferences of those groups may change. Alfred Kahn speaks to this point, when he concludes that "the revisionist literature has . . . been excessively simplistic, as well as static, in its characterization of the interests of the parties most directly affected by regulation. . . . As circumstances change, the component interests diverge."[47]

The revisionist literature also ignores cases where policy change occurs despite opposition from major interest groups. Noll and Owen note that recent regulatory experiences suggest that too much confidence is placed in interest group theory as an explanation for regulatory reform.[48] Reforms at the Federal Communications Commission, Civil Aeronautics Board, Interstate Commerce Commission, and Environmental Protection Agency are proof that "while regulation can be responsive primarily to well-represented special interests, it need not be."[49] In cases where the interest group model does not fully explain events—where policy changes occur in opposition to strong interest group pressures—the political process culminating in policy change is not well understood.[50]

Shortcomings of the revisionist literature associated with its assumption of static interest group preferences do not justify a conclusion that interest group structure is unimportant to an understanding of policy development. What the preceding criticisms of the revisionist literature do suggest is that an explanation for regulatory policy development must go beyond a "billiard ball theory"[51] of the policy process whereby policy outputs are attributed to the mechanistic collisions of identifiable interest groups or other variables. As Wilson notes, "a complete theory of regulatory politics— indeed, a complete theory of politics—requires that attention be paid to beliefs as well as interests. . . . The need for assembling a majority coalition requires that arguments be made that appeal to the beliefs (as well as interests) of broader constituencies."[52] A framework should direct attention to patterns of behavior that are associated with the promotion of a policy preference and alteration of the policy choice of others.

In summary, a conceptual framework of regulatory policy development must not exclude the process characteristics of policy development. In Wilson's words, "politics must take into account the efforts made to change preferences. . . . Much, if not most, of politics consists of efforts to change wants by arguments, persuasion, threats, bluffs, and education."[53]

A STRATEGIC PERSPECTIVE

Incongruencies between the success of deregulation initiatives and revisionist assumptions about regulatory policy development suggest that more attention should be given to the behavior associated with the alteration and promotion of policy preferences. The importance of the preference-formation process is noted in particular by analysts who stress the role of ideology in policy making. James Q. Wilson, for example, concludes from a series of case studies that "the movement to deregulate domestic aviation and trucking arose, not because the airlines or trucking companies had changed, but because the beliefs of key political participants had changed."[54] Behavior designed to alter the policy preferences of existing interest groups provides more direct insights into the policy-development process than a change in composition or structure of interest groups in a policy area.

The lack of attention of revisionist studies to the preference-formation process is also characteristic of public interest explanations of regulation and, in fact, of interest group theory in general. Both public interest and revisionist theories give little attention to the process by which conflicts over competing definitions of the public interest are managed or resolved. For example, Richard Posner concludes that "a serious problem with any version of the public interest theory is that the theory contains no linkage or mechanism by which a perception of the public interest is translated into legislative action."[55] Douglas Needham also concludes that "a major weakness of the traditional public interest theory is that it does not explain the mechanism by which any particular perception of the public interest is translated into public sector decisions."[56]

Similar inattention to the preference-formation process is evident in the revisionist literature. A review of the studies seeking to explain the demand for regulation leads Needham to conclude that, like public interest theories, "a problem with most theories of regulation is that they do not explain how group demands for particular regulations are initially formulated or how these demands are transmitted to legislators and regulators."[57]

The analysis of airline regulation and deregulation presented in the foregoing chapters attempts to address the need for a more explicit focus on the process by which policy change occurs. Generally, we have approached the problem of policy change from a process perspective. More specifically, an attempt has been made to identify what James March refers to as the "mechanisms" for conflict resolution. The "mechanisms" were presented in terms of patterns of political behavior associated with the promotion of deregulation, i.e., deregulation strategies.

With passage of the Civil Aeronautics Act in 1938, a comprehensive policy was adopted to guide economic regulation of the commercial aviation industry. The policy realignment represented by the legislation signifies what Mintzberg refers to as the adoption of a "gestalt strategy" or general approach to a problem that subsequently patterns decision making in the policy area.[58] In effect, government decision-making behavior in 1938 coalesced around a policy framework that seemed to be the appropriate solution for industrial and social problems associated with unregulated competition.

The policy framework adopted in 1938 continued virtually intact for the next forty years. Regulatory policy changed incrementally in response to problems associated with the management of airline competition and the growth of commercial aviation. The politics of regulation and the impetus for incremental policy development in subsequent years revolved around two competing policies advanced by groups with a stake in how the CAB implemented its regulatory mandate. A set of procompetitive policies, including increased rate and route competition and subsidized service, were supported by various consumers of air services. On the other hand, other groups, especially financial institutions and the major trunk carriers, were more prone to support anticompetitive policies that included restrictions on rate and route competition.

The CAB responded to the competing prescriptions for regulation by developing two distinct strategies. The strategies varied in response to cycles in the financial condition of the industry. The strategies differed in terms of how the Board regulated the various forms of competition among carriers. In periods of fiscal stress, the CAB implemented anticompetitive policies in an effort to moderate downturns in the business cycle. The approach was abandoned in high-profit periods and competition among the carriers expanded by the Board in response to consumer demands for lower fares and charges that the CAB was responsible for excessive industry profits.

Revisionist studies of airline regulation[59] narrowly focus on the anticompetitive periods of CAB regulation, assuming that the associated politics and policies were typical of all CAB policy behavior. Policies that minimized carrier competition by segregating airline route systems, limiting the number of carriers on a route, and minimizing discount pricing supported an industry-protection model of economic regulation. However, an anticompetitive strategy was not the only approach the agency took in regulating the industry. Exclusive emphasis on the CAB's anticompetitive policies oversimplifies the politics of regulation by ignoring the long-standing political support for a procompetitive approach to regulation and the impact that support has had on regulatory policy development.

On the eve of the deregulation movement in the early 1970s, political demands pressed on the Board as well as its responses to those demands were not fundamentally different from those in previous periods of industry financial stress. The Board predictably adopted anticompetitive route and rate policies and approved rate increases in response to airline financial losses. The difference in Board actions in contrast to previous anticompetitive phases was measured in magnitude and not direction. As conditions in the industry worsened, the Board became more vigorous in its application of policies associated with its anticompetitive strategy. As in the past, consumer groups opposed the Board initiatives. Major carriers experiencing profit decline lobbied the CAB to apply its traditional remedies to industry problems.

The incremental period of regulatory policy development, with its cycle of procompetitive/anticompetitive strategies in CAB regulation, played a major part in the adoption by Congress of a new comprehensive policy regarding commercial aviation: deregulation. The Board's resumption of an anticompetitive policy phase in the early 1970s provided the opportunity for deregulation advocates and the traditional supporters of procompetitive regulation to discredit the regulatory regime. In other words, CAB regulation in the early 1970s more closely approximated a protectionist interpretation of regulatory politics facilitating the task of discrediting regulation as a policy.

Implementation of anticompetitive policies to stabilize the financial condition of the industry in the early 1970s was perhaps a necessary precondition for a successful deregulation effort. However, other factors were also responsible and critical to the overwhelming support for airline deregulation that developed by 1978. In the mid-1970s, executive and legislative staff members and political executives sympathetic to economic deregulation occupied strategic positions in government and played key roles in the deregulation movement. Economists were especially well represented in the group. A variety of conditions in addition to anticompetitive CAB enforcement developed in the 1970s that facilitated promotion of their policy preference.

The activities and influence of deregulation advocates occupying administrative positions in the 1970s correspond closely to Hugh Heclo's characterization of "policy politicians" whose interactions represent "issue networks" that develop outside the traditional triangular executive bureau–congressional committee–interest group clientele structure.[60] In the 1970s, the "political marketplace"[61] was favorable to deregulation advocates, and many enhanced their careers by moving among agencies in order to participate in deregulation initiatives at such places as the CAB and ICC. For example, Alfred Kahn's key staff members were recruited largely because they had demonstrated a commitment to economic deregulation while serving in other positions, and many subsequently secured other jobs related to their work as deregulators. Darius Gaskins, for example, one of Kahn's chief aides at the CAB, was appointed to the ICC and directed efforts to deregulate the trucking industry.

Airline deregulation can be attributed in part to the efforts of a group of "policy politicians" united by their commitment to deregulation. The analysis in chapters 5 and 6 of the policy realignment period (1975-78) in which deregulation was placed on the legislative agenda and eventually adopted suggests how deregulation supporters were able to overcome strong opposition from the traditional anticompetitive faction in the CAB's regulatory community.

The success of deregulation advocates and the accelerated character of the reform process was explained in terms of strategic political behavior. An analysis of the 1975–78 period suggested six strategies, or patterns of political behavior associated with the promotion of airline deregulation, namely, policy articulation and evaluation, political packaging, strategic compromise and staffing, and administrative deregulation. To review them briefly: The articulation strategy involves the specification of a policy which will be substituted for the incumbent policy; whereas policy evaluation refers to the use of policy analysis to discredit the existing policy framework and the arguments made against its termination. Political packaging involves the assessment of the interests affected by the proposed policy alternative and subsequent presentation of the proposal in terms that are relevant to those interests. Strategic compromise refers to the changes made in the policy proposal that serve to attract political support. Strategic staffing involves the recruitment of individuals who support the policy alternative and appointment to government positions where they can influence its adoption. Finally, administrative deregulation refers to the use of agency discretion to implement the policy alternative before it receives statutory approval.

A variety of conditions enhanced the efforts of airline deregulation supporters. The articulation of a policy alternative was facilitated by the extent of academic research on airline regulation prior to and during the 1975–78 period, the unity of opinion among economists on the issue, and their strategic positions within the Ford administration. Critiques of airline regulation were reinforced by CAB actions in the early 1970s. General disenchantment with regulatory intervention and the popularity of antitrust enforcement as a means for reducing inflation enhanced the political attractiveness of deregulation. The compromises negotiated during the reform process served to strengthen rather than weaken the termination thrust of reform bills and the prospects for deregulation. Deregulation advocates exploited the opportunity to appoint key officials who could influence the course of reform. Finally, the CAB embarked on its own campaign to deregulate the industry. The significant impact of administrative deregulation was due to the effectiveness of strategic staffing at the CAB, the timing of administrative initiatives, the bipartisan support in Congress for deregulation, and an upswing in industry profits that coincided with the CAB initiative.

The strategic process explanation of airline regulation and deregulation summarized above rests on the assumption that governmental policies are constantly in flux and in conflict. The approach assumes that there are competing definitions of the "public interest," because very few government policies satisfy some members of society without simultaneously reducing the satisfaction of others.[62] Because the "public interest" is usually a problematic notion, an important task of analysis is to examine the methods used by political actors to manage political conflict.

A strategic approach to the regulatory process is limited in that it is not able to determine directly what the "best" policy is in a specific situation. Its purpose is more exploratory in that it focuses its analysis on the process by which competing policy preferences are developed, communicated, and promoted. Its emphasis is on the process and not the product of the policy process in that the approach yields patterns of behavior, i.e., strategies, associated with policy development.

Though the approach does not resolve the question of what the "best" policy is in a given situation, it does provide useful information to anyone wishing to make such a judgment. A strategic approach to the policy process requires careful analysis of the arguments, rationale, evidence, and interests associated with a policy proposal. The analysis clarifies the basis for competing definitions of the public interest, as well as characterizing the interests in conflict and isolating the conditions relevant to the policy process.

The strategic approach replaces the dichotomy drawn between political behavior and "external" conditions typical of more structured approaches with a dynamic view of the actor-conditions relationship. Similarly, strategy is treated in process and not structural terms. A strategy is not just one among several variables factored into equations for explaining policy change. A process definition of strategy recognizes the importance of conditions in the policy process but not in an objective sense. Conditions are relevant to the analysis only to the extent that they are perceived to be significant by actors in the policy process. Conditions are defined and made significant by policy actors in statements they make about their policy preferences and in the arguments they develop to promote or oppose policy alternatives. The implication is that political actors both influence and are influenced by the conditions under which they pursue their policy preferences. The focus, of the strategic approach in other words, is on the dynamic relationship between policy actors and their circumstances.

In summary, a strategic perspective on the process of economic regulation is in accord with Douglas Needham's position that "regulation must be viewed as a dynamic process that results from people's attempts to improve their personal satisfaction in a world of uncertainty regarding the effects of regulatory and other instruments."[63] The regulatory process is dynamic because people revise their demands for regulation, conditions change, the effects of regulatory policies alter perceptions of what is good and bad regulation, different groups are affected in different ways at different times, and new groups emerge to become members of the regulatory community. The challenge in explaining the pattern of government intervention in the market lies in developing new approaches to the problems of economic regulation—approaches that capture the dynamic character of the regulatory process.

Notes

CHAPTER 1

[1] For discussions and critiques of the increase in national health, safety, and environmental regulation, see William Lilley III and James C. Miller III, "The New 'Social Regulation,'" *Public Interest* 47 (Spring 1977): 49–61; and Eugene Bardach, "Reason, Responsibility, and the New Social Regulation," in *American Politics and Public Policy*, ed. Walter Dean Durnham and Martha Wagner Weinberg (Cambridge: MIT Press, 1978), 364–90.

[2] For example, see Murray L. Weidenbaum, "The Changing Nature of Government Regulation of Business," *Business Environment—Public Policy: 1979 Conference Papers*, ed. Lee Preston (American Assembly of Collegiate Schools of Business, 1980), 77–103.

[3] Tom Alexander, "It's Roundup Time for the Runaway Regulators," *Fortune*, 3 Dec. 1979, 126.

[4] Paul W. MacAvoy, *The Regulated Industries and the Economy* (New York: Norton, 1979), 16.

[5] U.S. Congress, Senate, *Aviation Act of 1975, Report* of the Senate Committee on Commerce, Science and Transportation on S.2551, 94th Cong., 1st sess., 22 Oct. 1975.

[6] "Airline Deregulation Text," *Congressional Quarterly Weekly Reports*, 18 Oct. 1975, 2215.

[7] Louis M. Kohlmeier, "A Ripe Time for Airline Deregulation," *National Journal*, 18 Oct. 1975, 1458.

[8] *Congressional Quarterly Weekly Reports*, 12 Sept. 1978, 2598–99; 25 Nov. 1978, 3337.

[9] "Airline Deregulation Act of 1978: Remarks on Signing S.2493 into

Law," *Weekly Compilation of Presidential Documents* 14, no. 43 (24 Oct. 1978): 1837.

[10] The Civil Aeronautics Act of 1938 (52 Stat. 601) was later incorporated into the Federal Aviation Act of 1958 (72 Stat. 811).

[11] 92 Stat. 1705 (1978).

[12] The proposition draws on the extensive literature characterizing the politics of economic regulation. For a review see Douglas D. Anderson, *Regulatory Politics and Electric Utilities* (Boston: Auburn, 1981), ch. 1.

[13] Paul Weaver, "Unlocking the Guilded Cage of Regulation," *Fortune* (Feb. 1977): 179.

[14] James Q. Wilson, ed., *The Politics of Regulation* (New York: Basic Books, 1980), 360.

[15] "A Short History of Federal Economic Regulation of the Domestic Scheduled Passenger Air Transport Industry, 1925–1974," *Civil Aeronautics Board Practices and Procedures*, 1975, *Report* of the Senate Subcommittee on Administrative Practice and Procedure of the Senate Judiciary Committee, 94th Cong., 1st sess., Appendix B, 255.

[16] There are a number of political histories of early aviation legislation. For example, see Claude E. Puffer, *Air Transportation* (Philadelphia: Blakiston, 1941); John H. Frederick, *Commercial Air Transportation* (Homewood, Ill.: Irwin, 1955); and Henry Ladd Smith, *Airways: The History of Commercial Aviation in the United States* (New York: Knopf, 1942).

[17] 43 Stat. 128 (1925).

[18] 44 Stat. 13 (1925), 45 Stat. 603 (1926), and 46 Stat. 223 (1930).

[19] 44 Stat. 344 (1926).

[20] Paul D. Tillett, *The Army Flies the Mail* (University: Univ. of Alabama Press, 1954).

[21] 48 Stat. 466 (1934).

[22] For a summary of this problem see Richard E. Caves, *Air Transport and Its Regulators* (Cambridge: Harvard Univ. Press, 1962), 124.

[23] Puffer, *Air Transportation*, 93–96.

[24] Lucille S. Keyes, *Federal Control of Entry into Air Transportation* (Cambridge: Harvard Univ. Press, 1951), 211.

[25] PL 87–528, 10 July 1962, 76 Stat. 737.

[26] PL 89–670, 15 Oct. 1966, 80 Stat. 937.

[27] Bradley Behrman, "Civil Aeronautics Board," in *Politics of Regulation*, ed. Wilson, 408, 61n.

[28] There is, however, a growing literature on the politics of policy and program decline. Some representative examples include Douglas Bothun and John C. Comer, "The Politics of Termination: Concepts and Process," *Policy Studies Journal* 7, no. 3 (Spring 1979): 540–53; Peter deLeon, *A Theory of Termination in the Policy Process: Roles, Rhymes and Reasons*

(Santa Monica, Calif.: Rand, 1977); and Robert D. Behn, "Closing a Government Facility," *Public Administration Review* 38, no. 4 (July–Aug. 1978): 332–38.

[29] Herbert Kaufman, *Are Government Organizations Immortal?* (Washington, D.C.: Brookings, 1976).

[30] For an example see Lilley and Miller, "New 'Social Regulation.'"

[31] James Anderson, *The Emergence of the Modern Regulatory State* (Washington, D.C.: Public Affairs Press, 1962).

[32] Charles O. Jones, *An Introduction to the Study of Public Policy* (Belmont, Calif.: Duxbury, 1970), 139.

[33] James Q. Wilson, "The Rise of the Bureaucratic State," in *Public Administration: Concepts and Cases*, ed. Richard J. Stillman, 2nd ed. (Boston: Houghton Mifflin, 1980), 84.

[34] Emmette S. Redford, *The Regulatory Process: With Illustrations from Commercial Aviation* (Austin: Univ. of Texas Press, 1969), 18.

[35] Paul Weaver, "Regulation, Social Policy, and Class Conflict," *Public Interest* 50 (Winter 1978): 47.

[36] Peter deLeon, "Public Policy Termination: An End and a Beginning," essay prepared at the request of the Congressional Research Service as background for the Sunset Act of 1977 (mimeographed).

[37] Robert P. Biller, "On Tolerating Policy and Organizational Termination: Some Design Considerations," *Policy Sciences* 7, no. 2 (June 1976): 133–49.

[38] Ibid., 134.

[39] Eugene Bardach, "Policy Termination as a Political Process," *Policy Sciences* 7, no. 2 (June 1976): 123.

[40] For discussions of problems associated with managing decline see Herbert J. Gans, "Planning for Declining and Poor Cities," *Journal of the American Institute of Planners* (Sept. 1975): 305–7; and "A Symposium: Organizational Decline and Cutback Management," *Public Administration Review* 38, no. 4 (July–Aug. 1978): 315–57.

[41] William G. Scott, "Organization Theory: A Reassessment," *Academy of Management Journal* (June 1974): 242–53.

[42] Charles H. Levine, "Organizational Decline and Cutback Management," 317.

[43] Ibid.

[44] Analysis of the deregulation process increased dramatically in the 1980s in the wake of regulatory reform. Representative studies include Barry M. Mitnick, *The Political Economy of Regulation: Creating, Designing and Removing Regulatory Forms* (New York: Columbia Univ. Press, 1980), 416–47; Susan J. Tolchin and Martin Tolchin, *Dismantling America: The Rush to Deregulate* (New York: Oxford Univ. Press, 1983); Martha Derthick and Paul Quirk, *The Politics of Deregulation* (Washington, D.C.:

Brookings, 1985); and Roger Noll and Bruce M. Owen, *The Political Economy of Deregulation* (Washington, D.C.: American Enterprise Institute, 1983).

[45] For an explication of the model see David Braybrooke and Charles E. Lindblom, *A Strategy of Decision: Policy Evaluation as a Social Process* (London: Free Press, 1963).

[46] The explanations are presented respectively by Louis L. Jaffe, "The Effective Limits of the Administrative Process: A Reevaluation," *Harvard Law Review* 67 (May 1954): 1105–35; Marver Bernstein, *Regulating Business by Independent Commission* (Princeton: Princeton Univ. Press, 1955); and Samuel P. Huntington, "The Marasmus of the ICC: The Commission, the Railroads and the Public Interest," *Yale Law Journal* 61 (April 1952): 467–509.

[47] Mitnick, *Political Economy of Regulation*, 420–21.

[48] Weaver, "Regulation, Social Policy, and Class Conflict," 48.

CHAPTER 2

[1] Leonard W. Weiss and Michael W. Klass, eds. *Case Studies in Regulation: Revolution and Reform* (Boston: Little, Brown, 1981), v.

[2] Consumer Goods Pricing Act, 89 Stat. 801 (1975); Natural Gas Policy Act, 92 Stat. 3350 (1978); Railroad Revitalization and Regulatory Reform Act, 90 Stat. 29 (1976); Staggers Rail Act, 94 Stat. 1895 (1980); Motor Carrier Act, 94 Stat. 793 (1980); Household Goods Transportation Act, 94 Stat. 2011 (1980); and the Depository Institutions Deregulation and Monetary Control Act, 94 Stat. 132 (1980).

[3] Mel Dubnick and Alan R. Gitelson, "Regulatory Policy Analysis: Working in a Quagmire," *Policy Studies Review* 1, no. 3 (Feb. 1982): 423–35.

[4] Mitnick, *Political Economy of Regulation*, 418–19.

[5] William R. Herman, "Deregulation: Now or Never," *Public Administration Review* 36 (March 1976): 224.

[6] James R. Nelson, "A Pragmatic Approach to Deregulation," in *Salvaging Public Utility Regulation*, ed. Werner Sichel, (Lexington, Mass.: Heath, 1976), 39.

[7] Alan Stone, *Regulation and Its Alternatives* (Washington, D.C.: Congressional Quarterly Press, 1982), 10.

[8] Mitnick, *Political Economy of Regulation*, 9.

[9] Ibid., 418.

[10] Stephen Breyer, "Analyzing Regulatory Failure: Mismatches, Less Restrictive Alternatives and Reform," *Harvard Law Review* 92 (Jan. 1979): 560.

[11] Emmette S. Redford, *American Government and the Economy* (New York: Macmillan, 1965), 361.

[12] The classification and its description draws on the analyses in Breyer, "Analyzing Regulatory Failure"; Redford, *American Government*; and Stone, *Regulation and its Alternatives*.

[13] Policy associated with this method of regulation is referred to as "competitive regulatory policy" in Randall B. Ripley and Grace A. Franklin, *Bureaucracy and the Policy Implementation Process* (Homewood, Ill.: Dorsey, 1982), 72, 109.

[14] Redford, *American Government*, 588.

[15] On this point see John M. Pfiffner, "The Development of Administrative Regulation," *Annals* 221 (May 1942): 1–8.

[16] Max Neiman, "The Virtues of Heavy Handedness in Government," *Policy Implementation: Penalties or Incentives?* (Beverley Hills, Calif.: Sage, 1980), 19–42.

[17] The discussion of alternatives to regulation is based upon the analyses by Breyer, "Analyzing Regulatory Failure," 578–84; and Stone, *Regulation and Its Alternatives*, 61–166.

[18] The argument that deregulation does not mean the absence of any government control is also made by Hendrick Houthakker, "Economic Aspects of Deregulation," in *Deregulating American Industry*, ed. Donald L. Martin and Warren F. Schwartz (Lexington, Mass.: Heath, 1977), 1–20.

[19] Weidenbaum, "Changing Nature of Government Regulation," 85.

[20] Jesse W. Markham, "A Century After Munn v. Illinois: What Kind of Regulation Should We Have?" in *Salvaging Public Utility Regulation*, ed. Sichel, 21–35; and Herman, "Deregulation Now or Never!"

[21] Roger Noll, *Reforming Regulation: An Evaluation of the Ash Council Proposals* (Washington, D.C.: Brookings, 1971), 3.

[22] Ibid., 40.

[23] David M. Welborn, "Taking Stock in Regulatory Reform," paper presented at the Annual Meeting of the American Political Science Association, Washington, D.C., Sept. 1977. For a somewhat different typology see David R. Berman, "Consumerism and the Regulatory System: Paradigms of Reform," *Policy Studies Review* 1, no. 3 (Feb. 1982): 454–62.

[24] Comparisons of social and economic regulation are found in Lawrence J. White, *Reforming Regulation* (Englewood Cliffs, N.J.: Prentice-Hall, 1981), 27–44; Lilley and Miller, "New 'Social Regulation,'" 49–61; and Weaver, "Regulation, Social Policy, and Class Conflict," 45–63.

[25] James Landis, *The Administrative Process* (New Haven: Yale Univ. Press, 1938), 16–17, 22–23, 30.

[26] Historical trends in regulatory reform are reviewed in Redford, *American Government*, 568–90.

[27] For a review see Welborn, "Taking Stock in Regulatory Reform."

[28] Redford, *American Government*, 573.

[29] The reforms are summarized in A. Lee Fritschler and Bernard H. Ross, *Business Regulation and Government Decision-Making* (Cambridge, Mass.: Winthrop, 1980), 62–63. Reform efforts during the Reagan administration are discussed in George C. Eads and Michael Fix, *Relief or Reform?: Reagan's Regulatory Dilemma* (Washington, D.C.: Urban Institute Press, 1984) and Eads and Fix, eds., *The Reagan Regulatory Strategy: An Assessment* (Washington, D.C.: Urban Institute Press, 1984).

[30] Murray L. Weidenbaum, *The Future of Business Regulation* (New York: AMACOM, 1979), 62–66.

[31] For example, see Louis J. Hector, "Problems of the CAB and the Independent Regulatory Commissions," *Yale Law Journal* 69, no. 6 (May 1960): 926; and the response to his critique by Earl W. Kintner, "The Current Ordeal of the Administrative Process," *Yale Law Journal* 69, no. 5 (May 1960): 965.

[32] Weidenbaum, *The Future of Business Regulation*, 60.

[33] For a critical analysis of the school, see Harry M. Trebing, "The Chicago School Versus Public Utility Regulation," *Journal of Economic Issues* 10, no. 1 (March 1976): 97–123.

[34] White, *Reforming Regulation*, 23.

[35] Ibid., 18–25.

[36] Markham, "A Century After Munn v. Illinois," 29.

[37] Leonard W. Weiss, "State Regulation of Public Utilities and Marginal-Cost Pricing," in *Case Studies in Regulation*, ed. Weiss and Klass, 262–91; and Douglas D. Anderson, "State Regulation of Electric Utilities," in *The Politics of Regulation*, ed. Wilson, 3–41.

[38] Weidenbaum, *The Future of Business Regulation*, 61.

[39] Markham, "A Century After Munn v. Illinois," 26.

[40] Testimony of Mimi Cutler, Director of the Aviation Consumer Action Project, *Regulatory Reform in Air Transportation, Hearings* before the Senate Subcommittee on Aviation of the Committee on Commerce, 94th Cong., 2nd sess. (1976), 1058.

[41] See the testimony of Ralph Nader, *Oversight of Civil Aeronautics Board Practices and Procedures, Hearings* before the Senate Subcommittee on Administrative Practice and Procedure of the Committee on the Judiciary, 94th Cong., 1st sess. (1975), 1150.

[42] Markham, "A Century After Munn v. Illinois," 26.

[43] Testimony of Donald I. Baker, *Oversight of Civil Aeronautics Board*, 671.

[44] Mitnick, *Political Economy of Regulation*, 431.

[45] Bardach, "Policy Termination," 126.

[46] Walter Rosenbaum, *The Politics of Environmental Concern*, 2nd ed. (New York: Holt, Rinehart, Winston, 1977), 97.

[47] DeLeon, *A Theory of Termination*, 17–31.

[48] The approach is described in James G. March, "The Business Firm as a Political Coalition," *Journal of Politics* 24, no. 4 (Nov. 1962): 662–78; and in Paul J. Quirk, *Industry Influence in the Federal Regulatory Agencies* (Princeton: Princeton Univ. Press, 1981), ch. 2.

[49] March, "Business Firm as a Political Coalition," 666.

[50] DeLeon, *A Theory of Termination*, 36.

CHAPTER 3

[1] 49 U.S.C. 20, Sec. 1372(a), 1482(j), and 1373 (1976). For a discussion of the CAB's relationship to international transport see Puffer, *Air Transportation*, 101–2.

[2] Caves, *Air Transport*, 133–35.

[3] Unless otherwise noted, references to the statutory authority of the CAB are based upon 49 U.S.C. 20 (1976).

[4] Redford, *American Government*, 409.

[5] 49 U.S.C. 20, Sec. 1302 (1976).

[6] Caves, *Air Transport*, 127.

[7] Robert C. Fraser, Alan D. Donheiser, and Thomas G. Miller, Jr., *Civil Aviation Development: A Policy and Operations Analysis* (New York: Praeger, 1972), 67.

[8] Marver H. Bernstein, "The Regulatory Process: A Framework for Analysis," *Law and Contemporary Problems* 26, no. 2 (Spring 1961): 333–34.

[9] Report of the Antitrust Subcommittee (Subcommittee No. 5) of the Committee on the Judiciary, House of Representatives, 85th Cong., 1st sess. Pursuant to H.R. 107, Washington, 1957, as quoted in Samuel B. Richmond, *Regulation and Competition in Air Transportation* (New York: Columbia Univ. Press, 1961), 70–71.

[10] Richmond, *Regulation and Competition*, 2.

[11] Redford, *The Regulatory Process*, 29.

[12] Richmond, *Regulation and Competition*, 3.

[13] Aaron J. Gellman, "The Regulation of Competition in United States Domestic Air Transportation: A Judicial Survey and Analysis," *Journal of Air Law and Commerce* 28 (Winter 1958), 178.

[14] By 1970, the original 16 trunk carriers were reduced to 11 as the result of CAB-approved mergers. For a history of trunk mergers see George W. Douglas and James C. Miller III, *Economic Regulation of Domestic Air Transport: Theory and Policy* (Washington, D.C.: Brookings 1974), 121–22.

[15] Keyes, *Federal Control of Entry*, 178.

[16] Richmond, *Regulation and Competition*, 86.

[17] C.A.B. 447, 480 (1941).

[18] For an analysis of the program see George C. Eads, *The Local Service Airline Experiment* (Washington, D.C.: Brookings, 1972).

[19] *Civil Aeronautics Board Reports* 6 (July 1944–May 1946): 52–53, as quoted in Eads, *Local Service*, 77.

[20] Piedmont Certificate Renewal Case, 15 C.A.B., 736, 810 (1952), as quoted in Barre Hall, "The Civil Aeronautics Board Policy Favoring Subsidy Reduction to Local Service Carriers: Its Role and Implementation in the Decision Process," *Journal of Air Law and Commerce* 34 (Autumn 1968): 576.

[21] Richmond, *Regulation and Competition*, 87.

[22] Initially, the only restriction on irregular carriers was that they not advertise or hold out to the public the offer of scheduled service. Keyes, *Federal Control of Entry*, 177.

[23] Frederick C. Thayer, Jr., *Air Transport Policy and National Security: A Political, Economic and Military Analysis* (Chapel Hill: Univ. of North Carolina Press, 1965), 94.

[24] Eads, *Local Service*, 166–69.

[25] For accounts of the events leading up to certification of the supplementals see Keyes, *Federal Control of Entry*, ch. 5; and Thayer, *Air Transport Policy,* ch. 5.

CHAPTER 4

[1] I would like to thank the editors of *Social Science Quarterly* for permission to reprint materials in chapters 4 and 5 previously published as "The Regulatory Policy Cycle and the Airline Deregulation Movement" in vol. 66, no. 3 (Sept. 1985): 552–63.

[2] Caves, *Air Transport*, 280–82.

[3] Gellman, "The Regulation of Competition," 155.

[4] Fraser et al., *Civil Aviation Development*, 91.

[5] Redford, *American Government*, 409.

[6] Hall, "Civil Aeronautics Board Policy," 578.

[7] Leslie O. Barnes, "Airline Subsidies—Purpose, Cause and Control," *Journal of Air Law and Commerce* 26 (Autumn 1959): 319.

[8] Ibid.

[9] William K. Jones, "Licensing of Domestic Air Transportation," *Journal of Air Law and Commerce* 30 (Spring 1964): 128.

[10] Route-strengthening and airport consolidation are discussed in Ronald D. Dockser, "Airline Service Abandonment and Consolidation—

A Chapter in the Battle Against Subsidization," *Journal of Air Law and Commerce* 32 (Autumn 1966): 496–525. For a discussion of the internal subsidy issue, see Eads, *Local Service*, 169.

[11] Dockser, "Airline Service Abandonment," 504–6.

[12] Ibid., 516.

[13] Eads, *Local Service*, 89.

[14] For an account of CAB attempts to decertify some of the local carriers see ibid., 97–104.

[15] Ibid., 105.

[16] Ibid., 111.

[17] Ibid., 105–6.

[18] For an analysis of the reasons for subsidy increases see ibid., 106–7.

[19] Hall, "Civil Aeronautics Board Policy," 581–82.

[20] Eads, *Local Service*, 149.

[21] For a detailed analysis of the new program see ibid., 150–76.

[22] Hall, "Civil Aeronautics Board Policy," 584.

[23] Eads, *Local Service*, 161–63.

[24] Ibid., 105–6.

[25] Ibid.

[26] Ibid., 166–69; Virgil D. Cover, "The Rise of Third Level Air Carriers," *Journal of Air Law and Commerce* 37 (Fall 1971): 41–51, analyzes several cases involving route transfers from trunks and locals to air taxis.

[27] Richmond, *Regulation and Competition*, 93.

[28] Gellman, "The Regulation of Competition," 163–64.

[29] Thayer, *Air Transport Policy*, 94–113.

[30] Richmond, *Regulation and Competition*, 91.

[31] Jaap Kamp, "The Near Future of Air Charter Regulation: The Case for More Experimentation in Public Policy," *Journal of Air Law and Commerce* 41 (Autumn 1975), 406–7.

[32] Ibid., 407–11.

[33] Ibid., 441.

[34] 37 Fed. Reg. 20808 (1972), as quoted in Kamp, "The Near Future," 395.

[35] Richmond, *Regulation and Competition*, 98.

[36] Fraser et al., *Civil Aviation Development*, 76.

[37] Louis Jaffe, Book Review, *Yale Law Journal* 65 (1956): 1068, 1074, as quoted in Richard J. Barber, "Airline Mergers, Monopoly, and the CAB," *Journal of Air Law and Commerce* 28 (Summer 1961–62): 209.

[38] 49 U.S.C. 20, 1302(d).

[39] William E. Fruhan, Jr., *The Fight for Competitive Advantage: A Study of the United States Domestic Trunk Air Carriers* (Boston: Harvard Univ. Press, 1972), 112.

[40] Ibid., 111.

[41] Douglas and Miller, *Economic Regulation*, 191.

[42] Fruhan, *The Fight for Competitive Advantage*, 111–12.

[43] Douglas and Miller, *Economic Regulation*.

[44] Gellman, "The Regulation of Competition," 174.

[45] Ibid., 175.

[46] Fruhan, *The Fight for Competitive Advantage*, 146; Richmond, *Regulation and Competition*, 100, 104.

[47] Gellman, "The Regulation of Competition," 176.

[48] Richmond, *Regulation and Competition*, 114.

[49] Barber, "Ariline Mergers," 172.

[50] Fruhan, *The Fight for Competitive Advantage*, 146; Douglas and Miller, *Economic Regulation*, 114–15.

[51] Fraser et al., *Civil Aviation Development*, 81.

[52] Ibid., 83.

[53] Douglas and Miller, *Economic Regulation*, 200.

[54] Ibid.

[55] Gellman, "The Regulation of Competition," 149; Fruhan, *The Fight for Competitive Advantage*, 76.

[56] Redford, *The Regulatory Process*, 31.

[57] Fraser et al., *Civil Aviation Development*, 81.

[58] For an analysis of the General Passenger Fare Investigation see Redford, *The Regulatory Process*, ch. 5. Douglas and Miller, *Economic Regulation*, ch. 8, review the Domestic Passenger Fare Investigation.

[59] Fruhan, *The Fight for Competitive Advantage*, 79–82.

[60] In the Matter of an Authorization for Discussions of Methods for Increasing Domestic Carrier Revenue, June 9, 1954, Order Serial No. E-8421, as quoted in Gellman, "The Regulation of Competition," 177.

[61] Ibid.

[62] William A. Jordan, *Airline Regulation in America: Effects and Imperfections* (Baltimore: Johns Hopkins Univ. Press, 1970), 58.

[63] Alan H. Silberman, "Price Discrimination and the Regulation of Air Transportation," *Journal of Air Law and Commerce* 31 (Summer 1965): 245–57.

[64] Jordan, *Airline Regulation in America*, 60.

[65] Gellman, "The Regulation of Competition," 149–50.

[66] Ibid.

[67] Silberman, "Price Discrimination," 223.

[68] Gellman, "The Regulation of Competition," 148.

[69] Ibid., 153–54.

[70] Douglas and Miller, *Economic Regulation*, 97–98.

[71] Fruhan, *The Fight for Competitive Advantage*, 86.

[72] Jordan, *Airline Regulation in America*, 59–60, 63–65.

[73] Gellman, "The Regulation of Competition," 149.

[74] Fruhan, *The Fight for Competitive Advantage*, 86.
[75] Ibid., 86–87.
[76] Gellman, "The Regulation of Competition," 148.
[77] Ibid., 55.
[78] Ibid., 156.
[79] Ibid., 148.
[80] Ibid., 161.

CHAPTER 5

[1] Behrman, "Civil Aeronautics Board"; Elizabeth A. Bailey, "Reform from Within: Civil Aeronautics Board Policy, 1977–78," in *Problems in Public-Utility Economics and Regulation*, ed. Michael A. Crew (Lexington, Mass.: Heath, 1979), 19–40.

[2] Barry R. Weingast, "Regulation, Reregulation, and Deregulation: The Political Foundations of Agency Clientele Relationships," *Law and Contemporary Problems* 44, no. 1 (Winter 1981): 147–77; and Alfred Kahn, "Deregulation and Vested Interests: The Case of Airlines," in *The Political Economy of Deregulation: Interest Groups in the Regulatory Process*, ed. Roger Noll and Bruce Owen (Washington, D.C.: American Enterprise Institute, 1983), 132–51.

[3] Stephen Breyer, *Regulation and Its Reform* (Cambridge: Harvard Univ. Press, 1982).

[4] Ivor P. Morgan, "Toward Deregulation" and "Government and the Industry's Early Development," in *Airline Deregulation: The Early Experience*, ed. John R. Meyer et al. (Boston, Mass.: Auburn House, 1981), 41–52 and 13–37; LeRoy Graymer and Frederick Thompson, eds., *Reforming Social Regulation: Alternative Public Policy Strategies* (Beverly Hills, Calif.: Sage, 1982), 276–80; and Alfred Kahn, "The Political Feasibility of Regulatory Reform: How Did We Do It?" in *Reforming Social Regulation*, ed. Graymer and Thompson, 247–63.

[5] In addition to footnoted sources, the following chronology and analysis draws on interviews conducted in June 1980 with participants in the reform process. Interviews were open-ended and averaged one and one-half hours. A list of informants is included in the bibliography. In order to protect confidentiality, interview material is not attributed to any one individual. Unfootnoted quotations come from the interviews.

[6] Behrman, "Civil Aeronautics Board," 97–120, provides an excellent description of this period and the CAB's impact on the reform process.

[7] *National Journal*, June 15, 1974, 884.

[8] See Lucille Keyes, "Policy Innovations in the Domestic Passenger-Fare Investigation," *Journal of Air Law and Commerce* 41 (Autumn 1975):

75–100, for an analysis of the DPFI.

⁹ The charter controversy is examined in Gerald S. Reamy, "Charter Air Travel: Paper Airplanes in a Dogfight," *Journal of Air Law and Commerce* 42 (Spring 1976): 405–32.

¹⁰ *Aviation Week*, 11 June 1973, 31.

¹¹ *National Journal*, 23 Nov. 1974, 1777.

¹² Derthick and Quirk, *Politics of Deregulation*, 35–39.

¹³ Ibid., 36.

¹⁴ Ibid.

¹⁵ Ibid., 122.

¹⁶ See Kahn, "Deregulation and Vested Interests," 135–40, for a discussion of groups having an interest in regulation.

¹⁷ *National Journal*, 5 Oct. 1974, 1504.

¹⁸ *Weekly Compilation of Presidential Documents* 10 (8 Oct. 1974): 1241–42.

¹⁹ Derthick and Quirk, *Politics of Deregulation*, 40–45.

²⁰ *Oversight of Civil Aeronautics Board*, 1.

²¹ Ibid., 4–5.

²² Ibid., 109.

²³ *Weekly Compilation of Presidential Documents* 11 (28 April 1975): 457.

²⁴ Ibid., 455.

²⁵ *National Journal*, 7 July 1975, 1000; 19 July 1975, 1065.

²⁶ U.S. Civil Aeronautics Board, Committee on Commerce, Science and Transportation, *Regulatory Reform: Report of the CAB Special Staff*, July 1975, 2.

²⁷ *Regulatory Reform in Air Transportation* (1976).

²⁸ Ibid., 346.

²⁹ Ibid., 350.

³⁰ *National Journal*, July 24, 1976, 1045.

³¹ U.S. Congress, Senate, Committee on Commerce, Science and Transportation, *Regulatory Reform in Air Transportation, Hearings*, 95th Cong., 1st sess., 1977, Vol. 1, p. 2.

³² Ibid., 412.

³³ For a review of the policies, see Bailey, "Reform from Within."

³⁴ Deterioration of regulated carrier opposition to deregulation is discussed in Derthick and Quirk, *Politics of Deregulation*, 147–64.

³⁵ Behrman, "Civil Aeronautics Board," 118–19.

³⁶ *Congressional Quarterly Weekly Reports*, 25 March 1978, 772–74.

³⁷ *New York Times*, 24 April 1978, 16.

³⁸ Amendments to the Federal Aviation Act of 1958 mandated by the Airline Deregulation Act of 1978 are presented and discussed in U.S. Congress, House, *Conference Report on the Airline Deregulation Act of 1978*, H. Rept. 95-1779, 95th Cong., 2nd sess., 1978, 1–51.

[39] Ibid., 44.
[40] *Congressional Quarterly Weekly Report*, 9 June 1984, 1403.
[41] Ibid., 30 June 1984, 1595; 7 July 1984, 1614; 18 Aug. 1984, 2048.

CHAPTER 6

[1] DeLeon, *A Theory of Termination*, 28.
[2] Bardach, "Policy Termination," 127.
[3] Herman, "Deregulation: Now or Never!," 227.
[4] Jaffe, "Effective Limits of the Administrative Process," 1119.
[5] Lucille S. Keyes, *Regulatory Reform in Air Cargo Transportation* (Washington, D.C.: American Enterprise Institute, 1980), 23.
[6] Herman, "Deregulation: Now or Never!," 224.
[7] U.S. Congress, House, Committee on Public Works and Transportation, *Aviation Regulatory Reform, Hearings* before the Subcommittee on Aviation, House of Representatives, 95th Cong., 2nd sess., 1978, 122–23.
[8] Breyer, "Analyzing Regulatory Failure," 606.
[9] Theodore E. Keller, "The Revolution in Airline Regulation," in *Case Studies in Regulation*, ed. Weiss and Klass (Boston: Little, Brown, 1981), 66–67.
[10] Breyer, "Analyzing Regulatory Failure," 604.
[11] Keyes, *Federal Control of Entry*, 342.
[12] Caves, *Air Transport*, 433.
[13] Ibid., 445–46.
[14] Ibid., 447.
[15] Redford, *American Government*, 413.
[16] See Michael E. Levine, "Is Regulation Necessary: California Air Transportation and National Regulatory Policy," *Yale Law Journal* 75 (July 1965): 1416–47; and Jordan, *Airline Regulation in America*. Findings from these and other studies are summarized in Keller, "The Revolution in Airline Regulation," 60–66.
[17] D. Anderson, *Regulatory Politics*, 7.
[18] Interview, 17 June 1980.
[19] Interview, 18 June 1980.
[20] Air Transport Association, *Consequences of Deregulation of the Scheduled Air Transport Industry*, April 1975, reprinted in U.S. Congress, Senate, *Oversight of Civil Aeronautics Board*, 141–378.
[21] *New York Times*, 20 Feb. 1976, 66.
[22] Ibid., 27 Feb. 1977, 24.
[23] Ibid., 22 June 1975, 23.
[24] The committee had five members. Four were CAB staff members and all five were economists. They were: Roy Pulsifer, assistant director of the

Bureau of Operating Rights and committee chairman; Willard L. Demory; James A. McMahon; Paul Eldridge; and Lucille S. Keyes, who served as a special advisor to the committee.

[25] Breyer, "Analyzing Regulatory Failure," 608.

[26] *New York Times*, 22 Feb. 1976, 22.

[27] Eugene Bardach, *The Skill Factor in Politics: Repealing the Mental Commitment Laws in California* (Berkeley: Univ. of California Press, 1972), 189.

[28] DeLeon, *A Theory of Termination*, 36.

[29] Bardach, *The Skill Factor in Politics*, 185.

[30] Interview, 18 June 1980.

[31] The point is argued by Braybrooke and Lindlom in *A Strategy of Decision*.

[32] Bardach, *The Skill Factor in Politics*, 183.

[33] Interview, 18 June 1980.

[34] U.S. Congress, Senate, *Regulatory Reform in Air Transportation* (1976), 87.

[35] Ibid., testimony of Paul R. Ignatius, president of the Air Transport Association, 955.

[36] Herbert Kelleher, "Deregulation and the Practicing Attorney," *Journal of Air Law and Commerce* 44 (Summer 1978): 274.

[37] *National Journal*, 22 June 1974, 933.

[38] Ibid., 14 Sept. 1974, 1394.

[39] Ibid., 15 June 1974, 875.

[40] Ibid.

[41] Ibid., 10 Aug. 1974, 1207.

[42] Ibid., 15 June 1974, 882, 884.

[43] Interview, 18 June 1980.

[44] Bardach, *The Skill Factor in Politics*, 184.

[45] *National Journal*, 30 July 1977, 1193.

[46] DeLeon, *A Theory of Termination*, 30.

[47] Mitnick, *Political Economy of Regulation*, 425.

[48] U.S. Congress, Senate, *Regulatory Reform in Air Transportation* (1976), 355, 347.

[49] Statement by Edwin I. Colodny, Allegheny Airlines, in *Competition in the Airlines: What is the Public Interest?* (Washington, D.C.: American Enterprise Institute, AEI Forum 9, 1977), 4.

[50] U.S. Congress, Senate, *Regulatory Reform in Air Transportation* (1976), 355.

[51] Mitnick, *Political Economy of Regulation*, 428.

[52] Ibid., 429.

[53] Ibid., 425–31.

[54] Federal Aviation Act of 1958 (revised March 1, 1979), Sec., 102(a) (4).

[55] DeLeon, *A Theory of Termination*, 37–8.

[56] Alfred Kahn, "Applying Economics to an Imperfect World," *Regulation* (Nov.–Dec. 1978): 27.

[57] Bardach, "Policy Termination as a Political Process," 130.

[58] On the significance of equity considerations in the regulatory process, see Paul Feldman, "Why Regulation Doesn't Work," *Review of Social Economy* 29, no. 2 (Sept. 1971): 31–38.

[59] Kahn, "Applying Economics," 27.

[60] *National Journal*, 30 July 1977, 1194.

[61] *Congressional Quarterly Weekly Report*, 29 Oct. 1977, 2325–26.

[62] *National Journal*, 30 July 1977, 1194.

[63] *Congressional Quarterly Weekly Report*, 5 Nov. 1977, 2381.

[64] Federal Aviation Act of 1958 (revised 1 March 1979), Sec. 43.

[65] Essential service was later defined as no less than two daily round trips, five days per week, or the level of service actually received by the community in the 1977 calendar year.

[66] *National Journal*, 30 July 1977, 1194.

[67] Interview, 20 June 1980.

[68] Bardach, *The Skill Factor in Politics*, 184.

[69] *Commuter Airline Digest*, Feb. 1977, 7–9, reprinted in U.S. Congress, Senate, Select Committee on Small Business, *The Decline of the Supplemental Air Carriers in the United States, Hearing* before the Subcommittee on Monopoly, 94th Cong., 2nd sess., 1976, 647–52.

[70] U.S. Civil Aeronautics Board, *Report to Congress*, FY 1972, 11.

[71] Commuter Airline Association of America, *Time for Commuters*, 1976 Annual Report of the Commuter Airline Industry, 3, reprinted in U.S. Congress, Senate, *Decline of the Supplemental Air Carriers*, 643.

[72] *Congressional Quarterly Weekly Report*, 25 March 1978, 774.

[73] U.S. Congress, House, *Conference Report*, 106–7.

[74] U.S. Congress, Senate, *Regulatory Reform in Air Transportation* (1976), 560.

[75] For a review of this period, see U.S. Congress, Senate, *Decline of the Supplemental Air Carriers*.

[76] S.421, 94th Cong., 1st sess., 1975.

[77] Most restrictions on charter travel were terminated in 1978 by the Board in its Public Charter Rule. U.S. Civil Aeronautics Board, *Report to Congress*, FY 1978, 14.

[78] Federal Aviation Act of 1958 (revised 1 March 1979), Title IV, Sec. 401(n) (2).

[79] In World Airways v. CAB 547 F.2d 695 (C.A.D.C. 1976) the court

affirmed an earlier CAB decision denying World's request to provide scheduled low-cost transcontinental service, on the grounds that a carrier cannot hold a supplemental and scheduled certificate simultaneously.

[80] Federal Aviation Act of 1958 (revised March 1, 1979), Title IV, Sec. 401(c) (1). The provision would not become effective until 180 days after the legislation became law.

[81] Bardach, "Policy Termination as a Political Process," 130.

[82] In regard to the influence of presidential appointments on regulatory commission policies, see David M. Welborn, "Presidents, Regulatory Commissions, and Regulatory Policy," *Journal of Public Law* 15 (1966): 3–29.

[83] Charles Perrow, *Complex Organizations: A Critical Essay*, 2nd ed. (Glenview, Ill.: Scott, Foresman, 1979), 14.

[84] The resources available to chairmen of regulatory commissions to influence agency policy are examined in David M. Welborn, *Governance of Federal Regulatory Agencies* (Knoxville: Univ. of Tennessee Press, 1977).

[85] Interview, 18 June 1980.

[86] For a brief but broader discussion of the role of economists in the regulatory reform movement of the 1970s, see Weiss and Klass, *Case Studies in Regulation*, 2–10, and Derthick and Quirk, *Politics of Deregulation*, 35–9.

[87] Quirk, *Industry Influence*, 74.

[88] Ibid., 75.

[89] Interview, 18 June 1980.

[90] See Quirk, *Industry Influence*, 77–78, for a discussion of Carter appointments.

[91] *National Journal*, 19 Feb. 1977, 291.

[92] U.S. Congress, Senate, *Oversight of Civil Aeronautics Board*, 87; *Congressional Quarterly Weekly Report*, 11 June 1977, 1156.

[93] Interview, 19 June 1980.

[94] Interview, 17 June 1980.

[95] U.S. Civil Aeronautics Board, *Report to Congress*, FY 1977 and 1978, describe the reorganization.

[96] U.S. Civil Aeronautics Board, *Report to Congress*, FY 1977, 1.

[97] Marvin H. Kosters and Jeffrey A. Eisenach, "Is Regulatory Relief Enough?" *Regulation* (March–April 1982): 26.

[98] Christopher C. DeMuth, "A Strong Beginning on Reform," *Regulation* (Jan.–Feb. 1982): 18.

[99] For an example of the genre, see Theodore Lowi, *The End of Liberalism* (New York: Norton, 1979).

[100] Interview, 17 June 1980.

[101] DeMuth, "A Strong Beginning on Reform," 18.

[102] The proposition is supported in A. Lee Fritschler, *Smoking and*

Politics: Policymaking and the Federal Bureaucracy (Englewood Cliff, N.J.: Prentice-Hall, 1975); and Erwin G. Krasnow, Lawrence D. Longley, and Herbert A. Terry, *The Politics of Broadcast Regulation*, 3rd ed. (New York: St. Martin's, 1982).

[103] Landis, *The Administrative Process*, 61.
[104] *National Journal*, 8 Aug. 1978, 1359.
[105] Interview, 16 June 1980.
[106] See U.S. Congress, House, Committee on Public Works and Transportation, *Report on the Air Service Improvement Act of 1978*, H. Rept. 95–1211, 95th Cong., 2nd sess., 1978, 3–4.
[107] Interview, 16 June 1980.
[108] U.S. Congress, House, *Conference Report*, 56.

CHAPTER 7

[1] For a comparative study of the cases, see Derthick and Quirk, *Politics of Deregulation*.
[2] Richard A. Posner, "Theories of Economic Regulation," *Bell Journal of Economics* 5, no. 2 (Autumn 1974): 335–58.
[3] Public interest explanations of economic regulation are presented in E.P. Herring, *Public Administration and the Public Interest* (New York: McGraw-Hill, 1938); J.C. Bonbright, *Principles of Public Utility Rates* (New York: Columbia Univ. Press, 1961); H.J. Friendly, *The Federal Administrative Agencies: The Need for Better Definition of Standards* (Cambridge: Harvard Univ. Press, 1962); and Landis, *The Administrative Process*.
[4] For examples, see Bernstein, *Regulating Business*; and Gabriel Kolko, *Railroads and Regulation, 1877–1916* (Princeton, N.J.: Princeton Univ. Press, 1965).
[5] A more extensive list of deregulation initiatives can be found in Noll and Owen, *Political Economy of Deregulation*, 4.
[6] For discussions of the public interest theory, see Thomas K. McCraw, "Regulation in America: A Review Article," *Business History Review*, 49, no. 2 (Summer 1975): 159–83; Posner, "Theories of Economic Regulation"; and Mitnick, *Political Economy of Regulation*, 91–108.
[7] Posner, "Theories of Economic Regulation," 336.
[8] McCraw, "Regulation in America," 161. See Mitnick, *Political Economy of Regulation*, ch. 4, for a discussion of the various meanings of the public interest concept.
[9] Some classics in the revisionist genre are Bernstein, *Regulating Business*; Kolko, *Railroads and Regulation*; George Stigler, "The Theory of Economic Regulation," *Bell Journal of Economics* 2, no. 1 (Spring

1971): 3–21; Richard Posner, "Taxation by Regulation," *Bell Journal of Economics* 2, no. 1 (Spring 1971): 22–50; and William A. Jordan, "Producer Protection, Prior Market Structure, and the Effects of Government Regulation," *Journal of Law and Economics* 15, no. 1 (April 1972): 151–76.

[10] For a review of the relevant studies, see Mitnick, *Political Economy of Regulation*, 94–96.

[11] Ibid., 95.

[12] Posner, "Theories of Economic Regulation," 337.

[13] Ibid.

[14] Ibid., 343. The economic theory of regulation is presented in Stigler, "Theory of Economic Regulation." Earlier studies in the tradition include James Buchanan and Gordon Tullock, *The Calculus of Consent* (Ann Arbor: Univ. of Michigan Press, 1962); Anthony Downs, *An Economic Theory of Democracy* (New York: Harper, 1957); Mancur Olson, Jr., *The Logic of Collective Action* (Cambridge: Harvard Univ. Press, 1965).

[15] Posner, "Theories of Economic Regulation," 344.

[16] Bernstein, "Regulating Business"; Huntington, "The Marasmus of the ICC"; Avery Leiserson, "Interest Groups in Administration" in *Elements of Public Administration*, ed. F. Morstein Marx (New York: Prentice-Hall, 1946); and Harmon Ziegler, *Interest Groups in American Society* (Englewood Cliffs, N.J.: Prentice-Hall, 1964).

[17] Posner, "Theories of Economic Regulation," 343.

[18] McCraw, "Regulation in America," 164.

[19] Michael E. Levine, "Revisionism Revised?" Airline Deregulation and the Public Interest," *Journal of Law and Contemporary Problems* 44, no. 1 (Winter 1981): 185.

[20] March, "The Business Firm as a Political Coalition," 670.

[21] D. Anderson, *Regulatory Politics*, 3–6.

[22] For example see Huntington, "The Marasmus of the ICC;" Bernstein, *Regulating Business*; and Paul Sabatier, "Social Movements and Regulatory Agencies: Toward a More Adequate—and Less Pessimistic—Theory of Clientele Capture,'" *Policy Sciences* 6 (Sept. 1975): 301–42.

[23] See Roger Noll, "The Economics and Politics of Regulation," *Virginia Law Review* 57 (Summer 1971): 1016–32; Stigler, "Theory of Economic Regulation"; George Hilton, "The Basic Behavior of Regulatory Commissions," *American Economic Review* 62, no. 2 (May 1972): 47–54; and Sam Peltzman, "Toward a More General Theory of Regulation," *Journal of Law and Economics* 19 (August 1976): 211–40.

[24] For an analysis of the three hypotheses, see Quirk, *Industry Influence*.

[25] John Baldwin, *The Regulatory Agency and the Public Corporation: The Canadian Air Transport Industry* (Cambridge, Mass.: Ballinger, 1975), 5.

[26] The phrase is from Quirk, *Industry Influence*, 36.

[27] For example, see Matthew Holden, " 'Imperialism' in Bureaucracy," *American Political Science Review* 60 (Dec. 1966): 943–51.

[28] Mitnick, *Political Economy of Regulation*, 421, 432.

[29] March, "The Business Firm as a Political Coalition," 166.

[30] Ibid., 167.

[31] The assumption is discussed in William J. Keefe and Morris S. Ogul, *The American Legislative Process: Congress and the States* (Englewood Cliffs, N.J.: Prentice-Hall, 1968), ch. 13.

[32] Charles Lindblom, *The Policy Making Process* (Englewood Cliffs, N.J.: Prentice-Hall, 1968), 101–6.

[33] Paul Schulman, "Nonincremental Policy Making: Notes Toward an Alternative Paradigm," *American Political Science Review* 69, no. 4 (Dec. 1975): 1369, 1370.

[34] Four categories of decision making are identified by Braybrooke and Lindblom. Two represent variants of an incremental mode of policy making while the remaining two are forms of nonincremental policy making. Braybrooke and Lindblom, *A Strategy of Decision*, 71.

[35] Schulman, "Nonincremental Policy Making," 1370.

[36] Barry Weingast and Mark Moran, "Bureaucratic Discretion or Congressional Control? Regulatory Policy Making by the Federal Trade Commission," *Journal of Political Economy* 91, no. 5 (1983): 765–800.

[37] D. Anderson, *Regulatory Politics*, ch. 1.

[38] Paul Sabatier, "Regulatory Policy-Making: Toward a Framework of Analysis," *Natural Resources Journal* 17 (July 1977): 415–60; and Gary Wamsley and Meyer Zald, *The Political Economy of Public Organizations: A Critique and Approach to the Study of Public Administration* (Bloomington: Indiana Univ. Press, 1973).

[39] Levine, "Revisionism Revised?" 190.

[40] Bailey, "Reform From Within."

[41] Behrman, "Civil Aeronautics Board."

[42] Charles O. Jones, "Speculative Augmentation in Federal Air Pollution Policy-Making," *Journal of Politics* 36 (May 1974), 438–64.

[43] Weingast, "Regulation, Reregulation, and Deregulation."

[44] Breyer, *Regulation and Its Reform*.

[45] Morgan, "Toward Deregulation" and "Government and the Industry's Early Development."

[46] Wilson, *The Politics of Regulation*.

[47] Kahn, "The Political Feasibility of Regulatory Reform," 254.

[48] Noll and Owen, *Political Economy of Deregulation*, 272.

[49] Ibid., 157.

[50] Ibid., 7.

[51] Arthur F. Bentley, *The Process of Government* (Chicago: Univ. of Chicago Press, 1908).

[52] Wilson, *The Politics of Regulation*, 372.

[53] Ibid., 363.

[54] Ibid., 348.

[55] Posner, "Theories of Economic Regulation," 340.

[56] Douglas Needham, *The Economics and Politics of Regulation: A Behavioral Approach* on: Little, Brown, 1983), 13.

[57] Ibid., 19.

[58] Henry Mintzberg, "Patterns in Strategy Formation," *Management Science* 24, no. 9 (May 1978): 934–38.

[59] Jordan, *Airline Regulation in America*; Caves, *Air Transport*; and Douglas and Miller, *Economic Regulation* are some prominent examples.

[60] Hugh Heclo, "Issue Networks and the Executive Establishment," in *The New American Political System*, ed. Anthony King (Washington, D.C.: American Enterprise Institute, 1978), 87–124.

[61] D. Anderson, *Regulatory Politics*, 6.

[62] Needham, *Economics and Politics of Regulation*, 13.

[63] Ibid., 27.

Bibliography

BOOKS AND MONOGRAPHS

Anderson, Douglas D. *Regulatory Politics and Electric Utilities*. Boston: Auburn, 1981.

————. "State Regulation of Electric Utilities." In *The Politics of Regulation*, edited by James Q. Wilson, 3–41. New York: Basic Books, 1980.

Anderson, James E. *The Emergence of the Modern Regulatory State*. Washington, D.C.: Public Affairs Press, 1962.

Bailey, Elizabeth A. "Reform from Within: Civil Aeronautics Board Policy, 1977–78." In *Problems in Public Utility Economics and Regulation*, edited by Michael A. Crew, 19–40. Lexington, Mass.: Heath, 1979.

Baldwin, John R. *The Regulatory Agency and the Public Corporation: The Canadian Air Transport Industry*. Cambridge, Mass.: Ballinger, 1975.

Bardach, Eugene. "Reason, Responsibility, and the New Social Regulation." In *American Politics and Public Policy*, edited by Walter Dean Durnham and Martha Wagner Weinberg, 364–90. Cambridge: MIT Press, 1978.

————. *The Skill Factor in Politics: Repealing the Mental Commitment Laws in California*. Berkeley: Univ. of California Press, 1972.

Behrman, Bradley. "Civil Aeronautics Board." In *The Politics of Regulation*, edited by James Q. Wilson, 75–120. New York: Basic Books, 1980.

Bentley, Arthur F. *The Process of Government*. Chicago: Univ. of Chicago Press, 1908.

Bernstein, Marver H. *Regulating Business by Independent Commission*. Princeton, N.J.: Princeton Univ. Press, 1955.

Bock, Edwin O., ed. *Government Regulation of Business: A Casebook.* Englewood Cliffs, N.J.; Prentice-Hall, 1965.

Bonbright, J.C. *Principles of Public Utility Rates.* New York: Columbia Univ. Press, 1961.

Braybrooke, David, and Charles E. Lindblom. *A Strategy of Decision: Policy Evaluation as a Social Process.* London: Free Press 1963.

Breyer, Stephen. *Regulation and Its Reform.* Cambridge: Harvard Univ. Press, 1982.

Buchanan, James, and Gordon Tullock. *The Calculus of Consent.* Ann Arbor: Univ. of Michigan Press, 1962.

Caves, Richard E. *Air Transport and Its Regulators: An Industry Study.* Cambridge: Harvard Univ. Press, 1962.

Competition in the Airlines: What is the Public Interest? Washington, D.C.: American Enterprise Institute, AEI Forum 9, 1977.

Crew, Michael A., ed. *Problems in Public Utility Economics and Regulation.* Lexington, Mass.: Heath, 1979.

DeLeon, Peter. *A Theory of Termination in the Policy Process: Roles, Rhymes, and Reasons.* Santa Monica, Calif.: Rand, 1977.

Derthick, Martha, and Paul J. Quirk. *The Politics of Deregulation.* Washington, D.C.: Brookings, 1985.

Douglas, George W., and James C. Miller III. *Economic Regulation of Domestic Air Transport: Theory and Policy.* Washington, D.C.: Brookings, 1974.

Downs, Anthony. *An Economic Theory of Democracy.* New York: Harper, 1957.

Durnham, Walter Dean, and Martha Wagner Weinberg, eds. *American Politics and Public Policy.* Cambridge: MIT Press, 1978.

Eads, George C. *The Local Service Airline Experiment.* Washington, D.C.: Brookings, 1972.

Eads, George C., and Michael Fix. *Relief or Reform?: Reagan's Regulatory Dilemma.* Washington, D.C.: Urban Institute Press, 1984.

———, eds. *The Reagan Regulatory Strategy: An Assessment.* Washington, D.C.: Urban Institute Press, 1984.

Fraser, Robert C., Alan D. Donheiser, and Thomas G. Miller, Jr. *Civil Aviation Development: A Policy and Operations Analysis.* New York: Praeger, 1972.

Frederick, John H. *Commercial Air Transportation.* 5th ed. Homewood, Ill.: Irwin, 1955.

Friendly, H.J. *The Federal Administrative Agencies: The Need for Better Definition of Standards.* Cambridge: Harvard Univ. Press, 1962.

Fritschler, A. Lee. *Smoking and Politics: Policymaking and the Federal Bureaucracy.* Englewood Cliffs, N.J.: Prentice-Hall, 1975.

Fritschler, A. Lee., and Bernard H. Ross. *Business Regulation and Government Decision-Making*. Cambridge, Mass.: Winthrop, 1980.

Fruhan, William E. *The Fight for Competitive Advantage: A Study of the United States Domestic Trunk Air Carriers*. Boston: Harvard Univ. Press, 1972.

Graymer, LeRoy, and Frederick Thompson. *Reforming Social Regulation: Alternative Public Policy Strategies*. Beverly Hills, Calif.: Sage, 1982.

Heclo, Hugh. "Issue Networks and the Executive Establishment." In *The New American Political System*, edited by Anthony King, 87–124. Washington, D.C.: American Enterprise Institute, 1978.

Heffron, Florence, with Neil McFeeley. *The Administrative Regulatory Process*. New York: Longman, 1983.

Herring, E.P. *Public Administration and the Public Interest*. New York: McGraw-Hill, 1938.

Houthakker, Hendrick. "Economic Aspects of Deregulation." In *Deregulating American Industry*, edited by Donald L. Martin and Warren F. Schwartz, 1–20. Lexington, Mass.: Heath, 1977.

Jones, Charles O. *An Introduction to the Study of Public Policy*. Belmont, Calif.: Duxbury, 1970.

Jordan, William A. *Airline Regulation in America: Effects and Imperfections*. Baltimore: Johns Hopkins Univ. Press, 1970.

Kahn, Alfred. "Deregulation and Vested Interests: The Case of Airlines." In *The Political Economy of Deregulation: Interest Groups in the Regulatory Process*, edited by Roger G. Noll and Bruce Owen, 132–51. Washington, D.C.: American Enterprise Institute, 1983.

———. *The Economics of Regulation: Principles and Institutions*. Vols. 1 and 2. New York: Wiley, 1970–71.

———. "The Political Feasibility of Regulatory Reform: How Did We Do It?" In *Reforming Social Regulation*, edited by LeRoy Graymer and Frederick Thompson, 247–63. Beverly Hills, Calif.: Sage, 1982.

Kaufman, Herbert. *Are Government Organizations Immortal?* Washington, D.C.: Brookings, 1976.

Keefe, William J., and Morris S. Ogul. *The American Legislative Process: Congress and the States*. Englewood Cliffs, N.J.: Prentice-Hall, 1968.

Keeler, Theodore E. "The Revolution in Airline Regulation: Revolution and Reform." In *Case Studies in Regulation: Revolution and Reform*, edited by Leonard W. Weiss and Michael W. Klass, 53–85. Boston: Little, Brown, 1981.

Keyes, Lucille S. *Federal Control of Entry Into Air Transportation*. Cambridge: Harvard Univ. Press, 1951.

———. *Regulatory Reform in Air Cargo Transportation*. Washington, D.C.: American Enterprise Institute, 1980.

Kolko, Gabriel. *Railroads and Regulation, 1877–1916.* Princeton, N.J.: Princeton Univ. Press, 1965.

Krasnow, Erwin G., Lawrence D. Longley, and Herbert A. Terry. *The Politics of Broadcast Regulation.* 3rd ed. New York: St. Martin's, 1982.

Landis, James. *The Administrative Process.* New Haven: Yale Univ. Press, 1938.

Leiserson, Avery. "Interest Groups in Administration." In *Elements of Public Administration*, edited by F. Morstein Marx, 314–38. New York: Prentice-Hall, 1946.

Lindblom, Charles. *The Intelligence of Democracy.* New York: Macmillan, 1964.

————. *The Policy Making Process.* Englewood Cliffs, N.J.: Prentice-Hall, 1968.

Lowi, Theodore J. *The End of Liberalism: Ideology, Policy, and the Crisis of Public Authority.* New York: Norton, 1969.

Lowi, Theodore J., and A. Stone, eds. *Nationalizing Government: Public Policies in America.* Beverley Hills, Calif.: Sage, 1978.

MacAvoy, Paul W. *The Regulated Industries and the Economy.* New York: Norton, 1979.

MacAvoy, Paul W., and J.W. Snow, eds. *Regulation of Passenger Fares and Competition Among the Airlines: Ford Administration Papers on Regulatory Reform.* Washington, D.C.: American Enterprise Institute, 1977.

McCraw, Thomas K. *Prophets of Regulation.* Cambridge, Mass.: Belknap, 1984.

McKie, James W., ed. *Social Responsibility and the Business Predicament.* Washington, D.C.: Brookings, 1974.

Markham, Jesse W. "A Century After Munn v. Illinois: What Kind of Regulation Should We Have?" In *Salvaging Public Utility Regulation*, edited by Werner Sichel, 21–35. Lexington, Mass.: Heath, 1976.

Martin, Donald L., and W.F. Schwartz, eds. *Deregulating American Industry.* Lexington, Mass.: Heath, 1977.

Meyer, John R., and Clinton V. Oster, Jr. *Deregulation and the New Airline Entrepreneurs.* Cambridge: MIT Press, 1984.

————, eds. *Airline Deregulation: The Early Experience.* Boston: Auburn, 1981.

Mitnick, Barry M. *The Political Economy of Regulation: Creating, Designing and Removing Regulatory Forms.* New York: Columbia Univ. Press, 1980.

Morgan, Ivor P. "Toward Deregulation" and "Government and the Industry's Early Development." In *Airline Deregulation: The Early Experience*, edited by John R. Meyer and Clinton V. Oster, Jr., 13–37 and 41–52. Boston: Auburn, 1981.

Needham, Douglas. *The Economics and Politics of Regulation: A Behavioral Approach.* Boston: Little, Brown, 1983.

Neiman, Max. "The Virtues of Heavy Handedness in Government." In *Policy Implementation: Penalties or Incentives?* Beverly Hills, Calif.: Sage, 1980.

Nelson, James R. "A Pragmatic Approach to Deregulation." In *Salvaging Public Utility Regulation*, edited by Werner Sichel, 37–51. Lexington, Mass.: Heath, 1976.

Noll, Roger G. *Reforming Regulation: An Evaluation of the Ash Council Proposals.* Washington, D.C.: Brookings, 1971.

Noll, Roger G., and Bruce M. Owen. *The Political Economy of Deregulation: Interest Groups in the Regulatory Process.* Washington, D.C.: American Enterprise Institute, 1983.

Olson, Mancur, Jr. *The Logic of Collective Action.* Cambridge: Harvard Univ. Press, 1965.

Perrow, Charles. *Complex Organizations: A Critical Essay.* 2nd ed. Glenview, Ill.: Scott, Foresman, 1979.

Phillips, Almarin, ed. *Promoting Competition in Regulated Markets.* Washington, D.C.: Brookings, 1975.

Preston, L.E., ed. *Business Environment—Public Policy: 1979 Conference Papers.* American Assembly of Collegiate Schools of Business, 1980.

Puffer, Claude E. *Air Transportation.* Philadelphia: Blakiston, 1941.

Quirk, Paul J. *Industry Influence in the Federal Regulatory Agencies.* Princeton, N.J.: Princeton Univ. Press, 1981.

Redford, Emmette S. *American Government and the Economy.* New York: Macmillan, 1965.

———. *The Regulatory Process: With Illustrations from Commercial Aviation.* Austin: Univ. of Texas Press, 1969.

Regulating Business: The Search for an Optimum. San Francisco: Institute for Contemporary Studies, 1978.

Richmond, Samuel B. *Regulation and Competition in Air Transportation.* New York: Columbia Univ. Press, 1961.

Ripley, Randall B., and Grace A. Franklin. *Bureaucracy and the Policy Implementation Process.* Homewood, Ill.: Dorsey, 1982.

Rosenbaum, Walter A. *The Politics of Environmental Concern.* 2nd ed. New York: Holt, Rinehart, and Winston, 1977.

Sichel, Werner, ed. *Salvaging Public Utility Regulation.* Lexington, Mass.: Heath, 1976.

Smith, Henry Ladd. *Airways: The History of Commercial Aviation in the United States.* New York: Knopf, 1942.

Stone, Alan. *Regulation and Its Alternatives.* Washington: Congressional Quarterly Press, 1982.

Taneja, Nawal K. *Airlines in Transition*. Lexington, Mass.: Lexington Books, 1981.

Thayer, Frederick C. *Air Transport Policy and National Security: A Political Economic and Military Analysis*. Chapel Hill: Univ. of North Carolina Press, 1965.

Tillett, P.D. *The Army Flies the Mail*. University: Univ. of Alabama Press, 1954.

Tolchin, Susan J., and Martin Tolchin. *Dismantling America: The Rush to Deregulate*. New York: Oxford Univ. Press, 1983.

Wamsley, Gary L., and Mayer N. Zald. *The Political Economy of Public Organizations: A Critique and Approach to the Study of Public Administration*. Bloomington: Indiana Univ. Press, 1973.

Weidenbaum, Murray L. "The Changing Nature of Government Regulation of Business." In *Business Environment—Public Policy: 1979 Conference Papers*, edited by Lee Preston, 77–103. American Assembly of Collegiate Schools of Business, 1980.

———. *The Future of Business Regulation*. New York: AMACOM, 1979.

Weiss, Leonard W. "State Regulation of Public Utilities and Marginal-Cost Pricing." In *Case Studies in Regulation: Revolution and Reform*, edited by Leonard W. Weiss and Michael W. Klass, 262–91. Boston: Little, Brown, 1981.

Weiss, Leonard W., and Michael W. Klass, eds. *Case Studies in Regulation: Revolution and Reform*. Boston: Little, Brown, 1981.

Welborn, David M. *Governance of Federal Regulatory Agencies*. Knoxville: Univ. of Tennessee Press, 1977.

White, Lawrence J. *Reforming Regulation: Processes and Problems*. Englewood Cliffs, N.J.: Prentice-Hall, 1981.

Wilson, James Q. "The Rise of the Bureaucratic State." In *Public Administration: Concepts and Cases*, edited by Richard J. Stillman, 68–84. Boston: Houghton Mifflin, 1980.

———, ed. *The Politics of Regulation*. New York: Basic Books, 1980.

Ziegler, Harmon. *Interest Groups in American Society*. Englewood Cliffs, N.J.: Prentice-Hall, 1964.

PERIODICALS

Alexander, Tom. "It's Roundup Time for the Runaway Regulators." *Fortune*, 3 Dec. 1979, 126–32.

Barber, Richard J. "Airline Mergers, Monopoly, and the CAB." *Journal of Air Law and Commerce* 28 (Summer 1961–62): 189–237.

Bardach, Eugene. "Policy Termination as a Political Process." *Policy Sciences* 7, no. 2 (June 1976): 123–31.

Barnes, Leslie O. "Airline Subsidies—Purpose, Cause and Control." *Journal of Air Law and Commerce* 26 (Autumn 1959): 311–22.

Behn, Robert D. "Closing a Government Facility." *Public Administration Review* 38, no. 4 (July–Aug. 1978): 332–38.

Berman, David R. "Consumerism and the Regulatory System: Paradigms of Reform." *Policy Studies Review* 1, no. 3 (Feb. 1982): 454–62.

Bernstein, Marver H. "Independent Regulatory Agencies: A Perspective on Their Reform." *Annals* 400 (March 1972): 14–26.

———. "The Regulatory Process: A Framework for Analysis." *Law and Contemporary Problems* 26, no. 2 (Spring 1961): 329–46.

Biller, Robert P. "On Tolerating Policy and Organizational Termination: Some Design Considerations." *Policy Sciences* 7, no. 2 (June 1976): 133–49.

Boorshin, David. "Regulatory Reform." *Editorial Research Reports* 1, no. 2, (16 Jan. 1976): 25–44.

Bothun, Douglas, and John C. Comer, "The Politics of Termination: Concepts and Process." *Policy Studies Journal* 7, no. 3 (Spring 1979): 540–53.

Bradley, John P. "The Restoration of Interstate Airline Service at Dallas Love Field." *The Municipal Matrix* [North Texas State Univ. Center for Community Services] 12, no. 4 (Dec. 1980).

Breyer, Stephen. "Analyzing Regulatory Failure: Mismatches, Less Restrictive Alternatives and Reform." *Harvard Law Review* 92 (Jan. 1979): 547–609.

Bruce, Peter, and D. Traynham. "Looking Back on Airline Deregulation." *National Review* 32, no. 10 (16 May 1980): 588–95.

Callison, James W. "Airline Deregulation—Only Partially a Hoax: The Current Status of the Airline Deregulation Movement." *Journal of Air Law and Commerce* 45 (Autumn 1980): 961–1000.

Cohen, Marvin S. "New Air Service and Deregulation: A Study in Transition." *Journal of Air Law and Commerce* 44 (Autumn 1979): 695–703.

"Controversy Over Proposed Airline Deregulation." *Congressional Digest* 57, nos. 6–7 (June–July 1978): 163–92.

Cover, Virgil D. "The Rise of Third Level Air Carriers." *Journal of Air Law and Commerce* 37 (Fall 1971): 44–51.

Deans, Ralph C. "Future of the Airlines." *Editorial Research Reports* 1, no. 4 (27 Jan. 1971): 65–80.

DeLeon, Peter. "Public Policy Termination: An End and a Beginning." Essay prepared at the request of the Congressional Research Service as background for the Sunset Act of 1977 (mimeographed).

DeMuth, Christopher C. "A Strong Beginning on Reform." *Regulation* (Jan.–Feb. 1982): 15–18.

"Dividends from Deregulation." *Time Magazine* 12 Nov. 1979, 113.

Dockser, Ronald D. "Airline Service Abandonment and Consolidation—A Chapter in the Battle Against Subsidization." *Journal of Air Law and Commerce* 32 (Autumn 1966): 496–525.

Dubnick, Mel, and Alan R. Gitelson. "Regulatory Policy Analysis: Working in a Quagmire." *Policy Studies Review* 1, no. 3 (Feb. 1982): 423–35.

Feldman, Paul. "Why Regulation Doesn't Work." *Review of Social Economy* 29, no. 2 (Sept. 1971): 31–38.

Gans, Herbert J. "Planning for Declining and Poor Cities." *Journal of the American Institute of Planners* (Sept. 1975): 305–7.

———. "A Symposium: Organizational Decline and Cutback Management," *Public Administration Review* 38, no. 4 (July–Aug. 1978): 315–57.

Gellman, Aaron J. "The Regulation of Competition in United States Domestic Air Transportation: A Judicial Survey and Analysis." *Journal of Air Law and Commerce* 28 (Winter 1958): 148–81.

Hall, Barre. "The Civil Aeronautics Board Policy Favoring Subsidy Reduction to Local Service Carriers: Its Role and Implementation in the Decision Process." *Journal of Air Law and Commerce* 34 (Autumn 1968): 566–609.

Harrigan, Kathryn, and Daniel Kasper. "Senator Kennedy and the CAB." *Harvard Business Case Study No. 4–378–055* (Jan. 1978).

Hector, Louis. "Problems of the CAB and the Independent Regulatory Commissions." *Yale Law Journal* 69, no. 6 (May 1960): 931–64.

Herman, William R. "Deregulation: Now or Never! (Or Maybe Someday?)." *Public Administration Review* 36, no. 2 (March–April 1976): 223–28.

Hilton, George. "The Basic Behavior of Regulatory Commissions." *American Economic Review* 62, no. 2 (May 1972): 47–54.

Holden, Matthew J. "'Imperialism' in Bureaucracy." *American Political Science Review* 60, no. 4 (Dec. 1966): 943–51.

Huntington, Samuel P. "The Marasmus of the ICC: The Commission, the Railroads and the Public Interest." *Yale Law Journal* 61, no. 4 (April 1952): 467–509.

"Inside the White House." *Aviation Daily*, 4 Sept. 1979, 4–6.

Jaffe, Louis L. "The Effective Limits of the Administrative Process: A Reevaluation." *Harvard Law Review* 67 (May 1954): 1105–35.

Jones, Charles O. "Speculative Augmentation in Federal Air Pollution Policy-Making." *Journal of Politics* 36 (May 1974): 438–64.

Jones, William K. "Licensing of Domestic Air Transportation." *Journal of Air Law and Commerce* 30 (Spring 1964): 113–72.

———. "Licensing of Domestic Air Transportation." *Journal of Air Law and Commerce* 31 (Spring 1965): 89–125.

Jordan, William A. "Producer Protection, Prior Market Structure, and the Effects of Government Regulation." *Journal of Law and Economics* 15, no. 1 (April 1972): 151–76.

Kahn, Alfred. "Applying Economics to an Imperfect World." *Regulation* (Nov.–Dec. 1978): 17–27.

Kamp, Japp. "The Near Future of Air Charter Regulation: The Case for More Experimentation in Public Policy." *Journal of Air Law and Commerce* 41 (Autumn 1975): 389–417.

Kaus, Robert M. "The Dark Side of Deregulation" *Washington Monthly* (May 1979): 33.

Kelleher, Herbert D. "Deregulation and the Practicing Attorney." *Journal of Air Law and Commerce* 44 (Summer 1978): 261–96.

Keyes, Lucille. "Policy Innovations in the Domestic Passenger Fare Investigation." *Journal of Air Law and Commerce* 41 (Spring 1975): 75–100.

Kintner, Earl W. "The Current Ordeal of the Administrative Process." *Yale Law Journal* 69, no. 5 (May 1960): 965.

Kosters, Marvin H., and Jeffrey A. Eisenach. "Is Regulatory Relief Enough?" *Regulation* (March–April 1982): 20–27.

Levine, Charles H. "Organizational Decline and Cutback Management." *Public Administration Review* 38, no. 4 (July–Aug. 1978): 316–25.

———, ed. "A Symposium: Organizational Decline and Cutback Management." *Public Administration Review* 38, no. 4 (July–Aug. 1978): 315–57.

Levine, Michael E. "Is Regulation Necessary? California Air Transportation and National Regulatory Policy." *Yale Law Journal* 75 (July 1965): 1416–47.

———. "Revisionism Revised?" Airline Deregulation and the Public Interest," *Journal of Law and Contemporary Problems* 44, no. 1 (Winter 1981): 179–95.

Lilley, William, III, and James C. Miller III. "The New 'Social Regulation.'" *Public Interest* 47 (Spring 1977): 49–61.

Lindblom, Charles. "The Science of Muddling Through." *Public Administrative Review* (1959): 79–88.

Loving, Rush, Jr. "How the Airlines Will Cope With Deregulation." *Fortune*, 20 Nov. 1978, 38–41.

———. "The Pros and Cons of Airline Deregulation." *Fortune* (Aug. 1977), 209–17.

McCraw, Thomas K. "Regulation in America: A Review Article." *Business History Review* 49, no. 2 (Summer 1975): 159–83.

March, James G. "The Business Firm as a Political Coalition." *Journal of Politics* 24, no. 4 (Nov. 1962): 662–78.

Mintzberg, Henry. "Patterns in Strategy Formation." *Management Science* 24, no. 9 (May 1978): 934–38.

Mitnick, Barry M. "Deregulation as a Process of Organizational Reduction." *Public Administration Review* 38, no. 4 (July–Aug. 1978): 350–57.

Noll, Roger G. "The Behavior of Regulatory Agencies." *Review of Social Economy* 29 (March 1971): 15–19.

———. "The Economics and Politics of Regulation," *Virginia Law Review* 57 (Summer 1981): 1016–32.

Peltzman, Sam. "Toward a More General Theory of Regulation." *Journal of Law and Economics* 19 (Aug. 1976): 211–40.

Pfiffner, John M. "The Development of Administrative Regulation." *Annals* 221 (May 1942): 1–8.

Posner, Richard A. "Taxation by Regulation." *Bell Journal of Economics and Management Science* 2, no. 1 (Spring 1971): 22–50.

———. "Theories of Economic Regulation." *Bell Journal of Economics and Management Science* 5, no. 2 (Autumn 1974): 335–58.

Reamy, Gerald S. "Charter Air Travel: Paper Airplanes in a Dogfight." *Journal of Air Law and Commerce* 42 (Spring 1976): 405–32.

"Regulation—the First Year." *Regulation* (Jan.–Feb. 1982): 19–40.

Sabatier, Paul. "Regulatory Policy-Making: Toward a Framework of Analysis." *Natural Resources Journal* 17 (July 1977): 415–60.

———. "Social Movements and Regulatory Agencies: Toward a More Adequate—and Less Pessimistic—Theory of 'Clientele Capture.'" *Policy Sciences* 6, no. 3 (Sept. 1975): 301–42.

Schulman, Paul. "Nonincremental Policy Making: Notes Toward an Alternative Paradigm." *American Political Science Review* 69, no. 4 (Dec. 1975): 1354–70.

Scott, William G. "Organizational Theory: A Reassessment." *Academy of Management Journal* (June 1974): 242–53.

Silberman, Alan H. "Price Discrimination and the Regulation of Air Transportation." *Journal of Air Law and Commerce* 31 (Summer 1965): 198–260.

Stigler, George. "The Theory of Economic Regulation." *Bell Journal of Economics and Management Science* 2, no. 1 (Spring 1971): 3–21.

Thomas, W.V. "Deregulating Transportation." *Editorial Research Reports* 1, no. 23 (22 June 1979): 443–60.

Trebing, Harry M. "The Chicago School Versus Public Utility Regulation." *Journal of Economic Issues* 10, no. 1 (March 1976): 97–123.

Weaver, Paul H. "Regulation, Social Policy, and Class Conflict." *Public Interest* 50 (Winter 1978): 45–63.

———. "Unlocking the Gilded Cage of Regulation." *Fortune* (Feb. 1977), 179–88.

Weingast, Barry R. "Regulation, Reregulation, and Deregulation: The Political Foundations of Agency Clientele Relationships." *Law and Contemporary Problems* 44, no. 1 (Winter 1981): 147–77.

Weingast, Barry, and Mark Moran. "Bureaucratic Discretion or Congressional Control? Regulatory Policy Making by the Federal Trade Commission." *Journal of Political Economy* 91, no. 5 (1983): 765–800.
Welborn, David M. "Presidents, Regulatory Commissions, and Regulatory Policy." *Journal of Public Law* 15 (1966): 3–29.
Williams, R.J. "Politics and the Ecology of Regulation." *Public Administration* 54 (Autumn 1956): 319–31.
Wilson, James Q. "The Dead Hand of Regulation." *Public Interest* 25 (Fall 1971): 39–58.
Worsnop, Richard L. "Federal Regulatory Agencies: Fourth Branch of Government." *Editorial Research Reports* 1, no. 5 (5 Feb. 1969): 83–102.

NEWS JOURNALS, PAPERS, AND BROADCASTS

Aviation Week. Jan. 1973–Nov. 1981.
Congressional Quarterly Weekly Report. Jan. 1974–Dec. 1978.
McNeil-Lehrer Report. Television broadcasts, 18 March 1980.
National Journal. Jan. 1974–May 1979.
New York Times. Jan. 1974–Dec. 1978.
Wall Street Journal. Jan. 1974–Dec. 1978.

CONGRESSIONAL HEARINGS AND REPORTS

Congressional Record. 95th Cong., 2nd sess., 19 April, 14 and 21 Sept. and 14–15 Oct. 1978.

A. House of Representatives:

Air Service Improvement Act of 1978. Report of the House Committee on Public Works and Transportation, H. Report 95–1211, 95th Cong., 2nd sess., 1978.
Airline Deregulation, Message from the President. H. Doc. 95–92, Public Works and Transportation Committee, 95th Cong., 1st sess., 1977.
Aviation Act of 1977 Message from the President. H. Doc. 95–45, Public Works and Transportation, 95th Cong., 1st sess., 1977.
Committee on the Budget. *Economic Aspects of Federal Regulation of the Transportation Industry. Hearings* before the Task Force on Tax Expenditures, Government Organization and Regulation, House of Representatives, 95th Cong., 1st sess., 1977.

Committee on Public Works and Transportation. *Aviation Economics. Hearings* before the Subcommittee on Investigations and Review and the Subcommittee on Aviation, House of Representatives, 94th Cong., 2nd sess., 1976.

————. *Aviation Regulatory Reform. Hearings* before the Subcommittee on Aviation, House, 95th Cong., 1st sess., 1977, and 2nd sess., 1978.

————. *Legislative History of the Airline Deregulation Act of 1978.* 96th Cong., 1st sess., 1979.

————. *Reform of Economic Regulation of Air Carriers. Hearings* before the Subcommittee on Aviation, House, 94th Cong., 2nd sess., 1976.

————. *Report on the Air Service Improvement Act of 1978.* 95th Cong., 2nd sess., 1978.

Conference Report on the Airline Deregulation Act of 1978. H. Report 95–1779, 95th Cong., 2nd sess., 1978.

B. Senate:

Amending the Federal Aviation Act of 1958. Report of the Senate Committee on Commerce, Science and Transportation on S.2493, 95th Cong., 2nd sess., S. Report, 95–631, 1978.

Aviation Act of 1975, Report of the Senate Committee on Commerce, Science and Transportation on S.2551, 94th Cong., 1st sess., 22 Oct. 1975.

Civil Aeronautics Board Practices and Procedures. Report of the Subcommittee on Administrative Practice and Procedure of the Senate Judiciary Committee, 94th Cong., 1st sess., 1975.

Committee on Commerce, Science and Transportation. *Impact of Airline Deregulation. Hearings* before the Subcommittee on Aviation, 96th Cong., 1st sess., 1979.

————. *Regulatory Reform in Air Transportation. Hearings* before the Subcommittee on Aviation, 94th Cong., 2nd ses., 1976, and 1st sess., 1977.

Committee on the Judiciary. *Oversight of Civil Aeronautics Board Practices and Procedures. Hearings* before the Subcommittee on Administrative Practice and Procedures, 94th Cong., 1st sess., 1975.

Report on Regulatory Agencies to the President-Elect [Landis Report]. Report to Subcommittee on Administrative Practice and Procedure, 86th Cong., 2nd sess., 1960.

Select Committee on Small Business. *The Decline of the Supplemental Air Carriers in the United States. Hearings* before the Subcommittee on Monopoly, 94th Cong., 2nd sess., 1976.

OTHER DOCUMENTS AND REPORTS

Air Transport Association. *Consequences of Deregulation of the Scheduled Air Transport Industry*. Prepared at the request of the Senate Subcommittee on Administrative Practice and Procedure. April 1975.

Commuter Airline Association of America. *Time for Commuters*. Annual Report of the Commuter Airline Industry. Oct. 1976.

Domestic Council Review Group on Regulatory Reform. *The Challenge of Regulatory Reform*. Washington, D.C. Jan. 1977.

Harbridge House, Inc. *A Proposed Means of Evaluating the Consequences of Changed Approaches to Economic Regulation of the Domestic Commercial Air Transportation System*. Prepared for the U.S. Civil Aeronautics Board. July 1975.

Lazarus, S., M. Schuman, and H. Wellford. *Opinions on Airline Regulatory Reform*. Report presented to President-Elect Carter. Dec. 1976.

President's Advisory Council on Executive Organization (Ash Council). *A New Regulatory Framework: Report on Selected Independent Regulatory Agencies*. Washington, D.C., 1971.

President's Committee on Administrative Management (Brownlow Committee). *Report of the Committee With Studies of Administrative Management in the Federal Government*. Washington, D.C.: U.S. Government Printing Office, 1937.

Simat, H., and Eichner, Inc. *An Analysis of the Intrastate Air Carrier Regulatory Forum*. Prepared for the Department of Transportation. Jan. 1976.

U.S. Civil Aeronautics Board. *The Domestic Route System: Analysis and Policy Recommendations*. Washington, D.C.: CAB. Oct. 1974.

———. *Regulatory Reform: Report of the CAB Special Staff*. Washington, D.C.: CAB, July 1975.

———. *Report of the CAB's Advisory Committee on Procedural Reform*. Washington, D.C.: CAB, 1972.

———. *Report to Congress*. Washington, D.C.: CAB. Annual.

———. *Service to Small Communities*. Washington, D.C.: CAB, 1972.

U.S. Department of Transportation. *Air Service to Small Communities*. Washington, D.C.: Department of Transportation. March 1976.

U.S. General Accounting Office. *Comments on the Study, "Consequences of Deregulation of the Scheduled Air Transportation Industry."* Washington, D.C., 1977.

———. *Lower Airline Costs Per Passenger Are Possible in the United States and Could Result in Lower Fares*. Washington, D.C., 1977.

Weekly Compilation of Presidential Documents. 8 Oct. 1974–24 Oct. 1978.

INTERVIEWS AND UNPUBLISHED MATERIALS

Barclay, C.M. Counsel, Senate Subcommittee on Aviation. Personal interview. Washington, D.C., June 1980.

Behrman, B.G. "Airline Deregulation: A Test Case for Fundamental Reform." Senior thesis, Harvard College, 1978.

Breyer, S. Chief Counsel, Senate Judiciary Committee. Personal interview. Washington, D.C., June 1980.

————. "From Candidate to Reform." Manuscript, June 1980.

————. "Mismatch: Excessive Competition: The Example of Airlines." Manuscript, June 1980.

Cohen, R.E. Analyst, Government Research Corporation (National Journal). Personal interview. Washington, D.C., June 1980.

Ditano, R. National Air Carrier Association of America. Personal interview. Washington, D.C., June 1980.

Heymsfeld, D. Assistant Counsel (Aviation), House Committee on Public Works and Transportation. Personal interview. Washington, D.C., June 1980.

Jackman, W. Public Relations Director, Air Transport Association of America. Personal interview. Washington, D.C., June 1980.

Kahn, A.E. Chairman, Civil Aeronautics Board, 1977–78. Personal interview. Washington, D.C., June 1980.

Landry, J.E. "Airline Deregulation in the United States: The First Ten Months." Informal remarks at the Annual Meeting of the Canadian Bar Association, Calgary, August 27, 1979. Mimeographed.

McInnis, M.S. General Counsel, Civil Aeronautics Board. Personal interview. June 1980.

Morris, S.E. Deputy Associate Director of Regulatory Policy and Reports Management, Office of Management and Budget. Personal interview. Washington, D.C., June 1980.

Robertson, R.B., III. Director, Bureau of Consumer Protection, Civil Aeronautics Board. Personal interview. Washington, D.C., June 1980.

Saunders, J. Chief Administrative Law Judge, Civil Aeronautics Board. Personal interview. Washington, D.C., June 1980.

Sullivan, R.J. Chief Counsel. House Committee on Public Works and Transportation. Personal interview. Washington, D.C., June 1980.

Welborn, D.M. "Taking Stock in Regulatory Reform." Paper presented at the Annual Meeting of the American Political Science Association, Washington, D.C., Sept. 1977.

Index

Act to Regulate Commerce, 47
Adams, Brock, 115
Ad Hoc Committee on Aviation
    Reform, 139, 156
administrative deregulation. *See*
    deregulation
Administrative Procedure Act,
    34, 118
agency capture. *See* capture
    theory
air carriers, types of, 54–59
Air Commerce Act, 6
air fares: discount, 88; ex-
    perimental approach, 68;
    level of, 85–86; presumption
    doctrine, 83; structure of, 85–
    86; types of, 88
airline: capacity, 99–100; competi-
    tion, 65; management, 103–
    104; performance standards,
    101
airline deregulation: conditions
    facilitating, 176–77; conse-
    quences of, 104, 108–109;
    and consumer groups, 156;
    explanations for, 170–71,

177–79; historical significance
    of, 5–10; and inflation, 139;
    as nonincremental policy,
    168–70; opponents of, 104–
    106, 138–39; phases of, 97–
    99; and Senate, 110–15; stud-
    ies supporting, 109–10; sup-
    port for, 102–104; theoretical
    significance of, 10–18; transi-
    tion to, 3, 123–25; and west-
    ern states, 147
Airline Deregulation Act of 1978,
    2, 3, 5, 10, 18, 45, 145, 161;
    and administrative deregula-
    tion, 157–58; and CAB anti-
    trust authority, 124–25; and
    commuter airlines, 148–50;
    compared to other reform
    bills, 112; conference com-
    mittee on, 121–23, 147–48;
    and courts, 117; and design
    compromises, 142–44; and
    equity issues, 138, 145–48;
    and House of Representa-
    tives, 119–21; labor protec-
    tion, 105, 146; provisions,

Quirk, Paul, 102, 103, 153

Railroad Revitalization and Regulatory Reform Act, 111
Rapp, Dennis A., 154
rate regulation, 48–49; and Airline Deregulation Act of
1978, 124; of charter fares,
100–101; CAB dilemma in, 91–
92; CAB policy on, 85–92,
117; CAB procedures for, 85–
88; and competition, 65, 85–
92; and discount fares, 89–90,
117; discrimination approach
to, 68, 89; and route regulation, 82; termination of, 125;
and zone of reasonableness,
29, 113, 117, 143
Reagan, Ronald, 125–26, 186
n.29
recreational travel, 79, 95
Redford, Emmette, 23, 24, 34,
53, 80, 134
regional airlines. *See* local service
airlines
regulation: alternatives to, 25–27,
131; anticompetitive
approach to, 4; and behavior
of regulators, 165–67; cartel,
31; classical, 23; competitive
approach to, 4; consumer,
31; definitions of, 22, 24–25;
economic, 30–32, 111; economic theory of, 164; and error by design, 29; and error
by incompetence, 28–29; expansion of, 181 n.1; instruments of, 23–25; and interest
group theories, 164; new-
style, 31; old-style, 31; policing type of, 31; politics of, 3,
182 n.12; and propensity to
regulate, 16; public interest

theory of, 160–62, 173; revisionist theory of, 161; social, 30–31, 111; types of, 32–
33; vertical, 31
regulatory policy: cycle of, 3–4,
67–93, 174–75; determinants
of, 170–71; development of,
173–79; and revisionist
theory, 167–70
regulatory politics, 5, 16, 17–18
regulatory process: conventional
wisdom about, 4–5, 12–13;
efficiency of, 34; equity of,
33–34
regulatory reform: and decrementalism, 4, 29, 102–15;
deregulation as, 29; history
of, 33–37; and incrementalism, 4, 28, 38; and interest
group theory, 172; paradigms
of, 29–30; politics of, 4, 5;
and Reagan administration,
186 n.29; types of, 28–29
revisionist theory of regulation,
173; and determinants of regulatory policy, 170–71; incremental bias of, 168–69;
and policy change, 171–72;
and regulatory behavior, 165–
66
Richmond, Samuel B., 53, 77, 80
Rizley, Ross, 84
Robertson, Reuben, 116, 154
Robson, John, 98; and Cannon
hearings, 113, 142–43; CAB
appointments of, 152–53; CAB
policies under, 112, 116–17,
151, 156, 171; resignation of,
116; and Wolff Committee,
136
Roosevelt, Franklin D., 5, 8
Rosenbaum, Walter, 38
route regulation: and Airline De-

regulation Act of 1978, 123–
24; and airline profits, 81, 91;
and airline subsidies, 69–76;
anticompetitive approach to,
82, 83–84; and automatic entry, 124; CAB policies for, 47,
68, 79–84, 117; and de facto
deregulation, 118; and dormant authority, 124; and
monopoly routes, 84; and
over-capacity, 81; and parallel service, 81; and "Realignment of System" program,
74; and route abandonments,
74; and route moratorium,
68, 81, 91, 99; and route
strengthening program, 71–
72; and show-cause order,
118; termination of, 125;
transition to, 121–22; and
"use-it-or-lose-it" policy, 74–
75
rural states, 105

scheduled airlines, 69; *see also*
local service airlines and
trunk airlines
Schulman, Paul, 169
Scott, William, 15
Sears Roebuck and Co., 103
Securities and Exchange Commis-
sion, 35
Senate bill 292, 114; 689, 115;
2551, 114; 3364, 114; 3536,
114
Senate Commerce Committee,
115, 146, 147, 156
Senate Commerce Subcommittee
on Aviation, 106, 110; and
Cannon hearings, 113, 138–
39
Senate Judiciary Subcommittee on
Administrative Practice and

Procedure, 98, 101–102; and
CAB policy changes, 112; and
deregulation, 114; and evaluation of airline regulation,
135–36; hearings of, 105, 108,
107–10, 141; and airline reform debate, 131, 138; and
small community service, 147
service regulation, 26, 28, 65, 68,
93
shippers, 95
small community airline service,
124, 146–47
Southern Service to the West
Case, 82–83
Staggers Rail Act of 1980, 161
standard industry fare level, 124
state and local organizations, 105
Stone, Alan, 23
strategic compromise, 129, 140–51
strategic staffing, 129, 151–54
sunset legislation, 15, 139
supplemental airlines, 55, 56, 58;
certification of, 9, 188 n.25;
and CAB policies, 76–79, 100–
101, 112, 117, 150–51; and
deregulation, 104, 150; dual
certification of, 151, 195 n.79;
origin of, 59, 76–77; and subsidies, 76; and trunk airlines,
76–79
survival hypothesis, 166

targeted benefit compromises,
148–51
termination: of CAB, 3; politics of,
130
Texas, 40, 134
third-level carriers, 75; *see also* air
taxi operators and commuter
airlines
Timm, Robert, 111, 112, 153; and
anticompetitive policies, 99;